Christianity entered history as a new social order, or
rather a new social dimension. From the very
beginning Christianity was not primarily a "doctrine," but
exactly a "community." There was not only a "Message"
to be proclaimed and delivered, and "Good News"
to be declared. There was precisely a New
Community, distinct and peculiar, in the process of growth
and formation, to which members were called and
recruited. Indeed, "fellowship" *(koinōnia)* was the basic
category of Christian existence.

GEORGES FLOROVSKY
*"EMPIRE AND DESERT: ANTINOMIES
OF CHRISTIAN HISTORY"*

Because the gospel the church has to proclaim
concerns the announcement of the fact and
possibility of renewed human community in the love
of God, "the teaching of the church" is,
basically, the church herself, as the sign and the beginning
of this renewed community. The verbal
proclamation of the message is merely the
articulation of the community's self-consciousness,
of the community's reality.

NICHOLAS LASH
HIS PRESENCE IN THE WORLD

The work of God is the calling of a people, whether in the
Old Covenant or the New. The church is then
not simply the bearer of the message of reconciliation,
in the way a newspaper or a telephone
company can bear any message with which it is entrusted.
Nor is the church simply the result of a message,
as an alumni association is the product of a school or
the crowd in a theater is the product of the reputation of
the film. That men and women are called
together to a new social wholeness is itself the work of
God, which gives meaning to history.

JOHN HOWARD YODER
"A PEOPLE IN THE WORLD"

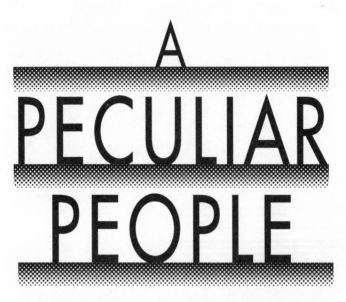

A PECULIAR PEOPLE

the church
as culture
in a post-
christian
society

Rodney
Clapp

IVP

InterVarsity Press
Downers Grove, Illinois

InterVarsity Press® is the book-publishing division of InterVarsity Christian Fellowship®, a student movement active on campus at hundreds of universities, colleges and schools of nursing in the United States of America, and a member movement of the International Fellowship of Evangelical Students. For information about local and regional activities, write Public Relations Dept., InterVarsity Christian Fellowship, 6400 Schroeder Rd., P.O. Box 7895, Madison, WI 53707-7895.

Scripture quotations, unless otherwise noted, are from the New Revised Standard Version of the Bible, copyright 1989 by the Division of Christian Education of the National Council of the Churches of Christ in the USA. Used by permission. All rights reserved.

Excerpt from "Manifesto: The Mad Farmer Liberation Front" in THE COUNTRY OF MARRIAGE, copyright © 1973 by Wendell Berry, reprinted by permission of Harcourt Brace & Company.

ISBN 0-8308-1990-8

Printed in the United States of America ♾

Library of Congress Cataloging-in-Publication Data

Clapp, Rodney.
  A peculiar people: the Church as culture in a post-Christian society/by Rodney Clapp.
     p.   cm.
  Includes bibliographical references.
  ISBN 0-8308-1990-8 (pbk.: alk. paper)
    1. Church.   2. Christianity and culture.   I. Title.
  BV600.2.C554   1996
  262—dc20   96-20803
                                                         CIP

20	19	18	17	16	15	14	13	12	11	10	9	8	7	6	5	4	3	2	1
13	12	11	10	09	08	07	06	05	04	03	02	01	00	99	98	97	96		

So long as women do not go cheap
for power, please women more than men.
Ask yourself: Will this satisfy
a woman satisfied to bear a child?
Will this disturb the sleep
of a woman near to giving birth?
Go with your love to the fields.
Lie easy in the shade. Rest your head
in her lap. Swear allegiance
to what is nighest in your thoughts.
As soon as the generals and the politicos
can predict the motion of your mind,
lose it. Leave it as a sign
to mark the false trail, the way
you didn't go. Be like the fox
who makes more tracks than necessary,
some in the wrong direction.
Practice resurrection.

from Wendell Berry,
"Manifesto: The Mad Farmer Liberation Front"

I dedicate this book to Sandy B., who has never gone cheap and has always corrected me with the moral gauge of the simplest, truest satisfactions and goes with me to the shade and has never denied me her lap and teaches me how to craftily lose my mind and with whom, I pray, someday to be resurrected.

Acknowledgments

One of the most pleasurable tasks of writing a book is thanking those who have helped it come to be. This book began as lectures at a retreat for the Episcopal clergy of the diocese of Iowa. I am grateful particularly to Bishop Christopher Epting for his invitation to speak.

Several people have read parts of the manuscript, have privileged me with their friendship, and remain in ongoing conversation about things theological, philosophical and cultural. They include Stanley Hauerwas, Philip Kenneson, Nancey Murphy, Tim Peebles, Jim Sire, Brian Walsh and David Wright.

Four other friends and conversation partners were prevailed upon to go even further and read the manuscript as a whole. I am grateful to Inagrace Dietterich for her criticisms, her boundless encouragement and her unflagging energy on behalf of God's church. Mark Nation did no less than read the manuscript on his honeymoon. While he assures me the reading did not interfere with more important matters, he offered helpful feedback and confirmed my reading of the work of John Howard Yoder. Greg Jones and Michael Cartwright read the manuscript quite closely, each delivering several helpful pages of comments. The book has been greatly improved via their generous critiques. They have done the additional service of keenly showing me where I need to think longer and harder—especially on the issue of authority.

For decades it was customary not to thank the editor of one's book. I am glad that custom has changed so that I can express my gratitude to my colleague Jim Hoover, who once again served as a faithful and sensitive editor. His encouragement and criticisms are not the less appreciated because they were offered in the line of duty. It has not, on the other hand, become customary to thank typesetters. Here justice and friendship demand departure from tradition so that I may acknowledge the irascible Gail Munroe, my surrogate big sister, who for a couple of weeks took time to typeset this book, and who every week assures that I never suffer a dull day at work.

This book is dedicated, with nary an exaggerated word, to Sandy, my spouse of nineteen years. Here I also thank my daughter, Jesselyn, who now is old enough to no longer claw imploringly on the closed door of Daddy's office. This summer, sweet girl, I promise more bike rides and hikes and trips to the pool.

Where
I'm Writing
From

eaders and writers are always in a relationship as complicated, and possibly as dangerous, as a blind date. After all, neither reader nor writer usually knows the other. Partly due to this, readers often find a writer maddeningly ambiguous. Sometimes they suspect the writer has an agenda he or she is less than forthcoming about. "What's he so angry over?" "Is she for or against [fill in whatever pet issues the book touches on]?" Such are the questions readers are forever asking themselves as they make their way through a book, much the way they would hack through a jungle full of mysteries both delightful and threatening.

Such uncertainty can weaken and distort the signal broadcast from author to reader. And such uncertainty may well be accentuated in a book like this one, wherein I will constantly call attention to context, to specific times and places, to distinctive identities and cultures. Given that I will mercilessly nag the reader not to forget that every perspective is particular and never simply universal, it seems fair enough that the reader might expect me to come clean about my own interests and location. In that spirit, and never presuming I know myself as truly as does my best friend or my worst enemy, I am willing to offer a few clues. If they do not put us on exactly the same wavelength, perhaps they will at least help you to better place my wavelength on your own tuning spectrum.

I write as a plebeian postmodern Christian. What in the world that means is exactly the burden of this book and, God willing, another one or two to follow. What it means more concisely is that I grew up a farm boy, on the dusty, treeless plains, in a region of Oklahoma once known as No Man's Land and mapped in the mid-nineteenth century as part of the "Great American Desert." In the language of a shipping company I once contacted to send some furniture there, my childhood home is a "beyond point."

Now if a colony is a people and a region whose resources are exploited to the advantage of a distant dominant order, all of rural America is today colonized. I no longer live in the colonies, but everything I most intensely care about has its origins, at least for me, in a particular colony. I am in that regard a plebeian, a commoner. I suppose I also resonate with plebeian interests because, though I am academically trained, I am not an academic. Holding no doctorate, I am not credentialed by or for the academy. My primary concern is for the church. If I am an intellectual, I am interested in thinking about issues that clearly impinge on and animate the "ordinary people" who, for the most part, make up the church.

Given that, though I will in this book devote attention to ideas, I do not see ideas as primary in Christian life and mission. What comes first is lived faith, or actual Christian community. Traditionally modern theology acts as if the church's main work is at the level of belief systems or worldviews. Evangelism and apologetics are then conceived of as intellectual combat, rational debate, dialectical dueling. Theologians working in this vein concentrate on philosophical concerns abstracted from material and political matters. The suffering of innocents, for example, then becomes a logical conundrum rather than a spiritual and ethical problem. I am barely animated by theology that fixates on such abstractions and cannot say what Trinity or eschatology has to do with sociocultural engagement. As a plebeian, I want theology that will help me survive, and survive Christianly, the Powers That Be.

In that postmoderns eschew as illusion the notion that there really is philosophy without perspective or theory without vested interests, I may be in this regard not only plebeian but also postmodern. In any event, I am convinced we live in a time of profound cultural change and that since this wild and woolly transitional period will certainly last the rest of my life, I might as well try to make the best of the ride. Put more specifically in terms of how this book will unfold, I am postmodern in that I have, by Christian motivation, renounced the longing for sure and certain, universal, once-for-all foundations to knowledge and action. I hope by such a move to build courage not to be cowed out of explicit Christian convictions by those who claim to speak for generalized "humanity" and to be in search of the "essential" truths—and who thereby may occasionally speak of an amorphous "God" but never finally of the distinctive "God the Father" of Jesus Christ.

Postmodernity brings with it the blurring of borders, the confusion of categories. This reassures me because I often find myself in between communities or categories. Put differently, I often find myself a member of two communities that true believers within each community regard as mortally opposed. My classical music CD club sometimes features, on the margin, some jazz and rock—but never, heaven forfend, any country music. Yet if I were being exiled to a desert island, I would pack Dwight Yoakam as well as Dvorak, Buck Owens as well as Bach, and the Mavericks as well as Mozart. Or to take another example, I am a member of the baby boom generation who is often more at home with so-called Generation Xers. Like the latter I am keen to meaning, more excited by relationships than possessions, and often happy to be cynical (not least because it seems that cynicism is the only faithful response to hypercommercialized Christianity).

In similar vein, I am trained academically in three fields often inimical to one another—theology, journalism and political science. Perhaps this is why I never became a doctrinaire respecter of disciplinary boundaries, and so am prone to borrowing from a number of disciplines. I would consider it a gross impoverishment not to read and learn from Renato Rosaldo as well as Karl Barth, Raymond Williams as well as John Calvin, Dostoyevsky as well as Reinhold Niebuhr. Maybe this results in work that is interdisciplinary, or maybe it just ends up undisciplinary. I am both plebeian and postmodern enough not to worry about it.

This reminds me of a song lyric by my favorite and patron Oklahoman, Woody Guthrie. It is not widely known that one of the verses of his "This Land Is Your Land" includes a reference to a "No Trespassing" sign. Woody observes that one side says "No Trespassing" but the other side is blank. So: the land on "that side was made for you and me." To those sociologists, anthropologists, literary theorists and others who may wonder what in the do-re-mi I'm doing wandering around in their fields in service of the Christian church, I can only say that I read the blank sides of your boundary notices.

But finally, and I pray most determinatively, I write as a Christian. My Christian background is certainly plebeian and perhaps also, in its eclecticism, postmodern. I grew up country-church United Methodist, where most of our pastors were former Nazarenes who had left that denomination in quest of salaries that would feed their families. In college I attended churches in the decidedly plebeian traditions of the Southern Baptist Convention and the Christian and Missionary Alliance. On a less plebeian note, I have for more than fifteen years been a confirmed Episcopalian. Through Donald Bloesch and especially my graduate school teachers Robert Webber and Lauree Hersch Meyer, I learned to appreciate the church in its depth and breadth, back to and beyond the Reformation to the church fathers. Thus perhaps the most formative "canonical" theologians for me have been Irenaeus, Athanasius, Augustine, Karl Barth, Dietrich Bonhoeffer and H. Richard Niebuhr. Growing appreciation of the church Catholic established me in sacramental and eucharistically centered worship and spirituality, through which I discovered sturdier resources of the faith than I had before ever imagined and finally made sense of the revivalistic/evangelical talk of a "personal relationship" with Jesus Christ. Later, in the work of John Howard Yoder and Stanley Hauerwas I was drawn to and profoundly influenced by Anabaptist theology and social ethics. Stanley's writing also introduced me to what has since come to be widely known as postliberalism—not least the work of George Lindbeck, William Placher and George Hunsinger. As the following pages betray, it is the neo-Anabaptists and the postliberals who, among contemporary theologians, I think most faithfully and adeptly fit us for the challenges of this day and place.

Of course, this book is published by a Protestant evangelical press—and, what's more, my entire professional (editorial) life has been spent at evangelical institutions. For inquiring readers of various sorts, this in itself leads to pressing questions about where I am writing from. Those outside what in North America is called evangelicalism may wonder how much I really care about the church beyond conservative Protestantism. Some within conservative Protestantism will be put on guard by professed friendliness to the "post" plagues of postmodernity and postliberalism, not to mention Karl Barth. To the reader with qualms from either direction, the best counsel is surely taste and see for yourself. Beyond that, I would again remind such readers that these really are days of blurred borders. Be careful whom you hate or dismiss out of hand. Tomorrow you may have to pass them the kiss of peace.

1

THE CHURCH AS UNCHURCH
How Christians Became Useless

P*riest and spiritual writer Henri Nouwen tells a significant story*
about what it means to be a Christian amid the late-twentieth-
century ruins of Christendom. Years ago, Nouwen was chaplain
of a Holland-America cruise line. He stood one day on the bridge of a
Dutch ship mucking its way through a thick fog into the port of
Rotterdam. "The fog was so thick, in fact, that the steersman could not
even see the bow of the ship. The captain, carefully listening to a radar
station operator who was explaining his position between other ships,
walked nervously up and down the bridge."

In the process of his nervous pacing, the captain collided with his
ship's chaplain. Adrift in anxiety as well as fog, the captain cursed the
chaplain and told him to stay out of the way. "But," says Nouwen, "when
I was ready to run away, filled with feelings of incompetence and guilt,
he came back and said: 'Why don't you just stay around. This might be

the only time I really need you.' "

Musing, Nouwen elaborates on how the experience is all too typical of ministerial—and, I would add, lay Christian—frustrations, on or off an ocean liner.

> There was a time, not too long ago, when we felt like captains running our own ships, with a great sense of power and self-confidence. Now we are standing in the way. That is our lonely position: We are powerless, on the side, . . . not taken very seriously when the weather is fine.

Father Nouwen concludes that Christians long to "touch the center" of men's and women's lives but instead find ourselves on the "periphery, often pleading in vain for admission." We seem no longer "to be where the action is, where the plans are made and the strategies are discussed."[1]

We live in times of dawning and sometimes bitter irony. A long story, the first chapter of which was written seventeen hundred years ago when Constantine made Christianity the official religion of the Roman Empire, now nears its end.[2] For the better part of recorded history, the church has been the sponsor of western civilization. Like gym-shoe manufacturers who win the right to advertise their wares with the world's most famous athletes, the church has coveted its association with Western civilization. Western civilization has been so powerful economically, militarily, technologically and culturally that the church, in sponsoring it, has seemed close to the center not merely of a few men's and women's lives but of history itself.

Yet exactly at this point the irony intrudes. Just when the Western inventions of capitalism, democracy and modernity reign over or are aspired to throughout the world; just when some declare that the West has won and history has reached its goal; just when America, the leading and pioneering capitalist, democratic and modern nation, becomes the world's sole superpower—just now the church is informed that its sponsorship is no longer needed or wanted. Western civilization (or, more accurately, Western civilizations) is no longer content with a single religious sponsor. Quite a few influential people, in fact, think they can do without any sort of religious sponsorship at all.

So here stands the Christian, chaplain on a ship with a destination sure and true, even if the surrounding fog sometimes gets pretty dense. The captain, the real mover and shaker in our world, wants the Christian out of the way. Let him, let her, goof off with the deckhands. Let the Christian divert and console these and other inconsequential people. And maybe, in a tight spot, let the Christian launch some prayers or perform some other hocus-pocus which at least will have the effect of calming and keeping the masses under control. But for crying out loud, keep the Christian off the bridge, out of the map room, away from the wheel. And when the ship has docked, don't let the religious fanatic in the corporate boardroom or the congressional chamber. There's work to be done in the real world.

Things to Do with Obsolete Chaplains

If all the genuinely significant work can be done just as well without them, no wonder Christians feel redundant or useless. One response is to decide Christianity and the church actually are redundant, depart the faith and get a truly honest line of work. Stay on the ocean liner, but retrain and serve as a chef or a counselor or maybe even a captain. Given the much-discussed rate of decline of mainline Protestant denominations in the United States and the United Kingdom, this must be an option often exercised by the sons and daughters of mainliners.[3]

Having grown up in the United Methodist Church myself, I distinctly remember Sunday-school curriculum that taught us Christians are people who are polite to the postman. If there is no more to it than that, Christianity is just archaic language and mystified formalities that get in the way. You can, indeed, counsel hurting people or do social action without being a Christian. A Christianity reducible to therapy or activism is, in the end, sentimentality. It is therapy and activism performed by people who could as easily do what they do without talk of Jesus and Israel and the kingdom of God, but who have mouthed these platitudes so long they can't quite let them go.

The family home is run down and uninhabited, but you can't just sell it, because after all you grew up there. Better, then, for this sort of Christian to keep going through the motions, as a bureaucrat or administrator, perhaps presiding at weddings and funerals, which seem vaguely more fitting if there is a religious air about them.

I would call this response to dying Christendom *sentimental capitulation*. It admits that in this modern (or postmodern), democratic, capitalistic world, the church has nothing distinctive to offer or to be. But it sentimentally hangs on to some Christian language and practice anyway. This option is rarely expressed with more candor or self-awareness than that of the Episcopal bishop John Shelby Spong, who has declared,

> The only churches that grow today are those that do not, in fact, understand the issues, and can therefore traffic in certainty. They represent both the fundamentalistic Protestant groups and the rigidly controlled conservative Catholic traditions. The churches that do attempt to interact with the emerging world are for the most part the liberal Protestant mainline churches that shrink every day in membership and the silent liberal Catholic minority that attracts very few adherents. Both are, almost by definition, fuzzy, imprecise and relatively unappealing. They might claim to be honest, but for the most part *they have no real message.*[4]

Note that this is not a critic of sentimental capitulation speaking from outside it. Spong identifies with this strategy. He believes the only genuine way to "interact with the emerging world" is to concede most of the game to it. This entails being "fuzzy" and "relatively unappealing." It means gaining honesty by admitting you "have no real message." But it avoids the unthinkable alternative of being fundamentalist or a "rigidly controlled" conservative Catholic.

And on the Bishop's Right . . .

One definition of the demonic is that it is that which we least want to become. During the Cold War communists were demonized: the worst thing imaginable was to be accused of being "Red." It's safe to say Bishop Spong's demons are fundamentalists. Call him a heretic, suggest he's not really a Christian, and he will only sell more books. But please, the bishop protests, never mistake him for a fundamentalist.

Repaying the favor, self-identified fundamentalists would never want to be mistaken for Bishop Spong's ilk. Yet I think both these camps fit in the same picture frame. The chaplain who capitulates but continues to fill ceremonial roles, providing a quaint if feckless presence at weddings and funerals—that chaplain blurs into the second and much more popular chaplaincy of the religious right.

The response of the religious right entails denying redundancy, sure enough, but it too wants to remain on ship as a chaplain. Like the bishop, the religious right wants to maintain close association with and sponsorship of Western civilization. But unlike Bishop Spong, it will act as a chaplain that has regained some (eventually all) the power the chaplaincy held in earlier Christendom. I will, then, call this option *retrenchment.*

Retrenchment occurs in several nations, including South Africa and Britain. We see an attempt at retrenchment when religious conservatives insist that theirs has been and should be again a Christian nation. In the United States, for example, *The Wall Street Journal* has reported on a California organization called Citizens for Excellence in Education, dedicated to restoring prayer to the schoolhouse and teaching the story of creation in the science classroom. The group works to elect Christian governmental officials, believing with one of its affiliates that government should be the "police department within the Kingdom of God on earth," ready to "impose God's vengeance upon those who abandon God's laws of justice."[5]

Better-known figures such as television evangelist and erstwhile presidential candidate Pat Robertson profess that America "was once a predominantly Christian nation." Calling for power politics that would "jam Capitol Hill phone lines and swamp congressional mailrooms," Robertson says, "I have enormous confidence in the strategy we've put together to change America and restore her moral strength, because there are an estimated 40 million eligible Christian voters nationwide."[6] Another well-known proponent of the religious right, Pastor D. James Kennedy, is even more straightforward than Robertson. Kennedy sees a battle for the soul of the nation, a battle waged by two armies: the secular humanists and the "Christian contingent that founded this nation and upon whose morality all of the laws originally were founded. . . . Our responsibility in the church is to insist that the laws of this Christian nation be consistent with God's Word."[7]

Others who would retrench hope to regain proximity to the wheel more subtly. Some are reluctant to let go of civil religion, which they often characterize as "Judeo-Christianity." (Strange faith, that has no actual living, card-carrying adherents—have you ever met anyone who called herself a Judeo-Christian?) These milder retrenchers remind those in power that religion can serve as a glue holding otherwise disparate parts of the nation together.

But perhaps the most popular form of retrenchment, at least in North America, is to ignore politics altogether and turn inward. Churches and pastors imitate the "helping professions," especially psychotherapy. To what we Americans oxymoronically call private citizens, these retrenchers suggest that Christianity is really about making people healthy and wealthy. It, or at least some religion, is a necessary component in the successful pursuit of happiness.

Therapeutic and marketing techniques are key for these retrenchers. They preach a kind of religious Reaganomics: "Ask yourself: Are you spiritually better off, more comfortable and tranquil and satisfied, than you were four years ago? If not, then you need our church." They read McDonald's ads more carefully than they do the Bible, then declare, "You deserve a break today, and the whole purpose of God's existence is to give it to you." What they present are, as one observer notes, the " 'Be-Happy Attitudes,' and they emanate not only from the Crystal Cathedral, but from a variety of religious edifices. They are not stances that question the dominant culture; instead they embody it."[8] Such declarations and practices, in other words, assert that there is still plenty for the Christian as chaplain—as sponsor and booster of an already existing culture—to do.

Emperor of the Imagination

As you may have guessed, I am not sympathetic to the option of retrenchment. Neither do I believe that the church and its work are in fact redundant or useless. Rather, I believe our imaginations have been entirely too circumscribed. Since the fourth-century emperor Constantine, too many Christians have too readily equated the church's work with religious sponsorship of the status quo. Both retrenchment and sentimental capitulation redefine the church and its mission on secular or worldly terms. And too many Christians continue to think these are our only options. Constantine remains the emperor of our imagination, even if he no longer rules our politics.

For centuries, most Christians have been eager to adapt the ways of the world and tell it that it is right. So doing, we make ourselves redundant. For then, as Stanley Hauerwas has said, the church "has nothing to bring to the dialogue; it announces to the secular world, as though by way of discovery, what the secular world has been announcing to it for a rather long time."[9] Indeed, philosopher Alasdair MacIntyre points out that the theist-atheist debate has been less and less interesting throughout modernity, since the theist in full retreat offers the atheist less and less to challenge.[10]

The sense of Christian and churchly uselessness is heightened as a society becomes secular not only in fact but more and more by its own confession. For a while there is an awkward period in which the society clings, with growing halfheartedness, to its Christian connection. So the captain on Nouwen's ocean liner first curses and banishes his chaplain, but then feels obscurely uneasy. There's still some sentiment and cloudy ceremony surrounding Christianity. Maybe Chaplain Nouwen should hang around, at least in case of the occasional storm. Such are the expectations when we sail in a world without the substance, but some remaining trappings, of Christendom. In these awkward, ambivalent times, many people seem to believe there is no God but it's prudent to pray to him from time to time.[11]

And yet if some ruins of Constantine's settlement still stand, I think it is clear that they are beyond repair. By one of God's mysterious and severe graces, we find ourselves in a pluralistic, postmodern world that forces us closer to a pre-Constantinian relation to the cultures around us.[12]

Let me put it this way: Christians feel useless because the church feels useless. And the church feels useless because it keeps on trying to perform Constantinian duties in a world that is no longer Constantinian. So the grace is this: Christians feel useless because they are no longer useful for the wrong thing, namely serving as chaplains in a sponsorial religion.

This, then, is a book about the mission and ministry of the church after Constantine. It best begins by accounting for how we got where we are.

The Constantinian Shift

Summing up the ambiguity of the Roman emperor Constantine, and what has come to be called Constantinianism, the classical scholar Charles Norris Cochrane writes that Constantine may have been unique, "the one human being to have enjoyed the distinction of being deified as a pagan god, while, at the same time, he was popularly venerated as a Christian saint."[13] Allegedly having seen a vision of Christ's cross in the sky as he rode into battle, Constantine was the first emperor to convert (at least ostensibly) to what had been a despised and dismissed "slave religion." For better and for worse, this conversion changed history.

What might be called the Constantinian shift began around the year 200 and took more than two hundred years to grow and unfold to full bloom.[14] Thus it began before Constantine's birth and matured after his death. Yet this monumental shift well deserves his name. Not only was he the first emperor to convert, he made his aim the legislation of Christ's millennial kingdom in a generation.[15] And indeed he enacted a number of laws that no doubt pleased the church of his day—making divorce difficult, aiding the poor and ending the gladiatorial games, for instance. Less grandiosely but more lastingly, Constantine was the first in what would be a long line of emperors, princes and presidents who saw Christianity as the unifying force that might bind and discipline their otherwise diverse subjects.

I do not want to pretend that the pre-Constantinian church was all good and the church after Constantine all bad. From Pentecost onward, the church has always lived in tension, never, as even a cursory reading of 1 Corinthians reminds us, being more than comparatively faithful. "Constantinianism," then, is not an excuse for ignoring or despising the history of the church beyond the New Testament. The significance of the symbol or concept of Constantinianism is to indicate that the pre-Constantinian church did not see itself as the sponsor of the world, with "world" here meaning the fallen and rebellious creation.

Sponsorship is a tricky affair, as soda pop and automobile makers nervously demonstrate when their celebrity commits a crime or loses the national championship. Etymologically, the word springs from the Latin *sponsus,* which has to do with guaranteeing and taking responsibility for the achievement of a desired outcome. The guarantor warrants, pledges or promises for that which is guaranteed. So guarantors are responsible for payment on a loan if the debtor defaults on it. Here is where sponsorship gets tricky. Whose identity and purpose are more determinant, the sponsor's or the sponsored's?

In baptismal sponsorship, the sponsor's identity and purposes are more fundamental and determinant than those of the baptismal candidate—often, as in my Anglican tradition, an infant with only the most nascent identity and purposes of its own. Here the candidate is sponsored into the Christian community and faith, on that community's and faith's terms. The sponsor will, in the Book of Common Prayer's words, "be responsible for seeing that the child you present is brought up in the Christian faith and life."[16]

But there are other kinds of sponsorship. Surely the most pervasive in our time is commercial sponsorship. In the commercial realm a sponsor wants to associate with an athlete, movie star, television program or celebrated event in order to gain prominence and favor through the sponsored's visibility and popularity. So Nike sponsored Michael Jordan, one of the most famous athletes in the history of any game. No one seriously believed it was Nike shoes that enabled Jordan to defy gravity, to slip Houdini-like through three defenders for the score, to consistently slacken spectators' jaws with amazement. In such a case the sponsor's identity and purposes are clearly less fundamental than the sponsored's. Visit Chicago's Niketown—a five-story shrine disguised as a department store—and you will find encased for adoration not only Jordan's footwear and jerseys but also a wall-sized poster of the shoe-god soaring through the sky. Nike quite successfully has aimed to get people to associate its goods with basketball magic: Michael Jordan Just Does It.

Similarly, with the Constantinian shift the church decided to derive its significance through association with the identity and purposes of the state. In the pre-Constantinian setting, the church saw the state as having a preservative function. It was "to serve God by encouraging the good and restraining evil, i.e., to serve peace, to preserve the social cohesion in which the leaven of the gospel can build the church" and render the present age more tolerable.[17] All this made the state important, but hardly central. The church considered itself, not the state, to be carrying the meaning of history. In the words of the letter to the Ephesians, it is "through the church" that "the wisdom of God in its rich variety" is "made known to the rulers and authorities" (3:10).

As theologian John Howard Yoder observes, the most "pertinent fact" of the Constantinian shift was not that the church was no longer persecuted but that the two visible realities of church and world were fused. There was, in a sense, no longer anything to call "world"—state, economy, art, rhetoric, superstition and war were all baptized.[18] This is much of what it means for Constantine to be credited, as Cochrane credited him, as the architect of the Middle Ages.[19]

Yet even if the distinction between church and world was blurred, and to a large degree eliminated, it was still necessary to distinguish true believers from nominal or false believers. St. Augustine, for example, thought that true Christians might make up as little as 5 percent of the visible church/world.[20] So he and other theologians constructed and refined the doctrine of the true *but now invisible* church. Yoder summarizes the reversal neatly. Before Constantine "Christians had known as a fact of experience that the Church existed, but had to believe against appearances that Christ ruled over the world. After Constantine one knew as a fact of experience that Christ was ruling over the world, but had to believe against the evidence that there existed a believing Church."[21]

Several important corollaries followed. With Constantine, Christian history begins to be told as the story of dynasties. The ruler, not the ordinary person, is made the model for ethical deliberations. The question is no longer "How can we survive and remain faithful Christians under Caesar?" but now becomes "How can we adjust the church's expectations so that Caesar can consider himself a faithful Christian?" Thus the ethical requirements of the church were adapted to the level of what might be called "respectable unbelief."[22] The statesman must be seen as Christian, but without significantly changing his statecraft. The morality of a statement or action is tested on the basis of whether or not the ruler can meet such standards (say, telling the truth, or not killing).

As Yoder writes, "The place of the church or of persons speaking for Christian morality . . . is that of 'chaplaincy,' i.e., a part of the power structure itself. The *content* of ethical guidance is not the teaching of Jesus but the duties of 'station,' 'office' or 'vocation.' "[23] Lawyers will play by the rules of the guild of lawyers, doctors by the guild of doctors, bankers by the guild of bankers and so forth. Christian lawyers, doctors and bankers may be different in some ways from their non-Christian colleagues, but they accept their professions as basically defined and regulated apart from the radical formative power of the Christian story.

In a real sense, then, it becomes fine and commendable for professing Christians to participate in the state and other realms of culture *as if* the lordship of Christ made no concrete difference. Even for Christians, culture begins to be seen as autonomous, as holding its own key to its establishment, maintenance and true purposes. The church, in other words, is in the process of creating secularism, a secularism that even Christians must laud and obey.[24]

Yet if early on the line between church and world was blurred, it was not entirely rubbed out. The Middle Ages retained some sense of distinctness between the church and the world. For instance, a higher level of morality was expected of clergy than of laypersons. Then there was the international character of the church hierarchy and the visibility of the church hierarch in occasional opposition to the princes. There were also occasional confrontations with the so-called barbarians, those beyond even nominal Christianity. Such things preserved some sense of what Yoder calls "the strangeness of God's people in a rebellious world."[25]

Lamenting the Reformation

But much of this changed with the advent of the Reformation. Of course the Reformation served in many respects as a vital corrective to the direction of Christian history and development. It issued a fresh and desperately needed call to return to our foundational story, the story of Israel and Jesus found in the Bible. And it instituted urgent changes that enabled all believers, not just an elite, to drink from the deepest and clearest springs of the faith. But, fatefully, between 1522 and 1525 the Reformers decided in favor of political conservatism, not to challenge the Constantinian settlement. As Yoder puts it, "The Reformers knew very well of the 'Fall of the Church'; but they dated this fall not in the fourth century but rather in the sixth and seventh. They did not see that the signs of fallenness to which they objected— papacy, Pelagianism, hagiolatry, sacramentalism—were largely fruits of the earlier confusion of Church and world."[26]

Thus the Reformers abandoned many of the very things that had continued to distinguish the church from the world: the international hierarchy of the church, the higher ethical commitments of the monastic orders, the international missionary character of the Roman Catholic Church. In the face of monasticism, the Reformation affirmed the ethical value of secular vocations. There was, of course, something to applaud in this. But the imprecision of terms, as Yoder notes, "amounted to the claim . . . that every calling has its own norm."[27] Despite the Reformers' intentions, the autonomy of the state and vocations was furthered by what they said and did.[28]

It is also extremely significant that as the Reformers strove to carry through their reforms, they did not call on an abstract "state" to assist them. They called on actual, particular, territorial states and their representatives, such as the Elector of Saxony and Milords of Zurich. Consequently particular, territorial states were loosed from the check or challenge of the overarching, transnational church hierarchy. At this point, Yoder notes,

> the conviction that the center of the meaning of history is in the work of the Church, which had been central in the pre-Constantinian Church and remained half-alive in the Middle Ages, is now expressly rejected. . . . The Church confesses in deed and sometimes in word that not she, but the State, has the last word and incarnates the ultimate values of God's work in the world. What is called "Church" is an administrative branch of the State on the same level with the Army or Post Office. Church discipline is applied by the civil courts and police. It is assumed that there is nothing wrong with this since the true Church, being invisible, is not affected.[29]

Again, this is not what the Reformers intended. They wanted to renew the visible, faithful body of believers. But in looking to the princes for support, they unleashed "the drives toward autonomy which exist in the State and other realms of culture" and which were "too strong to be controlled once they had been let loose."[30] The Reformers were emphatically right to appeal to the scriptural Word, to hail the divine ordination of the "secular" order. But they did not reexamine the Constantinian synthesis itself and thus inadvertently "created modern secularism."[31] What this means, to borrow the words of theologian John Milbank, is that the Reformation "completely privatized, spiritualized and transcendentalized the sacred" and at the same time "reimagined nature, human action and society as a sphere of autonomous, sheerly formal power."[32]

The Trajectory from Constantinianism to Deism

Now some Christians, namely those in the Anabaptist tradition in which Yoder does theology, have worried over these developments for centuries. But for those of us in other traditions, the pitfalls of Constantinianism have come clear only with more recent history. Reformed

Protestants have been particularly comfortable in the United States of America, where, in the earliest days, "the overwhelming majority of Americans were self-consciously rooted in variations of Reformed theology."[33] Even as Christianity was officially disestablished, the quasi-establishment of Protestantism endured well into the nineteenth century. It was, for instance, safely assumed that most Americans were leery of Roman Catholicism and abhorred marital infidelity. Protestantism influenced law, not too subtly shaped and suffused public education, founded colleges and provided agendas for social reform.

But from the 1830s onward came a massive influx of Catholic and Jewish immigrants. This caused significant problems for the Protestant majority, but eventually Catholics and Jews were in sufficient number that they had to be heard. Thus came the innovation and rise of "Judeo-Christianity," so that well into the twentieth century the country continued to see itself unified around a sure if vaguely defined biblical center. As Rabbi Solomon Schechter declared in 1903, "This country is, as everybody knows, a creation of the Bible, particularly the Old Testament."[34] And indeed the Bible provided important symbols of national identity—such as the adaptation of the imagery of the exodus and the linking of American destiny with the kingdom of God.

The Constantinian habit is hard to break, especially in America. So over the history of the United States, historians Robert Linder and Richard Pierard write, the "umbrella" of nominally Christian civil religion "has been enlarged from evangelical consensus to Protestantism-in-general, to Christianity-in-general, to the Judeo-Christian-tradition-in-general, to deism-in-general."[35]

Inarguably, at least when we have arrived at deism-in-general, we are talking about a gross distortion of the Christian God and the Christian faith. Constantinian culture appears to promise much in return for the church's sponsorship, but the contract carries terms that actually, if subtly at first, require the church to stop being the church, a people who worship and follow not the amorphous god of deism but the quite specific God of Abraham, Isaac, Jacob and Jesus. Perhaps most important for our current situation, the Constantinian settlement demands that the Christian faith be privatized and individualized. As Yoder comments,

> Interiorization and individualization [of the faith] . . . were not purely philosophical invasions which took over because they were intellectually convincing. They did so also because they were functional. They explained and justified the growing distance from Jesus and his replacement by other authorities and another political vision than that of the Kingdom of God.[36]

Pluralization and the Problem of Umbrellas

Since Constantinianism bears such fruit (and I will argue in more detail in the next chapter that it does), I think it clear enough that it is a theological and missiological mistake. I doubt it would be too provocative at this juncture in history to say that the near-identification of Christianity with the nation-state has been nothing short of disastrous.

This unfortunate marriage meant, among other things, that the "other" or stranger had now to be responded to violently. The pre-Constantinian church saw the outsider as in some sense privileged, as a kind of test of one's love (Mt 5:43-48; Lk 6:32-36). The church in the Middle Ages had largely ignored the outsider as "barbarian" or heretical. But with the Constantinian wedding of church and territorial state enabled by the Reformation, the outsider became the "infidel," the incarnation of antifaith. And destroying the outsider became a "positively virtuous undertaking."[37]

Most Christians can now see this was a tremendous error, harmful both to the world and to the mission and credibility of the church. But Constantinianism is a hard habit to break, and so a significant number of Christians can still fall into a barely diluted version of it. In January of 1992, President George Bush addressed the National Association of Religious Broadcasters, wanting to say "thank you for helping America, as Christ ordained, to be 'a light unto the world.' " He linked this with the Persian Gulf War, a war he characterized in distinctly black-and-white crusade terms as a conflict of "good versus evil" and "right versus wrong." Sadly, as Richard John Neuhaus writes, "thousands of Christian leaders, mainly evangelicals, responded with standing ovations."[38]

In this light, and that of many other examples that could be accumulated, we can hardly overestimate the tenacity of Constantinianism. And yet it has progressively eroded, taking more and more attenuated forms. To cite again historians Linder and Pierard, the "umbrella" of Constantinian civil religion in the United States "has been enlarged from evangelical consensus to Protestantism-in-general, to Christianity-in-general, to the Judeo-Christian-tradition-in-general, to deism-in-general."[39]

And since World War II Americans have arrived at a place where even something as foggy as "deism-in-general" can no longer serve as the unofficial religious sponsor of the nation. What has happened, in a word, is pluralization.

Perhaps the reality of pluralism is most vividly captured with a question. Where is North America's oldest Islamic mosque? Not in New York or Chicago, but in Cedar Rapids, Iowa. In the middle of middle America, in a part of the country where baseball, hot dogs, apple pie, Mother and other things quintessentially American remain as important as ever, Muslim immigrants in 1934 built their first North American place of worship. Now there are seventy-two hundred Muslim families in Iowa, plus five thousand Muslim college students. Fewer than sixty years after the first was built, there are six hundred mosques in the United States. As one of those Muslim Iowans, Mohammad Kahn, understates the matter, "It shows there here in a small place in Iowa, in a place practically nobody knows about, we have made a lot of progress, and that this nation has changed in [a few] years."[40]

Of course other faiths such as Hinduism, Buddhism and a host of "new religions" have grown rapidly as well. And we cannot overlook the swelling numbers of professing secularists. Now the fastest-growing community of "moral conviction" in America, this group grew from 2 percent of the population in 1962 to nearly 11 percent by the end of the eighties.[41]

Introducing a Third R

These are cultural circumstances that those who would retrench toward a robust Constantinianism can acknowledge only with regret. Some retrenchers would aggressively turn the clock back. More moderate retrenchers see that as hopeless and even undesirable. Yet, short of such aims and measures, they are left with a Christianity so diluted, so unspecified, so instrumentalized that there seems little justification in retaining the Christianity itself. (So it is that the retrenchment of a Pat Robertson and the sentimental capitulation of a Bishop Spong are strategies that differ only in degree, not in kind. Given their common pedigree of Constantinian Christianity, the prince of the religious right and the avant-garde bishop are actually twins separated at birth.) If the church is nothing more than, for instance, a volunteer social work force or political lobby, then why fool with liturgy, the Bible and other encumbrances of the Christian tradition? Why not just form volunteer social work forces and political lobbies? And if the pastor is, in the end, nothing more than a psychotherapist, why have her preach at us in the hoary language of sin and redemption? Why not skip theology and church history and get thoroughly trained as a competent counselor?

These are questions that could have been asked some time ago, but they are pressed on us by the pluralistic ethos of postmodernity.[42] They push Christians toward the options of retrenchment, relinquishment (sentimental capitulation) or, to add a third R, *radicalization.*

From the viewpoint of the radical Christian, postmodernity carries its pains and challenges, but also its promises. For radicals, postmodern pluralism is a social condition in which the Constantinianism that has always been a theological dead end now becomes a political and sociological dead end. There is a place for Christians in the postmodern world, not as typically decent human beings but as unapologetic followers of the Way. There is a place for the church in the postmodern world, not as a sponsorial prop for nation-states but as a community called by the God explicitly named Father, Son and Holy Spirit.

The radical option is nothing more or less than for the church to be a way of life. But what could that mean? In a word, salvation and life itself. In more than a word—well, that demands at least a book.

2

THE CHURCH AS PRIVATE CLUB
Irrelevant for Constantine's Sake

What can it mean for the Christian church to be a way of life? Briefly, it means seeing and practicing church as itself a culture and a political community. But what could *that* possibly mean? I will begin to unpack that constructively in chapter four. But here and in chapter three, I will unpack it critically or negatively by contrasting it with the predominant strategies of retrenchment today.

One of those strategies (the subject of chapter three) is to make the nation-state America the church. The subject of this chapter is that mode of retrenchment that privatizes Christianity. This strategy conceptualizes faith as opposite of the social and cultural, but very much as individualistic. It flees and denies any sort of politics. Such a strategy is Constantinian. As I have noted, drawing from John Howard Yoder, "Interiorization and individualization . . . were not purely philosophical invasions which took over because they were intellectually convincing. . . . They explained and justified the growing distance from Jesus and his replacement by other authorities and another political vision than that of the Kingdom of God."[1]

In fact, I want to argue that America has so eagerly and thoroughly been Constantinian that it does have a true "old-time" and civil religion, but this religion is not Christianity. It is instead that eminently interiorized and individualized faith called gnosticism.

The Gnostic Temptation

Gnosticism, of course, dates from the second century—making it one of the oldest and most persistent enemies of Christianity. In saying that America's real old-time religion is gnosticism, I do not mean George Washington or Thomas Jefferson looked directly to Valentinus, Manichee or any other self-declared ancient Gnostic. And certainly most current-day Americans have never heard of these characters. Rather, what Americans have long been interested in is the gnostic *type* of religion, the tendency to believe and act as if faith and salvation were essentially private, acultural and ahistorical.

As Philip J. Lee notes, "The gnostic escape, in the last analysis, is an attempt to escape from everything except the self."[2] The world, history and community are ultimately viewed with suspicion. The gnostic believes faith is a solitary affair between himself or herself and God. As Harold Bloom puts it, "Salvation, for the American, cannot come through the community or congregation, but is a one-on-one act of confrontation" with God. The American Jesus, Bloom suggests, "cannot be known in or through a church, but only one on one." This Jesus "is not so much an event in history . . . as he is a knower of the secrets of God who in turn can only be known by the individual."[3]

In this regard I think of popular American hymnody, shot through with images such as coming to the garden "alone," where Jesus "walks with me and talks with me." I think of a song we sang lustily in my high-school church group, to the effect that "me and Jesus got our own thing going." I think, more recently, of speaking at a convention about the necessity of the church to Christian family formation, and being approached afterward by an American Muslim woman who asserted I should affirm instead "the Jesus within all of our hearts, no matter what our religion."

These are indeed gnostic encounters with a gnostic Jesus. As New Testament scholar N. T. Wright notes, once we grasp a distorted and overemphasized "*pro me* of the gospel, the idea that God is 'being gracious to *me*,' we no longer need Jesus to be too firmly rooted in history."[4] Indeed, concentrating on the self and its individual salvation, we do not want a Jesus rooted in history, for that would be a particular Jesus who might reveal a particular God with a character and purpose different from our own. Nor do we want a Jesus who might be known in community or through the activities of a culture. All this runs against the American grain of discovering God within the self, a direction set at least since the early 1800s.

Consider Ralph Waldo Emerson's classic essay "Self-Reliance." Emerson forthrightly defines self-reliance as "a new respect for the divinity in man." Again and again he makes it clear that the divinity he seeks is found in the individual "man." Society, he says, is "everywhere in conspiracy against the manhood of every one of its members. . . . Whoso would be a man, must be a nonconformist." He counsels, "Trust *your* emotion," for the "primary wisdom" is the individual's intuition. But what if your impulses and intuition are evil? Emerson, here unafraid of the hobgoblin of consistency, answers, " 'They do not seem to me to be such; but if I am the devil's child, I will live from the devil.' No law can be sacred to me but that of my nature." It becomes nothing short of sacrilege to suggest that the individual might conform his or her faith to the Bible, tradition or the church:

> The relations of the soul to the divine spirit are so pure that it is profane to seek to interpose helps. . . . Whenever a mind is simple and receives a divine wisdom, then old things pass away,—means, teachers, texts, temples fall; it lives now, and absorbs past and future into the present hour. . . . If therefore a man claims to know and speak of God and carries you backward to the phraseology of some

old mouldered nation in another country [such as Israel?], in another world, believe him not.[5]

Bloom bluntly and correctly recognizes Emerson's "self-reliance" as "self-idolatry."[6] I think Bloom is also correct to see self-idolatry—or marked tendencies toward it—in such disparate American manifestations of faith as revivalism, the Southern Baptist Convention, Mormonism and that sometimes "charming parody" of the American religion dubbed the New Age movement.

It is the pervasive American understanding that faith is an individual concern, something that gives color to our private lives but is not publicly accountable. What I think or feel about God is between me and my conscience. "Spirituality" is an amorphous, ever mutable engagement between two isolated selves—the human individual and "God," both apart from the world, change, time, place and community.

A Homegrown Syncretism

We begin, then, to see how American Christians of all stripes could so easily and swiftly adopt a neutered, more or less totally psychologized faith, a faith that can profess with a straight face that God exists to "meet my needs." We have been quick to recognize the syncretism of Christians in, say, Africa or Indonesia, but blind to our own Constantinian gnosticism. To know our homegrown syncretism better, we might learn something of its past.

Historian Donald Meyer worries that over the last two centuries the Christian church in America has grown progressively less stimulating and challenging, becoming more and more of a reactive or merely reflexive institution. And he links this development with the church's— and the culture's—growing preoccupation with psychological therapy.[7]

Meyer observes that the nineteenth was a great century for (white) men. The nation was rapidly expanding, so there were railroads and telegraphs and entire towns to build. Banks and dozens of other businesses proliferated like weeds. Artisans, mechanics and engineers faced an abundance of energizing challenges. But with all the excitement going on beyond the front door of the family home, the nineteenth was not such a great century for women. Industrialization decisively moved them into the private sphere, with little of significance to do. Women, designated guardians of children, religion and morality, were rendered pure but ineffectual. They did not affect the "real world" of commerce, the arts and politics.[8]

Unable to do anything in the "real world," but dissatisfied, women turned inward. They assumed the cause of their dissatisfaction must rest in themselves. And so followed the rise of cultic illness and the creation of mind cure groups (such as the Christian Scientists) by women (such as Mary Baker Eddy) and largely for women. As Meyer argues, sickness was a route to meaning and significance for the "pure but weak"—a kind of escape enabling "a project which at the same time did not require one to wrestle with the world."[9] Mind cure groups were emphatically apolitical. They organized nothing for the society around them. And in a global sense they had a narrow appeal. There were, for instance, no converts in Naples or Calcutta. Outside the United States, Meyer notes, mind cure appealed only to ladies in the English upper middle class, women in a similar situation of affluence and privatization.[10]

With the mind cure movement, Americans first adapted a new definition of health. Before affluence, Meyer writes, health was understood only as a means to an end. Health was good because it was a necessary condition for anyone to accomplish worthwhile ends. You could not lay a railroad or missionize China without being of able body and sound mind. This attitude, of health as instrumental rather than an end in itself, is exemplified by the seventeenth-century Puritan divine Richard Sibbes. Sibbes declared, "This is a sign of a man's victory over himself, when he loves health and peace of body and mind . . . chiefly for this end, that he may with more freedom of spirit serve God in doing good to others."[11]

But with the inception of the new attitude, health as an end in itself, a "new style" of person emerges: he or she "who lives to avoid affliction."[12] I need hardly add how pronounced this style is in our day, when smokers are met with an opprobrium that can only be described as intense moral disapproval, when we religiously exercise and eliminate cholesterol from our diets—always, always that we might live longer. Period. Not live longer to find a cure for cancer or help lift a neighborhood out of poverty or "serve God in doing good to others," but simply live longer. Long life has become an end in itself.

In this atmosphere, says Meyer, an emphasis on inner equilibrium unconnected to the world around us can thrive. Mind cure was one of the early American forms of this emphasis. Its genius was discovering how the weak "might feel strong while remaining weak," while not even attempting to affect or change anything other than oneself. This attitude became more and more attractive—and overwhelmed both sexes—as the United States moved into the twentieth century. The economy continued to evolve into giant, cumbersome and impersonal bureaucracies. Individuals were beaten down, feeling they could do nothing but what these giants demanded of them. Now spreads psychotherapeutical talk of "adjustment" and, says Meyer, "attitudes of passivity, moods of indifference to social power."[13] (We might add that bureaucracy also overtook government—thus leading to the spread of the defeatist attitude that "you can't fight city hall.")

At the same time, Americans remained bound to the notion that in their nation business and the market are foundational. Woodrow Wilson, for instance, declared that "business underlies every part of our lives; the foundation of our lives, of our spiritual lives included, is economic."[14] Meyer holds that commercial mass culture, like a rising tide, swept away the last vestiges of a distinctive Christian identity. In the terms I have been using, we might say that Constantinianism now consummates its victory in the grand experiment called America. Spiritual authority is transferred to the system, with its gospel of consumption. In centralized, technologized, bureaucratized America, the good life, as Meyer writes, equals consuming from above and beyond. It amounts to consuming from "distant, concealed processes and sources like a transcending God who could nevertheless be known in His true character by His works, by His products, and therefore also was an immanent God being consumed, and who, of course, existed simply in terms of the desires that he satisfied."[15]

It remains only to see this attitude officially anointed, or explicitly baptized, by the church. Meyer indicates that Harry Emerson Fosdick, a prominent liberal pastor also remembered for squaring off against early fundamentalists, was one of the earliest clergy to link religion and therapeutic psychology. Following Fosdick, a long line of clergy and other Christian leaders have psychologized the faith. Now, in fact, the most prominent psychologizers are probably evangelicals.

But notice what happens when Christianity is psychologized. When this is done, the focus shifts from social change to how the individual can "adjust" to the status quo. Unasked is the question whether it is genuinely healthy to adjust to a system that may itself be sick.

Again, in the terms I have been using, this is the full Constantinianization of the church. The Constantinian church is *by definition* reactive and reflexive to the surrounding culture. It completely forgets the church's own culture-forming and sustaining capabilities. It denies any real tension between the church and the world; it overlooks the biblical awareness of Christians as nomads and resident aliens who will never be completely at home in a fallen world—even an affluent and exceedingly comfortable fallen world. And it aligns the church with power, against those out of power. As the early African-American liberationist Howard Thurman wrote,

> Too often the price exacted by society for security and respectability is that the Christian movement in its formal expression must be on the side of the strong against the weak. This is a matter of tremendous significance, for it reveals to what extent a religion that was born of a people acquainted with persecution and suffering has become the cornerstone of a civilization and of nations whose very position in modern life too often has been secured by a ruthless use of power applied to . . . defenseless peoples.[16]

But to return to Meyer's terms: in reality religion and psychology have been joined to promote ego surrender rather than ego strength.[17] After Fosdick, Norman Vincent Peale redefined Christian faith so that it did not provide challenges but satisfied "needs." "Religion was doctoring, and like the doctor-patient relationship, it was a private affair."[18] This promoted ego surrender because, as Meyer writes, "telling legitimately discontented people to find the source of their discontent in themselves was to tell them to shrink further from testing their powers in the society around them."[19]

"Without politics," Meyer concludes, "man and God dissolve into each other, leaving neither a standard of psychological well-being nor an image of divine incitement by which to measure and criticize the powers of the world."[20] Or as literary critic Roger Lundin puts it, "The social world dissolves and life becomes a matter of 'every one for himself; driven to find all his resources, hopes, rewards, society and deity within himself.' "[21]

The God of Gnostic Consumerism

So matters now stand. Pastors and other church leaders face enormous pressures to concentrate on ministry as marketing and psychotherapy—both tendencies that concentrate the practice of faith on the individual. Seminarians all too seriously suggest that the study of theology is "impractical," while demanding more counseling courses. People routinely depart churches with the complaint that their "needs weren't being met" or they "weren't being fed." Recently I asked an acquaintance about his church, and he expressed dissatisfaction, then sighed, "Oh well, you know the average church only has a shelf life of three years."

This attitude is gnostic to the extent that it leads Christians to focus on private, inner equilibrium unconnected to the world around us. Yet the gospel of Jesus Christ is about the salvation not of monadic, isolated individuals but of the world, of the entire groaning creation (Rom 8:22). And this attitude is gnostic to the extent it models our relationship to God on the doctor-patient relationship. As we understand the matter in the modern, liberal West, you have no place to ask me what went on in the confines of the sanctum known as the doctor's office. And you certainly have no business suggesting that I pursue one course of therapy instead of another: that is something for my doctor and me to decide. Likewise, and even more strongly, gnosticized Christians insist that their spirituality is a private matter—who are you, what is a community or tradition, to stand between an individual and his or her God? Yet again, how unlike this is the sort of spirituality and discernment Paul practiced, looking as he did to gifts given to individuals as "the manifestation of the Spirit for the common good" (1 Cor 12:7).

And this attitude is gnostic to the extent—the devastating extent—that it turns the good life and the gospel itself into a technique facilitating consumption. Then God is He Who Meets My Felt Needs. This is a God known only by his products, who exists merely in the terms of the desires he satisfies.

I am not arguing that in genuine Christianity individuals gain nothing from a relationship with the God of Israel—Jesus himself was hardly bashful about God-given rewards to the faithful servant. But our nearly exclusive focus on the individual and felt needs pushes us to ignore or distort entire vistas of the biblical terrain.

How can such a God be holy in any remotely biblical sense of the word? This question came home to me some time ago in my role as an editor. Writing and editing in the evangelical world for over ten years, I have seen our language increasingly forced away from the language of the Bible and toward that of religious consumerism. The issue crystallized one day when two authors submitted book manuscripts on the same topic—the holiness of God.

Both manuscripts worked directly, explicitly and consistently from the biblical text. Both were well written and, on their own terms, interesting. I saw value in both and moved to the editorial task of conceiving how the authors might draw in the widest possible readership. I needed, in other words, to start translating their work into "marketable" language.

But here was a translating headache. The authors had begun with God; I would now have to push them to begin with the individual human. They had addressed needs theologically perceived, fitting humanity onto God's agenda; I would push them to write about felt needs, fitting God onto the individual human's agenda. At the heart of what these authors had to say, in fact, was the conviction that humanity is in deep trouble exactly because it tries to use God to its own ends. So if I pushed these authors to speak in the gnosticized, consumerized idiom of the day, I would push them to say exactly the opposite of what they wanted to say!

They wanted to say—quite rightly—that God's holiness is not for my use or self-interest (though the gnostic language of consumerism can leave me to imagine no other purpose for it). It is the other way around. Apart from God I am lost, without direction and purpose, unable to know my true worth—the worth of a creature among creatures wrought and redeemed by a transcendent God.[22] Gnostic consumerism leads me (leads us) to a very different picture of God and the world, and indeed, to a very different God. Philip Lee is right that the gnostic approach "can reveal only a God who is a reflection of self or, more accurately, fantasized self."[23] Without politics—without a God who wrestles with a people in time and space—God and individual dissolve into one another.

The Dead End of Privatizing Faith

The psychologizing and marketizing strategy of retrenchment certainly addresses many of the fears and frustrations we all feel. So many aspects of the modern-verging-on-postmodern world make individuals or organizations feel impotent. Our world is a juggernaut—"a runaway engine of enormous power which . . . threatens to rush out of our control and which could rend itself asunder."[24] As theologian Nicholas Lash summarizes our circumstances, we now feel ourselves to be

incapable of countering chaos by constructing, in fact or even in imagination, a human world. Political cynicism expresses our sense of practical impotence, and the poverty of our imagination is evident in the collapse of any common grammar of ends and means, of value and virtue. Instead, we talk of "freedom," but the rhetoric rings hollow, and we have no means of deciding whether "pluralism" prescribes a solution or merely names a predicament. . . . And so, numbed by terror and acknowledged impotence, we retreat into varieties of personal and moral individualism, places of private feeling and individual "experience."[25]

But this retreat into individualism is a kind of Constantinian retrenchment (if ultimately capitulation) via privatization. For as Lash observes,

> however energetically we try to regress into the privacy of "pure experience," we cannot *entirely* disguise from ourselves the recognition that our abdication of social and intellectual responsibility, our attempts individually to tune in to an order beyond the present darkness of our imagination, merely serve to deepen the darkness in the *real* world in which people starve and nuclear policy is pursued.[26]

To repeat myself: Constantinianism has always been a dead end theologically. Now we live in a time and place that are showing it up as a dead end sociologically as well. The purpose I hope this résumé of Donald Meyer's work has served is to help us see how Christians have come to feel impotent and useless, and that further psychologization and marketization, attractive as they may seem in the short run, will only deepen our impotence and uselessness. They are, in the end, only a gnostic escape into the besieged self.

Meyer's account may be even more valuable in another respect: it shows us that the paralysis we are now caught in is due to cultural developments. And culture, however hard it may sometimes be to change, is not "natural" or inevitable. Where there is no inevitability, there can be hope.

3

THE CHURCH
AS NATION-STATE
*Why America
Is Not the Issue*

◧

Gnosticism of the sort I have been discussing is popular across much of the Western world's cultural spectrum. We see it manifested among religious liberals and conservatives alike in the psychologizing of the faith. It serves a Constantinian agenda by privatizing and etherealizing the church. The Constantinian-gnostic church, rather than recognizing itself as a culture embodying the communal stories of Israel and Jesus Christ, promotes the wholly unseen faith of individuals. It readily agrees that the true church is invisible and so outside time, space, history, politics and culture. This, I have said, is a paradoxical—and fatal—sort of retrenchment that is actually capitulation, actually relinquishment of true Christianity. It plays along with "the Enlightenment's central achievement," the secularization of public life. Although the God of the Bible is the Creator and Redeemer of the world, the Lord of the nations, the Constantinian-gnostic church cannot "tell us why a speaker's depth of spirituality is more relevant to her participation in public debate than her hobby or her hair-color."[1]

In this chapter I want to turn toward another form of Constantinian retrenchment. This is retrenchment that makes the nation-state into a kind of church. Such Constantinianism can occur in any number of nations, such as pre-Marxist Russia or apartheid South Africa. But I will focus on the United States, both because I know it best and because the tendency to create (or re-create) a Christian nation-state is today probably nowhere so strong as it is in America.[2]

G. K. Chesterton is often quoted to the effect that America is the nation with the soul of a church. This is typically cited by Christians who happily affirm his statement. But I think the dangers of this attitude become clearer when we invert Chesterton's aphorism: The U.S. church is the church with the soul of a nation. Because we have so readily privatized faith, we find that the institutional or corporate expression of our faith can occur only through the indisputably political entity called the United States of America. In a way, then, this is another aspect of gnosticizing the Christian church.

Christianity has its inescapably "public" and "political" elements—what else to do with a God against whom the nations and kings of the earth conspire, but whom they had better learn to serve with fear (Ps 2)? When the church itself is atomized and faith entirely interiorized, would-be worshipers of this quite public God must turn to other historical, political institutions to see and do the public and political will of the Lord. And just as the gnostic privatizing of faith is practiced by Christian liberals and conservatives alike, so too Christian liberals and conservatives have made America their church.[3]

Stanley Hauerwas writes, "Christian ethics, as a field, began as part of the American progressivist movement which assumed that the subject of Christian ethics in America is America."[4] Thus on the liberal or mainstream Protestant side we can call into the dock such witnesses as social gospeler Walter Rauschenbusch, who blurred Christianity with American democracy, and Reinhold Niebuhr, who justified American realpolitik as "Christian realism."

It is probably fair to say that those nearer the liberal end of the spectrum have been more subtle (and therefore more dangerous?) in treating America as a church than those grouped at the conservative end. Jerry Falwell, Tim LaHaye, James Kennedy, Pat Robertson and a host of other leaders of the religious right make it no secret that they want America to be a Christian nation. One way the religious right can be read, in fact, is as the latest manifestation of the evangelical refusal to admit the passing of American Constantinianism—which basically means evangelicalism's own hegemony over the culture.

A Constantinian, imperial church spread from Europe to early North America, where ten of the original thirteen colonies had state churches.[5] Evangelical Protestantism officially dominated. Even after the state church was dissolved in the eighteenth century, an informal establishment church reigned. The predominating evangelical Protestants shaped laws, started and sustained the country's elite colleges and so forth. This hegemony began to erode in the late nineteenth century, with increasing influxes of Roman Catholic immigrants. Ever more pluralization has followed, and the establishment church and most of its vestiges have washed away. Yet the religious right tenaciously, if sometimes vaguely, holds to the memory of a time when evangelicals dominated. Perhaps this is why Constantinianism is an especially hard habit for American evangelicals to break.

So, albeit in a variety of ways, some more blatant than others, both liberal and conservative Christians hold to a vision nicely (though not approvingly) summarized by H. Richard Niebuhr: "The Kingdom of the Lord . . . is in particular the destiny of the Anglo-Saxon race, which is destined to bring light to the gentiles by means of lamps manufactured in America."[6]

In coming chapters I will show that the church, not America (or any other nation-state), is itself the political and cultural body meant to bring light to the Gentiles. In this chapter I will lay the groundwork for that claim by arguing that America is no more "real," "public" or "visible" than the church. This is not a matter of despising America any more than it is a matter of lauding America. The whole point is simply that when it comes to *Christian* culture and politics, America is not the issue.

Making Maps and Making War

What I want to get at is the too easy American assumption that this nation is somehow more tangible and concrete than the church. Because the church has been so severely gnosticized, I realize this statement will strike many as counterintuitive. After all, Christian faith is supposed to be about heaven and unseen matters of the individual heart. The true church is not supposed to be locatable on any map. But America (we think) is different. It has a flag and an army. It has mountains and plains and rivers. America is the skyscrapers of Chicago and New York. It is men and women and goods streaming down the quite concrete (and asphalt) freeways of a sprawling, magnificent land. America is most certainly on the map.

Given all this, America seems as plain and natural as anything could be. But what is particularly plain or natural about a map? It is something, after all, created by people at a specific time and place for specific purposes. For instance, we can now locate on many maps an area designated as "Southeast Asia." But this area has existed as such only since World War II. Prior to 1942 there were no standard—or mapped—boundaries grouping together the countries we now regard as Southeast Asia. It was during World War II, as an engrossed American public followed Allied military maneuvers, that such a territory was delineated. As political scientist Michael Shapiro puts it, "Making war meant making maps. The National Geographic Society made them in unprecedented numbers, making nearly twenty million in 1941-42, including for the first time a Society map of 'Southeast Asia' to enable Americans to 'follow every move by our land, sea, and air forces to crush the Japanese.' "[7]

In fact, those peoples that American maps group together as "Southeast Asians" do not necessarily see themselves as any such monolithic unit. For example—and putting it mildly—many Chinese do not appreciate being taken as Vietnamese, and vice versa. Their descriptions of themselves and their countries, in short, differ from the descriptions portrayed by American maps. Maps are always drawn from specific vantage points, for specific purposes. The maps of nations, like nations themselves, serve political ends.

The world map Westerners grew up with, and still most often refer to, was created by the sixteenth-century Flemish geographer Gerhardus Mercator. As John Fiske observes,

> The maps produced by Mercator's projection, his scientific way of representing a globe on a flat surface, have become part of Western common sense because they represent not just the world, but Western power in and over it. To flatten the curvature of the earth, Mercator made the meridians parallel and so progressively widened the distance between them as they travelled northwards. To compensate for this, he enlarged the distances between the parallels proportionately. . . . Representationally, the projection enlarged Europe. Flattening the curve of the earth entailed enlarging the northern land masses which "happened" to be the ones occupied by Europeans. But this was not Mercator's only representational technique. Because most of his customers needed to know about and sail about the northern hemisphere, he dropped the equator to almost two thirds of the way *down* his map. He also standardized the idea that the north should be on top—in the position of discursive as well as political and economic power. Europe became the enlarged center of the world.[8]

Mercator's location and interests are further emphasized by the realization that his birth name was Gerhard Kremer. He not only Latinized it to identify himself with the classically educated class but chose a Latin name meaning "merchant," thereby allying himself with the emerging and powerful bourgeois, or shopkeeper, class.[9]

So maps and the descriptions they represent are always disputable, always open to change.[10] Shapiro offers the example of the territory we now know as Guatemala. This nation's most numerous population is the "Indians." The Indians have lived there since before the Spanish "discovery" (or "invasion"—again, the description depends on your vantage point) of their land. Yet the Indians are not those who have chosen to call their land "Guatemala" or even agree to the borders of Guatemala. Instead it is the descendants of the Spanish conquistadors, and those who cooperated with them, who have determined these boundaries, their significance and their protection.

America off the Map

But we need not resort to such "exotic" examples as Southeast Asia and Guatemala. All of our home places have a history, and it is often a history of strife. It is a history about land whose ownership and significance are, or at least have been, under dispute.

As I made clear in the introduction to this book, I grew up on a marginalized, wind-blasted piece of soil called the Oklahoma Panhandle. It has not always been called such. In the spring of 1874, Native Americans who roamed the region including the present-day Oklahoma Panhandle attacked several buffalo hunters. At Adobe Walls, the site of the battle, the Indians later erected a marker commemorating their fallen, including Best-Son-in-Law, Wolf-Tongue and Soft-Foot of the Cheyennes. The plaque read:

> They died for that which makes life worth living—Indian's liberty— freedom—peace—on the plains which they enjoyed for generations.[11]

I have no idea what the Cheyenne, Comanche and Kiowa who lived there called that country. After all, they were vanquished and their "maps" were not passed on. But I do know that by the time of the Adobe Walls battle, the territory had long been under dispute between Mexico and Texas. At the conclusion of the Mexican War in 1848, the northern and western boundaries of Texas were not settled with Mexico. Texans were ready to return to arms in order to end the argument. Mexico, meanwhile, used the region as a trading route and would not give it up easily. The U.S. Congress intervened to prevent further fighting, and because the appearance of new, undesignated but potentially American territory renewed angry debate over the slavery question then before Congress—would the new territory allow or prohibit slavery?

To stabilize the situation rapidly, Congress passed a bill setting Texas's boundaries so that the area in dispute (now the Oklahoma Panhandle) was not claimed by Texas, and paid Texas ten million dollars to accept the arrangement.[12]

Just five years later, in 1853, the territory of Kansas was officially demarcated. Its border was not extended southward to include the land under dispute with Mexico. What is now the Oklahoma Panhandle became an ungoverned rectangle of land 35 miles wide and 210 miles long, variously called No Man's Land, the Neutral Strip or Public Lands. For the next fifty years the country was under contention, occupied mostly by Indians. It was also occupied by outlaws, who exploited the region as a haven beyond the reach of any organized legal system. It was not at all clear who, if anyone, "owned" the land. In fact, as late as 1913, six years after Oklahoma statehood and the inclusion of No Man's Land as Oklahoma's Panhandle, an elderly frontiersman could argue that the land still partly belonged to Mexico. L. A. Allen, a former comrade of Kit Carson, wrote in the *Kansas City Star:*

> It was stipulated in the treaty with Mexico that this zone should be "neutral" forever. Mexico has never relinquished her rights under this treaty, so as a matter of fact Oklahoma has no right to this strip of ground because the United States of America had no legal right to cede it to the State of Oklahoma. It is today as much Mexican Territory as it is United States territory and neither the United States nor the State of Oklahoma has any right to give title to the farms there.[13]

The point of this short, if involved, historical excursion is simple. Maps are really little more than political snapshots. They capture a moment in time from a particular vantage point. Yet we often use them in a such a way that they obscure complicated, dynamic and still unfolding history. We too easily take them for an objective, once-for-all or final representation of the region they depict.

Growing up in the Oklahoma Panhandle, I was presented with maps and other documents that taught me to identify the Panhandle's heritage with the United States of America and the European legacy of the white Anglo-Saxons who now overwhelmingly occupy it. But my heritage, the heritage of the Oklahoma Panhandle, is much richer—and more conflicted—than that: it is not just European but also Indian and Mexican and Texan and anarchic (of course, the last two may be pretty much the same thing).

Multiply this diversity and conflict fifty, a hundred or more times, and you have the United States of America. In fact, America is so diverse and conflicted that it is not even clear when it began. We can say the United States of America began thousands of years ago, with the native Indians who fished its streams and hunted its forests. We can say it began in 1492, with the arrival of a fortune-seeking Spaniard named Columbus. Or we can start with the story of the English colonists, in the 1600s. Yet again, we can justifiably put the United States's inception at 1776, with the Declaration of Independence. But even then it could be said that the United States of America as a single, unified people did not yet exist. Historians emphasize that before the Civil War the United States of America *were*—*they* remained separate and plural. After the Civil War the United States of America *is*—the states are one and, defying proper grammar, singular. It was the event of the Civil War, with the victory of those favoring union, that consolidated and made whole a vast territory and different peoples.

Yet so varied and elusive and disputed—indeed, so dependent on war—is America's identity that even 1865 may not mark the true beginning of the United States. Political scientist Jean Bethke Elshtain argues that "a *united* United States is a historical construction that most visibly comes into being as cause and consequence of American involvement in the Great War [World War I]. Prior to the nationalistic enthusiasm of that era, America was a loosely united federation with strong and regional identities."[14]

Now, reconsider the church. We look at it, stretched across a long and controverted span of history, splintered into hundreds of pieces, and too quickly assume that the "true church" must be some ethereal essence, some invisible and spiritual reality outside time and space. Then, in the rough-and-tumble of our mundane (that is, quite earthly and historical) lives, this ethereal essence is *in practice* shoved aside in favor of the supposedly more concrete, less disputable, less abstracted, more real United States of America. Yet to the contrary of these tendencies, America is no more concrete and real than the church, and every bit as disputable and abstracted as the church. In these senses it is every bit a work in continual flux, no more finished or final or obvious than the church.

Oh Say Can You See? The Difficulty of Finding America

America, after all, is in the final analysis nothing more than an "idea" or "experiment." It is not rooted ethnically, unlike the French with Gallic ancestors, the Germans with Teutonic ancestors, the English with Anglo-Saxon ancestors, the Italians with Roman ancestors or the Irish with Celtic ancestors. In the United States only Indians can claim ancient native origins.[15] (In fact, before the War of 1812 *Americans* was generally used to designate Native Americans; only after it did the word denote European Americans.)[16] Americans have a mixed ethnic, political and religious heritage. We have no unique national language, though earlier Americans talked of inventing a new language by compounding Native American tongues, or of using Hebrew, Greek or Latin.[17] Likewise, our art and cultural forms are largely borrowed. We had no full-blooded, original American music, for instance, until Sousa's marches.[18]

What, then, does it mean to be a citizen of a country relatively young, ethnically unrooted, linguistically indistinct, made and remade via war—a nation that even a relatively conservative essayist presents as nothing more concrete than "a construction of mind" and a "collective act of imagination"?[19] Or to put it another way: How, given all these qualifications, do you determine a true American?

The question is important since, again, we too often and too easily render the church invisible, ahistorical, acultural and apolitical because there are many and competing ideas about what makes for a true Christian. I remember the wisecrack of my first philosophy teacher, a skeptic who taunted, "If anyone who goes to church is a Christian, does that mean anything you put in a garage is a car?" I do not deny the complexity and conflict of Christian identity. But I insist that American identity is also complex and conflicted. It is no easier to identify a true American than to identify a true Christian.

We cannot simply or finally say that anyone is an American because he or she meets the legal requirements of citizenship any more than we can simply or finally claim someone is a Christian because he or she occasionally shows up for worship. After all, spies and other traitors can hold legal citizenship. In fact, as historian David Potter writes, "almost every trait, good or bad, has been attributed to the American people by someone, and almost every explanation, from Darwinian selection to toilet-training, has been advanced to account for the attributed qualities."[20] How, then, do we gauge someone's genuine American-ness? By level of patriotism? By the ability to speak English? By tendencies to appreciate individualism, equality and progress? Something might be said for all these tests, but taken separately or together, they raise hordes of disputable and confusing points.

Some years ago, in a justly praised book, the neoconservative Richard John Neuhaus proposed a "carefully nuanced" definition of the true American. The true American is someone who affirms that, "on balance and considering the alternatives, the influence of the United States is a force for good in the world."[21] But even this "carefully nuanced" gauge leaves the seeker of the true American with plenty of difficulties and questions. For one thing, it faces the same problem as the utilitarian calculus on happiness. Utilitarians tell us we should seek the greatest good for the greatest number. But they have been criticized on this count, since it seems excruciatingly difficult to quantify, compare and tote up the "good." Putting a price on a bushel of apples is one thing, but how do we assign a "price" (or number) to my happiness or yours, especially when such disparate things make us happy? Likewise, how do we compare and tote up a person's degree of commitment to America? For instance, I love the variety and beauty of America's geography but abhor the consistently militaristic aspects of its history. How do these compare? Does appreciation of geography cancel out or exceed appreciation of militarism?

Or consider another, perhaps less significant comparison. Neuhaus has said there has been no excellent rock music after Simon and Garfunkel's "Bridge over Troubled Water." But many others of us usually classified as Americans think there is a good deal of fine (even better) rock music after "Bridge over Troubled Water." (I will mention only one artist: Bruce Springsteen.) We might affirm that on balance and alternatives considered, American influence has been to the good as regards rock music. And what could be more American than rock 'n' roll? So in terms of gauging Americanness, how much does this count against Neuhaus and for post-Simon-and-Garfunkel lovers of rock?

Once more, much depends on vantage point. I suspect, for example, that it is easier for an Anglo-Saxon like myself to affirm that the United State of America has been a force for good than it is for an African-American or Native American to do the same.[22] In the more colloquial terms of a frontier aphorism, "This country is all right for men and dogs, but it's hell on women and horses."[23] Just how you assess America's influence has much to do with whether you're a man or a woman, a dog or a horse.

Another difficulty arises if we are to take Neuhaus's proposition as the test of true American identity. Presumably there are countries that, on balance and alternatives considered, Neuhaus would believe have *not* been a force for good in the world. How, then, do we assess residents of such countries as Russia, Cuba or Romania? If Neuhaus's dictum were applied to their cases and some Russians, Cubans or Romanians answered it in the negative, would they no longer be true citizens of their homelands?

Or imagine a family that bears a long line of cruelty and scandal— say, the Rascalions. Now is born a generation of Rascalions that renounces the heritage of brutality, admits that Rascalions to date have not been a force for good in the world, and tries to live decently. Is this generation, despite genes and blood types and genealogy, not true Rascalions?

And in America, what of those who believe in life, liberty and the pursuit of happiness, but who feel the nation has not yet lived up to its ideals? In this sense Martin Luther King Jr. believed in America (what it stood for) against America (its actual racial policies and practices). Yet he is now seen as a true enough American to have his birthday declared a national holiday. Surely it is possible that someone might judge that America, *to this point,* has not been preponderantly a force for good—and yet also believe that America *could eventually be* a significant force for the good. And as with the likes of King, might not that person be a true American indeed?

After all (and this is another problem with assessment), the story has not yet finally unwound on America. It is possible that the standards of equality and technological progress that America has promoted for two centuries will somehow sweep the world and bring history to its peak. Yet America also gave the world the atom bomb and if, God forbid, there is yet a nuclear holocaust, later and remnant historians might very well look back and doubt that America was, on balance, a force for good in the world.

The Visibility of the Church

Once more, I want to be careful to make clear my point. My point is not that, in the end and after all, there really is no way to locate the true America or determine the true American. Though I can think of any number of given cases where it is hard to do either, I trust that we do have rough and workable (if evolving) notions about both. When historian David Potter, for example, says that Americans are mobile and adaptable and that the main American values are individualism, equality and progress, he has gotten at matters a great many usually considered American would affirm.[24]

My point, instead, is that the genuine United States is an entity every bit as elusive as the true church. Christians have disagreed and today disagree about many, many things—including what counts for faithful Christian identity. But Americans debate American identity. The church's history is long, varied and even sometimes contradictory. But so is America's history. The church's presence on maps has shifted constantly. But so has America's. Vast numbers of Christians have failed to live up to their high ideals. And so have many Americans.

Yet on all these counts the response has been asymmetrical. When thinking of the church, those making such criticisms have rendered the true church invisible, ahistorical, acultural. The same has not been done in response to America. I am insisting that the church is no less palpable than America. America is seen in its specific manifestations: Old Faithful at Yellowstone Park, or the Grand Canyon, or a flag, or apple pie, or one's parents and siblings, or an Independence Day celebration. Similarly, the church is manifest in particular congregations, in bishops, in lay ministries at work, in Christian friendships that span continents, in symbols such as the cross and stained glass, in its weekly liturgical celebration. In fact, according to Christian confession, the church is more palpable or tangible than America, since God is prepared to answer to the historical deeds and intentions of the church in a way he is not for those of America. (See, for instance, Matthew 18:15-20.)

Thus I am arguing that in important ways quite like the nation-state America, the church is a public, cultural, visible, political presence in the world. It is what theologian John Milbank calls "a new sort of universal society."[25] Relatedly, I reject the supposition that emphasizing the polity called church is somehow more sectarian and less universal than emphasizing the polity called America. Put differently, we should not assume that simply because the nation-state monopolizes violence (legal recourse to punish criminals and conduct war), it also monopolizes rationality and defines universality. If anything, in both age and geographic reach the church is considerably more nearly universal than the United States.

To recognize and reclaim this realness of the church, Christians must resist gnosticizing tendencies such as individualizing the faith. Theologian Bruce Marshall is quite right that the church's participation in God's life happens "not primarily in the minds and hearts of individuals . . . but in the public eucharistic celebration by which Christ joins individuals to himself and so makes them his own community." It is in fact through the eucharistic fellowship of the church that the "triune God visibly exhibits to and in the world his own single and eternal life."[26]

Of course there are aspects of the church and its work that are not visible or empirical. Someone's love for Jesus is no more (and no less) visible than her patriotism or affection for her spouse. "Love" and "patriotism" are not things you can see and point to as directly as you can a chair or wall. But both love and patriotism are seen or evidenced indirectly, in gestures such as a hug or saluting the flag. Similarly, the unity and genuineness of the church does not consist merely of invisible or inscrutable ties. Instead, as Marshall helpfully parses it, such matters of the heart or spirituality should

> be taken as interior or structural aspects *of* a visible, empirical community they help to unify. The church is not a community of inscrutable faith alone; indeed, it seems impossible that any community could be united only by invisible bonds—even its members would not know where to look for it. Still less is it two communities, one invisible, one visible, such that the latter is church only insofar as it (inscrutably) shares some members with the former. It is, rather, one public eucharistic community, which is in part united by factors not directly perceptible (that is, accessible apart from perception of the visible bonds they help create).[27]

In the end, Christians do not need a nation-state for the public, cultural and historical life of their faith. We do not so need a nation-state because we already have the church. Thus for Christians the more urgent political question is not "Will America (or some other nation-state) survive?" but "Will Christians from all over the world, in various communions, be able someday to eat the body and drink the blood of Jesus Christ together and in peace?"

4

THE CHURCH
AS TYPE
*Why Christians Should
Thank God
for the Culture Wars*

❑

or nearly two generations, seminarians and college students have gained
a framework for understanding the church's relationship to
culture from H. Richard Niebuhr's *Christ and Culture*. One of this
great theologian's greatest books, it was proclaimed as "without doubt
the one outstanding book in the field of basic Christian ethics."[1]
Dozens of textbooks have relied on Niebuhr's basic typology (Christ
against culture, of culture, above culture, in paradox with culture and
transforming culture) to describe various Christian traditions. Ever
since Niebuhr, Mennonites and other so-called separatists have been
said to represent Christ "against" culture, the medieval Catholic
Church to stand for Christ above culture, and so forth. For its influence,
but also for Niebuhr's insight, graceful phrasing and profound Christian commitment, *Christ and Culture* is indeed an extraordinary book.

We might expect, then, that in the midst of what are often touted as the "culture wars"—pitched battles over publicly sponsored art, multiculturalism, the definition of family and much else—Niebuhr's text would have as much value as ever. And in many quarters it does remain beyond criticism. Yet somehow, and to some extent, *Christ and Culture* is wearing thin in the culture wars. Thus the intrepid Methodist theologians Stanley Hauerwas and William Willimon have bluntly protested, "We have come to believe that few books have been a greater hindrance to an accurate assessment of our situation than *Christ and Culture.*"[2] Evangelical theologian David Wells, meanwhile, has publicly declared that the day for Niebuhr's book may be past.[3]

I believe the culture wars and the eclipse of Niebuhr's classic—if that is what we are indeed witnessing—are connected. The role of this chapter is to explain how such is the case. But more than that, I want to argue that just as *Christ and Culture* has obscured Christian vision, the culture wars can sharpen it. In short, *Christ and Culture* was the creature of a time when few Christians could conceive of the church as itself a culture. The culture wars are creatures of a different, more decisively post-Constantinian time, a time when the church may once again be capable of regarding itself as a "holy nation" (1 Pet 2:9).

A Short History of Culture

Much of *Christ and Culture*'s popularity has surely come from the fact that it seems so well to capture "culture," which is after all a slippery entity. It is one of those words, like *love* or *God,* that engulf and seem to use their users as much as we use them. Literary critic Raymond Williams thought "*culture* is one of the two or three most complicated words in the English language."[4] Yet the word and the concepts associated with it have a history, and it is a history of only about two hundred years.

Through the fifteenth century, *cultivate* was a word used solely to speak of the work of farmers and gardeners. Rice, wheat, grapes and flowers were cultivated—but not yet people. The word was first used to refer to people and societies in the early sixteenth century. By the mid-eighteenth century, many prominent European philosophers saw "culture" as synonymous with "civilization." Western European society was considered to be the height of civilization, the peak of the human developmental process. To be civilized was to be (Western) cultured, then, and those dwelling outside Western civilization were by definition uncultured.[5]

The idea of culture emerged at a time of massive social changes, not least the inception and growth of modern science. Initially, then, "culture" mediated between "man" and Nature, which science was supposedly bringing under control. Not long after, early science was applied, and the Industrial Revolution (centered, of course, in England) put a different spin on culture. Now culture was what stood between "man" and machine.[6]

Early on, then, a distinction was made between culture and something (nature or machine) seen in stark contrast to culture. Culture was not originally divided within itself, between the high and low, or elite and popular. The related term *literature*, for instance, covered all forms of writing. Any printed book, whether a supposed classic or a manual for building a sewage system, was "literature."[7] Nor was culture separated from everyday life: the balladeer strumming in a country tavern was as much of culture as the organist playing Bach at a cathedral festival. But as capitalism continued to unfold and industrialization seemed to pervade the workplace with a desperate if necessary ugliness, culture was separated from everyday life.[8] There arose the need to imagine culture as something higher and purer than the earthy, sometimes infernal business of the ordinary.

In the mind of nineteenth-century critic Thomas Carlyle, it was clear that industrialization had forced the partitioning (the apartheid, we might almost say) of culture and society. Carlyle's near contemporary Samuel Taylor Coleridge said that everyday life is not culture. His notion of culture was nearer that of the German *Kultur*, which pointed "exclusively to levels of excellence in fine art, literature, music and individual personal perfection." Given the necessity of (high) culture to human flourishing, and given that there was no longer a place for it in ordinary conduct, Coleridge called for an elite secular clergy (his "clerisy"), a cadre of artists and critics who might uphold and promote ennobling (high) culture.[9] All this culminated in the work of the Victorian literary critic and educator Matthew Arnold.

According to Arnold, culture was "the best that is known and thought" and would "nourish us in growth toward perfection." The sonnets of Shakespeare, the music of Mozart, the paintings of Da Vinci—these things would redeem people from all that was lowly and mortal in them. Culture was Arnold's secularized religious faith. As literary critic Roger Lundin puts it, Arnold saw culture as "the last hope for a world in which science had supplanted religion as the organizing force."[10] And indeed Arnold's England was in need of hope and stability. Racked by industrialization and the depression of the lower classes, the country seemed to many to be teetering on the knife's edge of revolution.[11]

At the same time Arnold narrowed "culture" to high culture, he decisively privatized it.[12] His famous *Culture and Anarchy* views culture as the expansion of the "gifts of thought and feeling." The "idea of perfection," which culture serves, "is an *inward* condition of the mind and spirit" and *"an inward spiritual activity."* By definition, people of culture are not people of "public life and direct political action." Instead it is their business to get "believers in action" to learn to think more clearly so they may act less confusedly.[13]

As literary critic Jay Clayton observes,

> In the nineteenth century, if a robber baron read poetry, the only social, economic, or political effects this activity could have were indirect; he might be humanized by the experience, and as a result, he might change his behavior toward his wife (social) or change the condition of employment for his workers (economic) or advise the President not to go to war (political). Improbable as this sequence might seem, it is the principal way that culture can be said to have had power in the modern era.[14]

So we have what Clayton calls the "liberal model" of culture. Culture is privatized (only indirectly public, if at all) and made a matter of private values (as opposed to public and "scientific" facts).[15] The model is also liberal in that it imagines truth is found outside any particular tradition or time and place. Arnold professed that study of the "best that is known and thought" would lead to the discovery of those prescriptions of reason that are "absolute, unchanging, of universal validity."[16]

The liberal model of culture, of course, often shows itself right up to our day. Consider John F. Kennedy's address at the dedication of the Robert Frost Library in 1963. Kennedy said poetry has power by virtue of its "disinterested" questioning of society. It is powerful exactly because it remains aloof from the social, the "sphere of polemics and ideology," which enables it to establish "basic human truths which must serve as the touchstones of our judgment." In Kennedy's own judgment, "Robert Frost coupled poetry and power. For he saw poetry as the means of saving power from itself."[17] Poetry (or any other manifestation of "culture") has nothing to do with the social and political; only so, in fact, may it remain pure enough to serve the social and the political, albeit indirectly.

Now what if culture is so understood and religion is considered part of culture? Working within his liberal model, Arnold sees them as exactly parallel. He declares: "Religion says: *The kingdom of God is within you;* culture, in like manner, places human perfection in an *internal* condition."[18] Culture, and religion like it, is confined to the private; both alike are idealized and etherealized. The liberal model ostensibly exalts culture and religion, yet in reality it marginalizes them. I would even go further and say it gnosticizes them. Culture and faith are redemptive, but redemptive only at the cost of being reduced to the knowledge and feelings of private individuals—individuals carefully removed from the world of the social, the economic and the political.

From Arnold to Niebuhr via Troeltsch

Returning now to Niebuhr's *Christ and Culture,* we can see the liberal model hard at work—this time at the level of shaping the renowned categories of Christ against culture, for it, transforming it and so forth. Perhaps the best way to uncover the influence of the liberal model is to dig beneath Niebuhr's architecture to the foundation of his work.

He made no secret of his reliance on the thought of his mentor, theologian Ernst Troeltsch. In fact, in the acknowledgments of *Christ and Culture*, Niebuhr confesses that his book "in one sense undertakes to do no more than to supplement and in part correct [Troeltsch's] *The Social Teaching of the Christian Churches.*"[19] It is exactly from *Social Teaching* that Niebuhr draws the basis for his famous five types.

Troeltsch works with only two categories, the church (institutional and even state churches) and the sect (voluntary churches).[20] For Troeltsch, the church type is clearly preferable to the sect type. This is the case because he cannot imagine the Christian church itself as a social power that might shape and form a distinctive people. Instead, Troeltsch insists that "State and Society . . . are still the main formative powers of civilization."[21] So his agenda is thoroughly Constantinian. Troeltsch expects the church to adjust itself to a political, social and economic order *predetermined* by state and society. His key question for the Christian church is "How can the church harmonize with these main forces [state and society] in such a way that together they will form a unity of civilization?"[22] Since the church, he believes, inevitably desires to "cover the whole life of humanity," it cannot keep from being an "overwhelmingly conservative" organization that must accept the secular order and help it "dominate" or "control great masses of men."[23]

That the liberal model holds sway here is evident when we turn to Troeltsch's discussion of religion, and the Christian gospel in particular. Troeltsch sees earliest Christianity as utterly asocial and apolitical. It "is of the utmost importance," he writes, "to recognize that the preaching of Jesus and the creation of the Christian Church were not due in any sense to the impulse of a social movement." The "values of redemption" preached by Jesus and the apostles were "purely inward, ethical, and spiritual, leading inevitably and naturally to a sphere of painless bliss." Jesus' "fundamental moral demand" is "the sanctification of the individual." Troeltsch can hardly state the matter emphatically enough: the gospel presents "an unlimited, unqualified individualism"; the Christian community exists only to promote this "absolute religious individualism." Religion itself, he writes again and again, is "inward" and "individual." And in this severely privatized, desocialized sense of religion, "the central problem of the New Testament is always purely religious" and the gospel is focused on the "religious value of the soul."[24]

Troeltsch's student Niebuhr is more subtle and certainly far less individualistic. But in the end he appropriates and builds on the liberal model represented by Troeltsch. So Niebuhr also separates Jesus from the social and the political. Early in his book, and along these lines, he approvingly quotes the thought and words of Rabbi Joseph Klausner:

> Though Jesus was a product of [Jewish] culture, . . . yet he endangered it by abstracting religion and ethics from the rest of social life, and by looking for the establishment by divine power only of a "kingdom not of this world." "Judaism, however, is not only religion and it is not only ethics: it is the sum-total of all the needs of the nation, placed on a religious basis. . . . Judaism is a national life. . . . Jesus came and thrust aside all the requirements of national life. . . . In their stead, he set up nothing but an ethico-religious system bound up with his conception of the Godhead."[25]

True to the liberal model, this vision sees Jesus' faith as "abstracting religion and ethics" from social life. In this model's view, Jesus supposedly threw over Judaism as "a national life" and set up an asocial, atemporal "ethico-religious system." So for Niebuhr, "Christ" is something to be grasped and understood in contrast to "culture" (thus the two poles of his book's title). Arriving, supposedly after putting aside culture, at who we consider Jesus to be and what we consider him to be about, we must then set this abstract "Christ" in some relation to culture. And the "culture" at hand is a monolithic whole: Niebuhr calls it "that total process of human activity and that total result of such activity to which now the name *culture,* now the name *civilization,* is applied in common speech."[26] So it is culture or civilization as a totalized block that Christians, depending on their stripe, must decide once for all to accept, dominate, transform—or reject. Yet what can it mean to reject culture if Christ is acultural and his work asocial? It can only mean becoming a sectarian, and sectarian in the sense of fleeing the "world"—the wider (and really only) social order. It means rejecting in toto nothing less than what is often called civilization.

Niebuhr's types are Constantinian in that within their conceptuality it is impossible to imagine or enact the church as itself a culture or a "nation." The church cannot be a distinctive, theologically formed public or culture but must instead conceive of itself as bringing an individualized, abstracted "ethico-religious system" to culture. Consequently Niebuhr, entering the fray with weapons bequeathed him by Troeltsch, actually disarms the church with Constantinian and liberal categories. Unlike Matthew Arnold, Niebuhr does not cut culture off from the social; for Niebuhr, culture is "the 'artificial, secondary environment' " that grouped people superimpose on the natural, and as such it is "always social."[27] But like Arnold and Troeltsch, Niebuhr privatizes Christianity and imagines that its truth is found outside any particular culture or time and place. Any social contribution the church has to make, then, cannot be made by the church itself but must be made through, and ultimately on the terms of, the society. Politics, likewise, can only be done through or by the state. Thus does *Christ and Culture* render the church safe for the world—or, to be more exact, for modern, liberal civilization.

What Happens When the Liberals Go Liberal

Though most church folk have never read Arnold, Troeltsch or Niebuhr, it will be evident to many that the liberal model has pervaded, and corrupted, our mainline denominations. For those who may doubt it, I offer the recent work of sociologists Donald Luidens, Dean Hoge and Benton Johnson.[28] They begin by observing that since the mid-1970s mainline Protestants have suffered a serious hemorrhaging of their membership rolls. The major reason for this decline is that rolls are not being replenished by the offspring of older members. Why is that the case? Our sociological trio's answer: liberalism of the exact sort crystallized by Matthew Arnold and accepted by Ernst Troeltsch and H. Richard Niebuhr.

Drawing from a survey of five hundred baby boomers, the sociologists learned that 92 percent of these describe themselves as religious, but only 62 percent claim to be church members and just 47 percent worship at least twice a month.[29] Among many of these boomers the nonnecessity of church involvement is almost an item of faith. Ninety-five percent of those who are unaffiliated but think themselves religious told the sociologists that "a person can be a good Christian or Jew [even] if he or she doesn't attend church or synagogue." More significantly, the same position is generally held among the churched. "Eighty percent of active Presbyterians and 72 percent of other mainline participants agree. Even among the fundamentalists this position is held by 45 percent of the Boomers."[30]

Many or most Christian boomers would agree, then, with the liberal atheist philosopher Richard Rorty, who avers that religion is "at its best, Whitehead's 'what we do with our solitude,' rather than something people do together in churches."[31] And the unwillingness to commit oneself to a particular church is matched by an unwillingness to consider Christianity itself as uniquely authoritative. As the sociologists report, "Few would agree that salvation is only through Jesus Christ or that Christ is the only source of absolute truth." These boomers, in effect, argue

> that their own Christianity is an accident of birth; had they been born to Muslim or Buddhist families, they would have been Muslims or Buddhists. Consequently, it would be presumptuous of them to stand on their accidental birthright and make claims on others' faith. Many Boomers go so far as to say that they would be content if their children adopted non-Western religions "as long as they are happy" and as long as they are moral citizens.[32]

I need hardly comment how these intuitions betray a deep liberalism: the sense that commitments other than those consciously chosen are merely "accidental" (and potentially if not actually prejudicial), the implied emphasis on personal autonomy, and the accordingly necessary privatizing of faith. As theologian Nicholas Lash puts it, modern and liberal Western culture allows religion "to be about the Beautiful; sometimes it is even allowed to be about the Good. What is quite excluded are suggestions that religion also has to do with public Truth."[33]

Consequently, the "strongly privatized faith" of these boomers is resistant to evangelism and mission—this might involve suggesting that the (private) faith of a Buddhist or Muslim or agnostic is inadequate or (paradoxically, since these boomers can only very gingerly affirm the truth of their own faith) untrue. As our sociologists observe, boomers are, in good liberal fashion, confused about any authority other than their own autonomy:

> In the footsteps of historic Protestantism, they give little credence to the pronouncements of the institutional church or to religious tradition. Moreover, in the wake of nineteenth-century challenges to biblical literalism, the Reformation's allegiance to *sola scriptura* holds little sway. . . . For many . . . the basis for religious authority narrows to personal experience, which becomes the touchstone of their religious and moral affirmations.[34]

In this light, I think Luidens, Hoge and Johnson are exactly right to label the phenomenon "lay liberalism" and suggest that it is

> very shifting sand on which to build a religious community. It has no inherent loyalty factor upon which institutions can depend for sustained support. Rather, it promotes an ethos in which church involvement is strictly optional, and the option is to be exercised solely at the discretion of the individual. As a result lay liberals become religious consumers, seeking the religious services that meet their personal wants.[35]

Evangelicals in the Liberal Cage

For those more closely identified with conservative Christianity, such liberalism and such effects may come as little surprise, and hardly seem directly threatening. For that reason if for no other, it is important to recognize that lay liberalism is no respecter of persons—even "conservative" persons. I can, of course, remind such readers that 45 percent of the fundamentalists surveyed by Luidens, Hoge and Johnson affirmed that one need not be churched to be a "good Christian." But the prison bars of liberal language confining us all are set much deeper than that. For evidence of how this conceptuality creeps into and crabs even our brightest "conservative" imaginations, I turn to statements by two outstanding evangelical writers.

Charles Colson and Philip Yancey are evangelical authors who not only have sold millions of books each but also mark their work with penetrating reflection and felicitous expression. Colson founded and leads a much-admired worldwide ministry to convicts, Prison Fellowship. Yancey has written sensitively and often brilliantly on issues of human suffering. The pair's stature within evangelicalism is indicated by the fact that they are regular columnists for the leading evangelical periodical *Christianity Today*.

Furthermore, both have written on the importance of the church, and have in fact emphasized one of the central Christian metaphors for the corporateness of faith, the body.[36] Certainly neither of them is obviously indebted to such theological liberals as Ernst Troeltsch. Here, if anywhere among conservative evangelicals, we might expect to find an alertness to the vagaries of "lay liberalism." Yet I am afraid both writers can betray a stark captivity to liberalism.

Addressing the National Press Club, for instance, Colson is admirably explicit about his faith in Jesus Christ. But he is quick to qualify this: "I would not be so presumptuous to say that only the gospel of Christ can bring about moral reformation. I'm happy about every effort where people are helped. But it is Jesus Christ who made a lasting difference in my life. And this is what I can offer to others."[37] If liberalism has validly reminded Christians of anything, it has reminded us that praiseworthy and moral behavior is not monopolized by Christianity. So I am sympathetic to Colson's clarification that he does not think only Christianity can, in some ways, better the world. But I fear liberal ears, at least, will too easily absorb his elaboration that Jesus Christ has made a difference in *"my* life." This puts faith right where liberals want it, in the category of the private and the emotive.

Matters worsen (or get better yet, if you are a liberal listening in) when Colson immediately adds, "Does it [Christianity in prison reform] work?" With this combination of moves, faith and its effects are put solidly in the liberal dock, first privatized and then bared to the judgment of the preeminent liberal criterion: pragmatism. Jesus is "my" thing and "works" for me. Any self-respecting liberal would ask for little more, or could say nothing more consistent with liberal views about religion or a religious figure.

Now Colson might understandably object that he would want to say much more on behalf of the faith, and that he is trying to use a language understandable and perhaps persuasive to a given audience. Yet he goes ahead to emphasize, in a manner that would come as sweetness and light to Matthew Arnold, that Christianity (and religion in general) is first of all an inward matter. Any public or social effect it has is indirect.

> Though George Will might argue that government can inspire and create public virtue—that statecraft is soulcraft—I respectfully disagree. I believe virtue is something that grows from within, not something enforced from above. The law does have a role in moral instruction. But the roots of our moral life go deeper than laws and bills. Government programs can feed the body; they cannot touch the soul. They can punish behavior; they cannot transform hearts.[38]

Colson swallows whole the liberal compartmentalization of the external and the internal, the body and the soul, behavior and the "heart." The life of faith is then primarily an individual, private concern. Furthermore, there appears to be no place in Colson's scenario for any polity between the state (with its coercive powers emphasized) and the individual. A liberal will consider this obviously true, if not self-evident. But Christians who are less fully committed liberals must ask: Where is the church? Is there no way station in the moral pilgrimage from the solitary heart to the achievement of virtue?

It is ironic, furthermore, that Colson at once criticizes an Aristotelian (pundit George Will) and resorts to the supremely Aristotelian language of virtue. Aristotle, after all (and George Will following him), famously considered the human a "naturally political animal."[39] This meant, among other things, that no real moral excellence (or virtue) could be achieved outside an excellent (or virtuous) community and without exemplars of excellence close to hand. As political philosopher Ronald Beiner writes, "Aristotle's most powerful insight is that in every society, moral life is based upon ethos, that is, character formation according to socially bred customs and habit."[40] For Aristotle, then, there can be no sharp separation of the "private" and the "public," nor of the inward "heart" and outward behavior. In fact, the student of politics must study the soul just as the physician must study the body.

The apostle Paul, I believe, has a similar social or corporate understanding of character in mind when he declares that Christians find and practice their gifts as "one body in Christ, and individually . . . members one of another" (Rom 12:5). But the point now is that inasmuch as Colson wants to keep faith and morality private and cannot countenance the primacy of social formation in the building of character, he remains consummately liberal.

Likewise, Philip Yancey would have us conceive of the Christian virtue of forgiveness in implacably liberal terms. Writing poignantly on Bosnia and other instances of "ethnic cleansing," he concludes, "I have difficulty even imagining forgiveness on a national or global scale." And similarly to Colson, he sees no possible forgiving polity (can a church forgive a member?) between the nation-state and, yes, the individual. Consequently:

> When I contemplate forgiveness, I find it easier to consider individual, personal acts. Politics deals with externals—borders, wealth, crimes. . . . Authentic forgiveness, lasting forgiveness, deals with the evil in a person's heart. Virulent evil (racism, ethnic hatred) spreads through society like an airborne disease; one cough infects a whole busload. But the cure, like a vaccine, must be applied one person at a time.[41]

Clearly, this abandons us in the heart of liberal territory. Politics is a matter of "externals"; forgiveness deals with the individual's "heart," and at least in regard to what Christians as Christians can do, evil must be fought like a virus, "one person at a time." Aristotle (and Paul?) would hardly agree.

Just how restricting these liberal categories can be comes front and center in another essay by Yancey, this time an earnest attempt to solve "The Riddle of Bill Clinton's Faith."[42] Yancey is understandably puzzled by a number of the president's policies—stances on the likes of abortion and homosexuality that have alarmed many evangelicals. But after interviewing and spending time with Clinton, he does not doubt the genuineness of his faith. He records that Clinton prays more since he assumed the office of the presidency, and that he "stayed up until 3 A.M. reading the Book of Joshua before the Middle East peace signing."[43] What is one to make of these apparent contrasts?

Yancey gets a clue when he and Clinton attend the National Prayer Breakfast and hear an address by Mother Teresa. Here the "consummate politician" meets the bona fide saint. And the saint, of course, takes occasion to speak movingly against abortion: "Please give it [the child] to me," she says to pregnant women who don't want their children. "I want it. I will care for it."

To Yancey, Mother Teresa, "like saints and prophets before her," views the world in "stark, binary terms." "In her talk," he observes, "she managed to reduce the abortion controversy to its simplest moral terms: life or death, love or rejection." But "ten feet away from her sat Bill Clinton, a politician stuck with the practical details of implementing policy on a contentious moral issue." Here, then, may rest the answer to the riddle of Clinton's faith. Yancey suspects "Mother Teresa probably would not make a very good politician: she would have little patience with public relations, compromise, and writing regulations." And Bill Clinton, ever running for office, "would not make a very good saint."[44]

These, I submit, are the stark, binary terms of liberalism. We are left with the choice between an irrelevant saint and a finally compromised politician. Yet why might it not be an act of *political* imagination for Christians to respond to abortion on demand by offering to adopt otherwise aborted children?[45] Why must the politician's faith be confined to lonely postmidnight Bible reading and the saint's politics limited to emotionally, though ineffectually, bringing tears to a president's eyes? What might it mean for there to be a polity in which Christians could be both saints and politicians? Was there ever such a polity, is there such a polity, might there be such a polity?

Such are the questions I think we must ask, and in fact live, at the close of the Constantinian age. Again, I comment at such length on the work of Charles Colson and Philip Yancey not out of disrespect, but exactly because they are so insightful and articulate, yet rarely if ever associated with liberalism. If even such as they are prone to fall, at last, into stifling liberal conceptual pits, what about the rest of us? If even the likes of Colson and Yancey find themselves in the hole with Matthew Arnold, all Christians are in need of new categories and fresh imagination. And that, I believe, is exactly what the culture wars can give us.

Culture: From the Art Museum to the Battlefield

Arnold, promoting a liberal model, puts culture in a removed and separate realm, outside "public life," politics and the world of "action." Any social, economic or political effect culture might have is indirect. Accepting the Arnoldian view, at least insofar as religion is an aspect of culture, Colson and Yancey also see saintliness assigned to the individual and the heart. For them, faith is at best indirectly related to the social, economic and political.

Aside from biblical and theological objections this assignment might meet, it raises severe ethical problems. Put briefly, Nazis read Goethe and listened to Beethoven.[46]

It is simply not enough, in other words, for the cultural to have a possible and indirect effect. If culture is privatized and compartmentalized, removed to a realm separate from the public and "real world," a Nazi can ponder "the best that is known and thought" all night long and then, at daybreak, go out and shoot a Jew in the face. Likewise, Christian faith that is privatized will exercise only a tenuous hold on much significant human conduct.

The late evangelical writer Joseph Bayly once remembered visiting with a German believer who had served in Hitler's Third Reich. This Christian proudly told how on one occasion his commandant ordered him to attend a dance, but since dancing was against his religious convictions, he refused the order at his own considerable peril. As Bayly mordantly commented, so it was that a Christian could assist Hitler in a genocidal cause but stand up to him on social dancing.[47] This is only a particularly ludicrous example of the end that the privatization of faith and culture can bring us to.

Ironic as it may seem, then, liberalism will leave Christians (and citizens in general) trapped in a way of life that provides us few or no resources to resist the nation-state even at its most diabolical. What the culture wars bring is a debate not only concerning such fractious issues as abortion, homosexual rights, the role of women and so forth but also *concerning the definition of culture itself.* No longer, in our actual and day-to-day life, is culture a "static repository of the best that has been thought and felt." Culture is now a "field of contention," as Jay Clayton has it, a forum of debate over identity, family, gender, class, technology, the environment, race—and faith.[48] Culture, we might say, is now not so much an art museum as a battlefield.

Of course I do not want to get cavalier about the intensity—and costs—of culture as battle. Yet I count it as gain that culture has decisively moved into public and everyday life and that it, like politics, "has become a readily available arena for reflecting, expressing, and debating differences."[49] The culture wars have forcefully reminded us that culture as ethos, as a way of life that forms character, is immensely powerful and not at all removed from any realm of life.

We have seen the power of (nonprivatized) culture in the change of women's roles despite the legislative failure of the Equal Rights Amendment. We have seen the power of culture in the growing acceptance of homosexuality, again despite few "public" legislative changes. And we have seen the power of culture in the guise of religion with Khomeini's Islamic ascent in Iran and with the Catholic-charged Solidarity movement in Poland—this despite thoroughgoing governmental, legal and media ignorance or denial of religion.

The culture wars come to us partly because we live in a changing, transitional period and partly because we live in what is often called the Information Society. In the Information Society "an important source of power is the ability to influence 'messages,' an ability one would traditionally describe as cultural."[50] Thus we are moving from an understanding (and practice) of culture as "high culture" or the fine arts to a definition that includes "low" as well as "high" culture. It takes in media, advertising, information technology, fashion, ritual, worship, academic disciplines, public symbols, lifestyles and everyday practices such as automobile commuting or childrearing.

This understanding of culture is drawn not so much from the fine arts as from anthropology. And I have seen few better encapsulated definitions of culture than that of anthropologist Renato Rosaldo:

Anthropology invites us to expand our sense of human possibilities through the study of other forms of life. Not unlike learning another language, such inquiry requires time and patience. There are no shortcuts. We cannot, for example, simply use our imaginations to invent other cultural worlds. Even those so-called realms of pure freedom, our fantasy and our "innermost thoughts," are produced and limited by our own local culture. Human imaginations are as culturally formed as distinctive ways of weaving, performing a ritual, raising children, grieving, or healing; they are specific to certain forms of life, whether these be Balinese, Anglo-American, Nyakyusa, or Basque.

Culture lends significance to human experience by selecting from and organizing it. It refers broadly to the forms through which people make sense of their lives, rather than more narrowly to the opera or art museums. It does not inhabit a set-aside domain. . . . From the pirouettes of classical ballet to the most brute of brute facts, all human conduct is culturally mediated. Culture encompasses the everyday and the esoteric, the mundane and the elevated, the ridiculous and the sublime. Neither high nor low, culture is all-pervasive.[51]

However much Christians despise the culture wars because certain culture "warriors" espouse positions some find disturbing (or even cataclysmic), the culture wars can be welcomed on the count that they help return us to a place where we can conceive of Christianity as a way of life, as a specific manner of being and doing in the world. And they make it possible for Christians, like those who inhabit other ways of life, to move more easily and directly into the public, the social, the political and the economic realms—and to do so *specifically as Christians.* The culture wars free the church of the Constantinian shackles that have confined it for seventeen centuries. They make it possible for the church not merely to be relevant to culture but to *be* a culture, a "cultivating process that produces people in a particular way"; not merely to contribute to politics from the sidelines but to *do* politics of a peculiar kind—a kind that once turned the world upside down (Acts 17:6).[52]

In short, the culture wars may not look very Christian or indeed be very Christian. Yet they return the church to an existence that can become distinctively, exhilaratingly Christian—a social and political existence quite like that of the church in its earliest days.

5

THE CHURCH
AS CHURCH
Practicing the
Politics of Jesus

◻

My argument thus far has been that the Constantinian church, melded
with such elements friendly to it as certain brands of gnosticism and liberalism, has domesticated itself by depoliticizing
itself. To this point I have largely only asserted that the church was once,
and should be again, "political." But we have now come nearly to the
midpoint this book, and it is fair enough for the reader to protest: "Put
up or shut up. When was Christianity not individualized and privatized?" This entire chapter will be my long answer. But the short answer
is: Christianity was not individualized and privatized at its origin, when
it was a Jewish sect.

In the last chapter I noted H. Richard Niebuhr's approving quotation of Rabbi Joseph Klausner, to the effect that though Jesus was a Jew,
he abstracted religion and ethics from the rest of social life. "Judaism,"
said Klausner, "is a national life," but Jesus supposedly came and "thrust

aside all the requirements" of such an irrefutably social and political faith.[1] What I am ready to say now is that much of the church's late Constantinian malaise comes from the fact that Christians all too quickly forgot how to be good Jews, *yet Jesus and the earliest, New Testament Christians did not.* They were all (even the Gentiles) good Jews in the sense that Klausner thought they were not.(That is, they saw themselves embodying a national, or social and political, way of life.) Israel's story was, in a profound sense, their story—and they did not psychologize and etherealize it to make it theirs.

Now that the long Constantinian age has all but passed, we Christians find ourselves in a situation much more closely analogous to that of New Testament Christians than to the Christendom for which some nostalgically long. The Bible, it turns out, offers abundant resources for living in a wildly diverse and contested world. With Constantine finally buried, theologians and biblical scholars find themselves able to reclaim, and present again to the church, the politics of Jesus.[2]

Jesus' World

Perhaps the main reason that the Bible has, at least in recent centuries, seemed to offer scarce political or cultural guidance is that Christians have read a "rank anachronism" back into its text. The strict split between "religion" and "politics" belongs to centuries much later than the first. As N. T. Wright remarks, "No first-century Jew . . . could imagine that the worship of their god and the organization of human society were matters related only at a tangent."[3]

Even the most rank anachronizer will not deny that there is much of the political, the physical, the social and economical throughout the Old Testament. Israel, after all, is a nation, an irrefutably political entity. And it is a political entity born of social, not merely psychological, rebellion—the revolt of slaves against what was then the world's most powerful empire, Egypt. The story of the nation Israel is, like that of all nations, one of conquest (the vanquishing of Canaan), of hierarchy and its power plays (the kingdom of David), of hope and striving for justice as well as security. Israel's story, furthermore, does not become apolitical the moment it loses its capital and its land and is sent into exile. The nation is scattered but still a nation, and now a nation whose prophets hope strenuously for the restoration of that capital and land. Isaiah, Jeremiah, Joel, Micah and Zechariah all cite Zion as the place of God's climactic (and clearly political) saving act.[4] So: "Hear the word of the LORD, O nations, and declare it in the coastlands far away; say, 'He who scattered Israel will gather him, and will keep him as a shepherd a flock' " (Jer 31:10).

Yet even if all this is recognized, there remains a strong tendency to imagine that the political and social dimensions of faith fell away at, or with, the birth of the church. A moment's pause reveals how untenable this assumption is. To make the earliest church asocial and apolitical is to suppose that suddenly the Jews of Jesus' day ceased worshiping a God that, for hundreds of years, their people had considered eminently involved with history and politics.

In fact, Jesus proclaimed his message and gathered his disciples in a politically charged context. His was a society grinding under the oppression of a distant, colonizing empire, that of Rome. The Jews of Jesus' day and place, although they were regathered in Palestine and had rebuilt the temple in Jerusalem, considered themselves still in exile, "since the return from Babylon had not brought that independence and prosperity which the prophets foretold."[5] The Pharisees and other parties vying for control were in no sense "religious" in such a manner that their aims excluded the political, the social and the economic. The political agendas of Jewish parties ranged from the most "conservative" (the Sadducees, most nearly allied with the occupying Romans and so least desirous of significant change) to the most radical (the dispossessed Zealots, who advocated violent revolution).[6]

To make good, faithful and biblical sense of Jesus, we simply must take into account the world in which he lived and the problems he (or any other religious figure) was expected to address. Wright summarizes the situation: "Jewish society faced major external threats and major internal problems. The question, what it might mean to be a good and loyal Jew, had pressing social, economic and political dimensions as well as cultural and theological ones."[7] As my exploration of the psychologization of America (in chapter two) suggested, it is perhaps only the most affluent, socially stable people who can ignore social, economic and political questions and concentrate on their abstracted inner well-being. Christian Science and other mind cure groups so popular in the nineteenth century made no converts in Naples or Calcutta. Outside the United States, they appealed only to the English upper middle class. I doubt that Christian Science, or for that matter Christianity as it is now profoundly psychologized by many liberals and evangelicals alike, would have found many converts—or even had made any sense—among first-century Palestinian Jews. You might just as well have entered into an argument with them that the world was really round or that the earth was not the center of the cosmos. The anachronism, whether drawn from our physical sciences or our preoccupation with individualistic psychology, is equally rank.

Wright emphasizes that "the pressing needs of most Jews of the period had to do with liberation—from oppression, from debt, from Rome." None of this is to suggest for a moment that Jewish (and Jesus') faith was exclusively political, whatever that might mean. But it does suggest that other issues "were regularly seen in this [political] light." This context—the actual context of Jesus' life and work—renders incredible Ernst Troeltsch's confident assertion that the "values of redemption" preached by Jesus were "purely inward" and led "naturally to a sphere of painless bliss."[8] The hope of Israel was, as Wright puts it, not for "disembodied bliss" after death "but for a national liberation that would fulfill the expectations aroused by the memory, and regular celebration, of the exodus. . . . Hope focused on the coming of the kingdom of Israel's God."[9]

Language Matters

Indeed, given such blatantly political language as *exodus* and *kingdom*, it can be difficult to comprehend how we have managed to so thoroughly privatize the New Testament faith. Of no less political provenance than *kingdom* is the term *gospel*, or *evangel*. In the Greco-Roman world from which the early church adopted it, "gospel" was a public proclamation of, say, a war won, borne by a herald who ran back to the city and, with his welcome political news, occasioned public celebration.[10] Christian ethicist Allen Verhey suggests that Mark, in calling what he had written a "Gospel," was meaning to evoke *evangel* as it was used within the Roman cult of emperor to refer to announcements of the birth of an heir to the throne, of the heir's coming of age, accession to the throne and so forth. If so, the writer of the Gospel is comparing the kingdom of God come in Jesus to the quite this-worldly and political kingdom of Caesar.[11] It would not be amiss to translate "The Gospel According to Mark" as "The Political Tidings According to Mark." In short, if Mark in his world had wanted to convey a privatistic and individualistic account of Jesus' life and death, he could have thought of many better things to call it than a Gospel (Mk 1:1).

No less political is the language used to describe the church's worship. Our word *liturgy* comes from the Greek meaning "work of the people," or, as we might put it now, a "public work." In Roman society, "to build a bridge for a public road across a stream on one's private property would constitute a liturgy." Military service at one's own expense was an act of liturgy. The wealthy sought favor by sponsoring lavish "liturgies"—huge dramas for the entertainment of the citizenry. *Leitourgoi,* or, very roughly, "liturgists," in the secular Greek usage of the times referred to government officials.[12] To modern, privatized Christian ears, *worship* too easily connotes escape from the world (we worship, after all, in a "sanctuary"), a removal from the political and the social. Yet inasmuch as we read such connotations onto the word in its New Testament context we are saying something oxymoronic like the "private public work" of the church. The New Testament Christians themselves, I submit, were not so confused.

No less cultural and political is the very word used to describe the new community of God. *Church* (the Greek *ekklēsia*) from the fifth century B.C. onward referred to an assembly of citizens called to decide matters affecting the common welfare.[13] The Hebrew *qāhāl* denotes a solemn, deliberative assembly of Israel's tribes. The assembly par excellence, for example, was at Mount Sinai, where the Law was received (Deut 9:10; 18:16). When the ancient Jews translated the Old Testament into Greek, *qāhāl* was rendered *ekklēsia*. This is the term Christians seized on to describe their own assemblies. Thus the "*Ekklēsia* of God*"* means roughly the same thing as what New Englanders might call the "town meeting of God."[14]

Given all this, it is unsurprising that early observers of Christianity were not struck by its "religious" (in our privatized sense) qualities. What struck outsiders, says Wright, was the church's "total way of life"—or in my terms, its culture.[15] The Romans called Christians "atheists" (they refused cultic emperor worship) and classified Christianity as a political society. This classification meant that Christianity was under a ban on corporate ritual meals, much as many governments down to the present ban the "free assembly" of those considered subversive. Christians, says Wright, "were seen not just as a religious grouping, but one whose religion made them a subversive presence within the wider Roman society."[16] There can be no doubt that Rome consistently saw Jews and early Christians as a social and political problem and treated them accordingly.

Of course we know that the Romans misunderstood both Jews and Christians on many counts. Did they also grossly misconstrue their intentions here? The thoroughly political language adopted by the church suggests otherwise. The clincher is that if the early church had wanted itself and its purpose to be construed in privatistic and individualistic terms, there were abundant cultural and legal resources at hand for it to do just that. The early church could easily have escaped Roman persecution by suing for status as a *cultus privatus,* or "private cult" dedicated to "the pursuit of a purely personal and otherworldly salvation for its members," like many other religious groups in that world.[17] Yet instead of adopting the language of the privatized mystery religions, the church confronted Caesar, not exactly *on* his own terms but *with* his own terms. As Wayne Meeks summarizes the matter, early Christian moral practices

are essentially communal. Even those practices that are urged upon individuals in the privacy of their homes . . . are extensions of the community's practice—indeed they are means of reminding individuals even when alone that they are not merely devotees of the Christians' God, they are members of Christ's body, the people of God. That was how the Christian movement differed most visibly from the other cults that fit more easily into the normal expectations of "religion" in the Roman world. The Christians' practices were not confined to sacred occasions and sacred locations—shrines, sacrifices, processions—but were integral to the formation of communities with a distinctive self-awareness.[18]

The original Christians, in short, were about creating and sustaining a unique culture—a way of life that would shape character in the image of their God. And they were determined to be a culture, a quite public and political culture, even if it killed them and their children.

Biblical Faith on the Ground

What I am suggesting is that the Constantinian church, for many centuries, responded to the world in such a manner that it lost sense of itself as an alternative way of life. Most immediately, the late Constantinian/modern belief in some (preeminently scientific) truths as acultural and ahistorical made it seem as if there was a neutral, nonperspectival viewpoint available to anyone, anywhere who was rational and well-meaning. In that atmosphere, much of the church thought it necessary to divide Christianity into (1) private truths, or values, to be confirmed by individuals apart from any communal and political context, and (2) public truths, or facts, which consisted of Christianity translated into acultural and ahistorical truths, "essences" more or less instantiated in all viable cultures.

But this was distorting, since Christianity, like Judaism, is historically based. It concerns what has happened with a particular people, namely ancient Israel, and through a particular man who lived and died in a specific time and place, namely Jesus the Nazarene, "crucified under Pontius Pilate." It is true that most religions posit a god who in no way can be pinned down or identified by time and place. But not so the religion of the Israelites. As Robert Jenson observes,

> Other ancient peoples piled up divine names; the comprehensive-
> ness of a god's authority was achieved by blurring his particularity,
> by identification of initially distinct numina with one another, lead-
> ing to a grandly vague deity-in-general. Israel made the opposite
> move. Israel's salvation depended precisely on unambiguous iden-
> tification of her God over against the generality of the numinous.[19]

The God of Israel simply is he who led Israel out of Egypt, established
it in the Promised Land, abandoned it to exile and promised someday,
somehow, to end that exile. Thus Israel's God can only be identified
narratively, by the telling of this story. That is why "in the Bible the
name of God and the narration of his works . . . belong together. The
descriptions that make the name work are items of the narrative. And
conversely, identifying God, backing up the name, is the very function
of the biblical narrative."[20]

Accordingly, when those not born into the heritage of Israel later
come to know and worship Israel's singular God, they can do so only
through this same story—but now extended and made more encom-
passing by the life, teachings, death and resurrection of the Jew Jesus.
Put bluntly, Christians "*know how* to pray to the Father, daring to call
him 'Father,' because they pray with Jesus his Son."[21]

In modernity, this particularity was such a scandal that many Christians acted as if (and sometimes outright argued) that everyone of all
and sundry faiths worshiped the same "God" and that the story of Israel
and Jesus was secondary to knowing this "God." Now in post-Constantinian postmodernity, all communities and traditions (including the
scientific) are called back to their inescapable and particular histories.[22] Christianity no longer need worry about its "scandal of particularity," since it is recognized that particularity "scandalizes" everyone.
The upshot for Christians is that the church does not have to aspire
anymore to a supposedly neutral language and story; now we can freely
speak our own language and tell our own story.

To phrase it only slightly differently, we can now embrace, more
wholeheartedly than we could under the modern regime, what might

be called the Bible's narrative logic. Modernity pushed us toward a logic, or way of seeing and thinking, concerned to find "universal" and "reasonable" principles that could be embraced apart from any historical tradition. Modern "logic" is at work in Matthew Arnold's eagerness to think that Greek philosophy, Jewish faith and indeed "all great spiritual disciplines" move toward the same goal. All alike, says Arnold, now quoting Christian Scripture, aim for the final end "that we might be partakers of the divine nature."[23] Yet there have been and are many divinities worshiped and admired by humanity. What divine nature do we aspire to? Will we partake of Zeus's caprice? the Mayan god's lust for human blood? And how do "great spiritual disciplines" that claim no divinity (such as Buddhism) then partake of this selfsame divine nature?

Biblical logic, by contrast, does not search for disembodied, abstracted essences. It is historical through and through. It deals with particular characters and events unfolding over time, and as such it is narrative, or story-based. Hence the God who will later elect Israel creates the heavens and the earth, then suffers its rebellion (Gen 1—3). Spiritual, political, familial and economic division and alienation ensue (Gen 4—11). Now this specific Creator God decides to reclaim the world. Yet this God is not a very good modernist, and so aims to reclaim the world not by calling the divided peoples to "principles" or "essences" that somehow reside within all of them. Instead God chooses a particular man, Abraham, and promises to make of him a "great nation" through which "all the families of the earth shall be blessed" (Gen 12:2-3).

The rest of the Old Testament is the story of this God's refusal to give up on a chosen, if often fickle and unfaithful, people. Israel is that strange and great nation elected to wrestle with the strange and great God Yahweh down through the centuries. This election is often not such an appealing privilege, since the God who has chosen Israel will judge Israel when it departs from its covenant (Is 7:9). Yet God, even if God sometimes judges, will not relinquish a sure grip on the descendants of Abraham and Jacob. As Ben Meyer writes, "Though any generation in Israel might fall victim to catastrophic judgment, Israel itself will never go under."[24] Once again biblical narrative logic is relentlessly particular. Thus most of Israel may stray, but God will snatch a remnant from the lion's mouth (Amos 3:12) and make it "the new locus of election and the seed of national restoration."[25]

Ultimately confident in God's election, Israel suffers its national ups and downs but persists in looking ahead to a new reign like glorious David's (Is 11:1-9; Jer 30:8-9; Amos 9:11-15). It hopes in a new and paradisal Zion (Is 2:2-4; 28:16), a new covenant (Jer 31:31-34) and vindication in the teeth of its national enemies (Ps 137). So:

Listen to me, my people,
  and give heed to me, my nation;
for a teaching will go out from me,
  and my justice for a light to the peoples.
I will bring near my deliverance swiftly,
  my salvation has gone out
  and my arms will rule the peoples. (Is 51:4-5)

As N. T. Wright memorably puts it,

This is what Jewish monotheism looked like on the ground. It was not a philosophical or metaphysical analysis of the inner being of a god, or the god. It was the unshakeable belief that the one god who made the world was Israel's god, and that he would defend his hill against all attackers or usurpers. To the extent that Israel thought of her god in "universal" terms, this universal was from the beginning made known in and through the particular, the material, the historical.[26]

The New Testament in the Light of Jewish Politics

It was according to the rules of this narrative logic that Jesus understood his mission and the early church interpreted its Lord and its life.[27] Exactly twelve disciples, one for each of the tribes of ancient Israel, were chosen. This is but one sign that the church saw itself as Israel's seed restored and that a crucial aspect of its early mission was to call on all Israel to claim its heritage.[28] The disciples were a flock (Lk 12:32) destined to be scattered (Mk 14:27; Jn 16:32) much as Israel had been scattered. But like Israel they would be regathered (Mk 14:28; Jn 16:17, 22) and enjoy kingly rule when God drew the world's drama to its end (Mt 19:28; Lk 12:32).[29]

Following the Bible's narrative logic, Israel and the disciple-remnant within it are saved in even more specific terms. Everything depends on the single man Jesus, who takes onto himself the history and destiny of Israel. Thus, like Israel, Jesus was the one called out of Egypt (Mt 2:15). Like Israel, Jesus wanders, is tempted and is fed by God in the wilderness. Like Israel, Jesus cares for the poor, the orphaned and the stranger.

Jesus of Nazareth, as he apparently understood himself and certainly as he is interpreted by the New Testament documents, was a living recapitulation of Israel's history. More precisely, Jesus did not merely copy the history of Israel but realized it afresh in terms of his own life and obedience. By so doing, he re-presented not only Israel's past but also its future, what it would come to be through Yahweh's mighty consummating works.[30] Hence Jesus (with and through his disciples) will build a new and unsurpassable temple.

Now it is crucial to recall how important the temple was to the biblical story. Within Israel the temple bore manifold social, spiritual, political, economic and cultural importance. In contemporary America it would be the equivalent of the entire range of our iconic political and cultural institutions: the White House, Capitol Hill, the National Cathedral, Wall Street and Hollywood.[31] More than this, Jerusalem, in a profound theological sense, was considered the center of the earth—the hill Yahweh would defend against all attackers. And at the center of Jerusalem was the temple, in whose inner chambers the King of the Universe was known to dwell with an especially awesome presence. To this temple's courts all the world would someday stream, bearing offerings and worshiping the earth's one true God—Israel's Lord (Ps 96:8-10).[32]

In this light it is hard to overstate the significance of Jesus' climactic few days in Jerusalem. His entry on a donkey identifies him with the lowly and peaceable king of Zechariah 9:9. His attack on the temple, if so it may be called, simultaneously critiques Israel theologically, culturally, politically, socially and economically. And since the temple was the center not only of Israel but indeed of the universe, the cleansing of the temple purifies not only Israel but the entire cosmos.[33] Jesus and the church together, furthermore, are the new temple, a temple whose splendor will exceed that of any built with human hands (Mk 14:58; compare 2 Sam 7:4-17; Hag 2:9).

But the new temple will be built in three days—the span of time between Jesus' crucifixion and his resurrection—which means it can be built only through Jesus' death. So Jesus proceeds to his death. Under covenantal dynamics, Israel is blessed when it responds obediently to God and cursed when it strays. Roman-occupied Israel, as I have noted, still considered itself in exile, under the curse. But Jesus the Christ (Messiah-King) represents Israel and so can take on himself Israel's curse and exhaust it.[34] He perishes as King of the Jews, at the hand of the Romans, whose oppression is "the present, and climactic, form of the curse of exile itself. The crucifixion of the Messiah is, one might say, the *quintessence* of the curse of the exile, and its climactic act."[35]

Narrative logic, then, reveals the significance of Jesus' resurrection. As David Hume was to observe many centuries later in impeccable modern terms, if Jesus was raised from the dead that *in and of itself* proves nothing except that a first-century man in a backwater country somehow survived death. It is only within the context of Israel's story that Jesus' resurrection assumes its supreme significance. For this was not just any man who died, but a man who took onto himself Israel's story. And within Israel's story, resurrection had long functioned as a symbol for the reconstitution of Israel, the return from exile, and the crowning redemption. In the Israel of Jesus' day, resurrection was seen as the divine reward for martyrs, particularly those who would die in the great and final tribulation and bring Israel to its own divine reward. The prophet Ezekiel, for instance, saw the return of Israel in the figure of bones rising and taking flesh (37:1-14). Since at least Ezekiel, the symbol of corpses returning to life not only denoted Israel's return from exile but also implied a renewal of the covenant and all creation. So Jesus' resurrection was nothing less than the monumental vindication (or justification) of Israel's hopes and claims. Israel has claimed throughout its history that its God is the single Creator God, and Jesus' resurrection at last redeems that claim.[36]

Recall one more time the Bible's narrative logic. Israel's God is universal, but is known as such only through the particular, the material, the historical. God elects Abraham, and from Abraham a nation, and from that nation Jesus. Now from Israel and Jesus flow God's blessings on all the world. God restores Israel; then, building on this event, God seeks the Gentiles. As Meyer writes, "This scheme is recurrent in Acts. First, the word is offered to the Jews, who split into camps of believers and unbelievers. The believers by their faith constitute restored Israel, heir of the covenant and promises. Now and only now may gentiles find salvation, precisely by assimilation to restored Israel."[37]

The early Christians saw themselves as continuing Israel's story under new circumstances. The church "understood itself now as messianic Israel covenanted with her risen Lord" (Acts 2:38; 5:30-32).[38] It, with Jesus' headship, is the new temple, the sanctuary of the living God. It in fact is nothing less than the firstfruits of a new humanity, reborn in the last Adam named Jesus. Thus the church was seen, by itself and others, as a "third race," neither Jew nor Gentile but a new and holy nation or people (*ethnos hagion*—1 Pet 2:9). Narrative logic drives home to a theological conclusion that is unavoidably cultural and political.

Consider Ephesians 2:11-22. Here the Gentile addressees of the letter are reminded that before Christ they existed in the political status of "aliens from the commonwealth of Israel" and as a consequence were "strangers to the covenants of promise, having no hope and without God in the world" (v. 12). But now "by the blood of Christ" the Gentiles—we members of disparate nations among whom Israel was sent as a light and an example—have been made part of the same humanity as Israel (vv. 13-15). Christ has broken down the dividing wall between the Hebrews and the Gentiles, for "he is our peace" (v. 14).

This is not a peace of mere inner, psychological tranquillity: it is the peace of two reconciled peoples, a peace made possible by the change wrought "through the cross" (v. 16), a change of nothing less than the political and cultural status of the Gentiles from "aliens" to "*citizens* with the saints" (v. 19).

All this reveals just how thoroughly modern and "liberal" the lay liberals noted in chapter four are. Christian faith, far from being a matter solely between the individual and God, amounts to being grafted into a new people. For the apostle Paul, those who are justified are justified because they believe the gospel and through it become God's covenant people. Gentiles, through baptism, are incorporated into the body and life of God's particular, historical people. Baptism is initiation into a new culture, a culture called church that now, exactly as a political and social entity, is poised at the pivot point of world history. As theologian John Milbank puts it, "The *logic* of Christianity involves the claim that the 'interruption' of history by Christ and his bride, the Church, is the most fundamental of events, interpreting all other events." The church claims to "exhibit the exemplary form of human community," and as such "it is *most especially* a social event, able to interpret other social formations, because it compares them with its own new social practice."[39]

In short, the church understands itself as a new and unique culture. The church is at once a community and a history—a history still unfolding and developing, embodying and passing along a story that provides the symbols through which its people gain their identity and their way of seeing the world. The church as a culture has its own language and grammar, in which words such as *love* and *service* are crucial and are used correctly only according to certain "rules." The church as a culture carries and sustains its own way of life, which includes

☐ a particular way of eating, learned in and through the Eucharist

☐ a particular way of handling conflict, the peculiar politics called "forgiveness" and learned through the example and practice of Jesus and his cross

☐ a particular way of perpetuating itself, through evangelism rather than biological propagation

In its existence as a culture, the church is eminently Jewish. Only in certain Constantinian, and peculiarly modern, terms could it regard its mission as acultural, its gospel as ahistorical, its existence as apolitical. Instead, what political scientist Gordon Lafer says of the Jewish nation and its witness is true as well of the church:

> [The Jewish emphasis on] social solidarity . . . helps to make sense of the concept of a "chosen people," which will be a "light unto the nations." The example that Jewish law seeks to set is one aimed not at individuals but specifically at other "nations." The institutions of solidarity that mark off Jews' commitments to one another from their more minimal obligations to outsiders are not designed to be applied as universal law governing relations among all people, but rather to be reiterated within each particular nation. This, then, is the universalist mission of Judaism: not to be "a light to all individuals," . . . but *rather to teach specific nations how to live as nations.*[40]

The Individual: A Modern Mystification

So: the church as what I am calling a culture is a manner and mode of church that is, as George Lindbeck says, "more Jewish than anything else. . . . It is above all by the character of its communal life that it witnesses, that it proclaims the gospel and serves the world." And such is why "an invisible church is as biblically odd as an invisible Israel."[41] Biblical narrative logic simply demands a specific, visible people, a society or societal remnant, a *polis.*

I realize all this will strike many readers as exceedingly strange. I too, after all, have been reared and shaped in late modernity, taught to conceive of persons and Christianity in liberal, individualistic terms. So I understand that what I am calling for is an arduous retraining of the imagination, the learning and practice of a new grammar or logic. But perhaps it will ease the difficulty to remember that much of this grammar is new only to us. In historical perspective, it is our individuated, isolated self that is exceedingly strange.

As rhetorician Wayne Booth notes, the self as "in-dividual" (literally "un-divided one") is barely more than two centuries old. The in-dividual was invented by a succession of Enlightenment thinkers and became, in its most extreme but perhaps also its most widespread interpretations, a view of the self as "a single atomic isolate, bounded by the skin, its chief value residing precisely in some core of in-dividuality, of difference." Thus it remains popular—almost second nature—to think we get at our "true self" by peeling away social ties like the skin of an onion. The "real me" is not my membership in the worldwide church, my shared kin with Clapps around the country, nor my connection—with three million other people—to the geography and culture of Chicago. The "real me" is my unique, in-dividual, core self. The in-dividual self values itself most for what is supposedly utterly different and unconnected about it. But, objects Booth, such an understanding of self is incoherent. Can we really believe that we are not, to the core, who we are because of our kin, our occupations, our political and social situations, our faith or philosophical associations, our friendships? And if our "true self" is whatever stands apart from those around us and is altogether unique about us, most of us are in trouble. The bizarre modern, liberal notion of the self means even the greatest geniuses have only minimal worth. "Goethe," says Booth, "was fond of saying that only about 2 percent of his thought was original."[42] Truly, as Philip Slater remarks, "the notion that people begin as separate individuals, who then march out and connect themselves with others, is one of the most dazzling bits of self-mystification in the history of the species."[43]

In fact, Booth continues, "people in all previous cultures were not seen as *essentially* independent, isolated units with totally independent values; rather, they were mysteriously complex persons overlapping with other persons in ways that made it legitimate to enforce certain kinds of responsibility to the community." In these settings, persons were not " 'individuals' at all but overlapping members one of another. Anyone in those cultures thinking words like 'I' and 'mine' thought them as inescapably loaded with plurality: 'I' could not even think of 'my' self as separated from my multiple affiliations: my family, my tribe, my city-state, my feudal domain, my people . . ."[44]

Are the biblical cultures part of the "previous cultures" Booth here remarks on? Scholars have again and again noted the Hebrew conception of "corporate personality," the understanding that families, cities, tribes and nations possess distinctive personalities and that individuals derive identity from and so might represent these social bodies.[45] We need no new frame when we extend this picture. Writing on the concept of personhood in New Testament times, Bruce J. Malina notes, "The first-century Mediterranean person did not share or comprehend our idea of an 'individual' at all." Rather, "our first-century person would perceive himself as a distinctive whole *set in relation* to other such wholes and *set within* a given social and natural background."[46]

When Paul spoke of the church as a "body," he borrowed the metaphor from a fable widely used in several cultures of antiquity. Just as "Israel" could serve as the name either of an individual (Jacob) or of a community (the nation), so could Paul use "Christ" to refer to an individual (Jesus of Nazareth) or a community (the church). In the words of New Testament scholar Charles Talbert, " 'Members' . . . is Paul's term for the parts of the body through which the life of the body is expressed (cf. 1 Cor 12:12, 14-26; Rom 6:13). Paul is saying then that individual Christians in their corporeal existence are the various body parts of the corporate personality of Christ through which the life of Christ is expressed."[47]

It is no simple matter to "translate" ancient understandings of self (or anything else) into our later, quite different setting. Yet I think this is another task that is made more feasible by our post-Constantinian, postmodern setting. As Booth comments, the in-dividuated self has been criticized from its beginning, and "it has been torn to pieces and stomped on by almost every major thinker in this century."[48]

Furthermore, freed from its distorting Constantinian "responsibility," the church no longer must support a view of the self as in-dividuated and able to determine the good apart from all "accidental" ties of history or community. We can reaffirm that just as there can be no individual Americans apart from the nation America, so can there be no Christians apart from the church. We can be like the apostle Peter, who "did not learn God's will by Socratic questioning and rational reflection, but as the member of a group who had been with Jesus 'from the beginning in Galilee.' "[49] We can be like the early followers of Christ the Way, who trained fresh imaginations and became a new humanity by devoting themselves "to the apostles' teaching and fellowship, to the breaking of bread and the prayers" (Acts 2:42). After Constantine, on the other side of modernity, we can regard and embrace the church as a way of life.

6

THE CHURCH
AS WORSHIPING
COMMUNITY
Welcome to the
(Real) World

◨

A culture, I have argued, is a way of life. It forms and shapes a people into a distinctive community. Culture takes the raw material of certain gross, biological givens—that we must eat and procreate, that we inevitably face conflict with others—and refines them in varied, multitudinous ways. Thus every culture has its own peculiar ways of eating, procreating and fighting. These ways, in turn, correspond with what a people understands to be the basic meaning and purpose of staying alive. Individuals stop living when they give up, when they decide life is just not worth the struggle any longer. Cultures also begin to die when their spirits falter and their inhabitants suspect existence is futile. At the core of culture is the immediate and ongoing intuition that staying alive is worth the trouble. So it is not just an etymological accident that the root of the word *culture* is *cultus,* or worship. Worship is about assigning and recognizing worthiness—and ultimate worthiness at that.

Yet Christians in the modernized Constantinian situation saw their worship marginalized. Christianity, like other "religions," was a private preference. What Christians did on Sunday was removed from what they did on Monday through Saturday. Worship was an opportunity to escape politics, business and conflict. Far from being a time of intense engagement with the world, it was moved to a "sanctuary." Far from being an opportunity for people to wrestle with the principalities and powers—to wage the war of the Lamb—worship was decided never to be controversial, always to be comfortable and sentimental.

Christians were taught that worship was preeminently their opportunity to be "fed." But it was rarely recognized that to be fed is to be infantilized. To say I go to church to be fed is the same as saying, "I go to church so I can act like a baby." And the irony of this marginalized, privatized worship is heightened when we realize that even our children find such worship boring and trivial. Will Willimon quotes a child psychotherapist in his congregation who complained that the problem with children's sermons was that they never dealt with any of the real concerns of children.

"Such as?" Willimon asked.

She responded, "Concerns like death, abandonment, fear of adults, adult injustice, violence."[1]

Christian worship has not always been removed from "real life." The biblical book of Revelation is a case study in how the early church audaciously confronted the world through its worship. John's vision comes on the Lord's Day—Sunday, the day of worship. Jesus is seen in the liturgical setting of praise and thanksgiving. And he is seen not only as the "firstborn of the dead" but as "the ruler of the kings of the earth" (1:5). Not only the angels of heaven but the merchants of the earth will bow before him (chap. 18). Rather than shy away from politics or commerce, then, John and the communities that embraced his writing celebrated their worship as an indication that the way (or culture) of the Lamb was the final and true way of life.

Despite the fact that they are ragtag, disenfranchised, often persecuted bands of believers, John's communities are bold enough to set their worship head-to-head with the worship of the mighty Roman Empire. Thus two of the seven churches John addresses in his early chapters are in the cities of Smyrna and Pergamum, strongholds of the imperial cult, or worship of the Roman emperor.[2] It is just such churches that John seeks to remind, in and through the mode of liturgy, that things are not as they seem. For all its power and apparent ability to name what is ultimately worthy, Rome's worship is really nothing more than a parody of the praise and service of Israel's God (chaps. 17—18). The real lord and lion turns out to be the Lamb who was led to slaughter (chap. 5); those slain by the beast that is Rome, like the Lamb they follow, are actually conquerors (7:14); those who now seem powerless will receive obeisance from those they fear (3:8-9); and those who suffer poverty are actually rich (2:9).

In short, the business of worship as it is depicted in Revelation is "to stand things on their heads in the perceptions of its audience, to rob the established order of the most fundamental power of all: its sheer facticity."[3]

Worship: Liberation from Common Sense

It is fair enough to say, then, that Christian worship is practice in learning to see through common sense. To the world of John's day, common sense was that Rome was invulnerable, that Rome's lord was lord of the earth. But the church in its liturgy recalled itself to a different, and true, lord. And worship is where we later Christians also learn to see the world as it really is: the wonderful, if now rebellious, creation of the God of Israel.

It is crucial to emphasize that the way people see the world is a matter of being inducted into a culture's language and practices. The Enlightenment (and gnostic) dream of escaping time, place and community and arriving at universally self-evident, acultural and ahistorical truths has failed. The botanist learns a precise language and set of practices that enable her to see aspects of a tree that the untrained onlooker quite literally cannot see. In a college geology class, until I learned some of the terminology and methods of that tribe called geologists, limestone and sandstone were indistinguishable to me. The farmer knows a complicated way of life that enables him to walk through a field of wheat, then tell you when it will be ready for harvest, how abundant its yield will be, if it needs to be treated for insect pests and whether it suffers from any fungal diseases. But the accountant who accompanies the farmer through the field can only tell you he has walked through wheat, not corn. The Alaskan Inuit looks at a seal and sees a rough number of meals, a certain amount of oil for fuel, a potentially useful hide. The tourist in Orlando looks at a seal and sees a cute zoo animal.

It is culture that gives us the context from which we see and the categories by which we see. As theologian Nancey Murphy writes,

Seeing itself is influenced by what one knows and by the language used to express that knowledge. . . . To see boxes, birds, rabbits, goblets, faces, x-ray tubes, is to have knowledge. One very important type of knowledge already present in seeing is knowledge of causes; for example, seeing a concavity as a crater is already to be committed to its origin. . . . Theories provide patterns within which data appear intelligible. A theory is not pieced together from observed phenomena; it is rather what makes it possible to observe phenomena as being of a certain sort and as related to other phenomena.[4]

In this light it is worth remembering that the grace of God is not something we naturally recognize. It is not a theory pieced together from neutrally observed phenomena. It is instead the result of God's reaching out to us in mercy. It is through our acceptance of and participation in that mercy that we are given the categories of creation, world, sin, reconciliation and kingdom of God—the categories by which we claim to see "reality" as it really is.

Far from being natural or automatic, learning to see reality this way requires induction and immersion into a controversial culture. Jesus Christ is confessed to be the fullest, clearest revelation of the God of Israel—and yet he was widely rejected. What can we compare this to? Imagine a foster child who cannot recognize love, who thinks her new father's extended hand is always a hand set to strike her. Or a man who has been reared (enculturated) to think a woman's every move to comfort is a sexual advance. Or a spy whose way of life has convinced her that even the most transparent gesture is an attempt to deceive or manipulate. Or, vice versa, imagine a naive innocent who thinks the prostitute's smile is only an indication of sisterly affection and who can never detect even the most obvious ploys to exploit him.

So it is that we must be molded in certain ways, trained in certain skills, in order to see rightly what is happening around us and to us. The cruciality of Christian enculturation is underscored by the biblical testimony that the world prefers illusion to the truth. So it is that we find the frequent mention of moral and spiritual blindness or deafness (as in Is 6:9-10; 28:9-13; 29:9-14; 30:10-11, as well as in Jesus' parables—"those who have hears to hear, let them hear"). The Israelites did not imagine the world could be seen truly apart from true practices, a faithful way of life. So where rulers rule with justice, the eyes that can see will not be clouded (Is 31:1, 3), and if you cease to pervert justice and "offer your food to the hungry . . . your gloom [will] be like the noonday" (Is 58:10).

The church is in fact surrounded, pressured from all sides to give up its faithful practices and renounce its confession. I think of the film *Serpico,* in which New York City policeman Frank Serpico refuses to go on the take. But so many other cops accept bribes, and resent Serpico's refusal, that he is the one made to "feel like a criminal." At one point, when he is on the verge of giving up, his girlfriend tells him the fable of a people who drank from a poisoned well and went crazy. Only the king did not drink from the well. He alone was sane. But now the crazed populace scorns their king's difference and declares him the insane one. Overcome, the king one night drinks from the polluted well, and the next day his subjects are delighted to find him as "sane" as they are.[5]

Like that king, Christians have a source of water other than the world's poisoned well. So it is against great odds and severe resistance that we are called to a holy madness. As Robert Inchausti observes, "To be insane is to reject the given universals, and in so far as those categories are the accepted intellectual currency of the age that produced Auschwitz, holy madness is the only true sanity."[6] And as I have insisted, the preeminent place and time for Christians to cultivate holy madness is worship. Craig Dykstra helpfully notes,

> In worship, we see and sense who it is we are to be and how it is we are to move in order to become. Worship is an enactment of the core dynamics of the Christian life. This is why worship is its central and focusing activity. It is paradigmatic for all the rest of the Christian life. . . . To grow morally means, for Christians, to have one's whole life increasingly be conformed to the pattern of worship. To grow morally means to turn one's life into worship.[7]

Hearing the story of God preached, through the exercise of praise, Christians learn and rehearse what it means to be Christians. Liturgy is the primary responsibility of the church because without worship there can be no people capable of seeing and witnessing to the God of Israel. Just as capitalistic Americans could never become such exquisite consumers apart from the rites of advertising and credit cards, so Christians can never achieve the skills and vision necessary to be the church without attention to baptism and Eucharist.[8]

After Constantinianism, beyond modernism, it is crucial that the church refuse the marginalization and privatization of its worship. Liturgy is not an escape from the real world. Rather, it is constitutive of the church or, as Aidan Kavanagh wonderfully expresses it, "the Gospel of Jesus Christ become a People."[9] There is much to be said, but I can comment on only a few aspects of the liturgy's culture-forming and sustaining power.

Baptism as Civil Disobedience

In some ways the practice of baptism is the rite most explicitly addressing our constitution and cultivation as a Christian people. It is readily understood that the family is an important agent of culture, one of the most important institutions that socialize and enculturate children— that is, persons in formation. The New Testament understands life in the church as a kind of resocialization, an enculturation according to the standards of the kingdom of God rather than this world. And so the New Testament uses familial metaphors to talk about baptism and initiation into the church.

Along these lines John's Gospel can speak of being "born again" in water and the Spirit. But Paul is the New Testament writer who most lengthily elaborates on baptism and its likeness to admission into a family. In Romans 6 he writes in language reminiscent of John's born-again lingo, seeing believers baptized into the death of Christ and so now able to live in Christ (vv. 1-11). But his emphasis falls on the language of adoption (as in Rom 8:15-17 and Gal 3:26—4:6). He reminds believers that they have a new identity because they have been baptized into Christ and adopted as his sisters and brothers. When children are adopted they take on new parents, new siblings, new names, new inheritances—in short, a new culture. And those who have been baptized into Christ, according to Paul, have been adopted by God. This baptism means that Christians' new parent is God the Father. Their new siblings are other Christians. Their new name or most functional identity is simply "Christians"—those who know Jesus as Lord and determiner of their existence. Their new inheritance is freedom and the bountiful resources of community. Their new culture, or comprehensive way of life, is the church.

It is in this profound sense that Paul can speak of conversion and baptism creating a new person—even a new world (2 Cor 5:17). The biological family, let alone the nation-state, is no longer the primary source of identity, support and growth.[10] Seen in this light, baptism is profoundly subversive. Anytime the church takes baptism seriously, which is to say on its own terms, the surrounding society cannot help but see it as at least potentially politically threatening. Indeed, sociologist Robert Nisbet has commented that here lay the deepest conflict between the church and the Roman Empire.[11] In its baptism the church boldly insisted that there was a kind of kinship, a particular allegiance, more significant and constitutive than that of the biological family or the state. And so it created and sustained a people that might challenge the family's or the state's understanding of reality and truth.

In the Constantinian setting, however, baptism was stripped of its political significance and subversive potential, because in that setting the church was no longer seen as a distinctive and challenging culture. But when the church recovers some sense of itself as a culture, baptism's political overtones are immediately apparent. Consider the case of the early Anabaptists, living—and all too frequently dying—at the time of the Reformation.

It is interesting to remember that at least for Luther, heresy alone did not merit the death penalty. But the "blasphemy" of the Anabaptists was taken more seriously because it was seen as seditious. And what seditious blasphemy, exactly, did the Anabaptists commit? Adult baptism, of course. As Dale Brown writes, "More than anything else baptism into voluntary faith communities was seditious because the Reformers could not conceive that the basic fabric of society would survive if one opened the door to freedom of religion and the resultant pluralism of religious perspectives." I will not dwell on this point, but must comment how similar the dynamics sound to our own post-Constantinian, postmodern situation. Though Christians are not now burning or drowning other Christians, those who would retrench into a Constantinian Christianity have a fear much like the Reformers'. They perceive pluralism as chaos. They seek to hold society together with a dominant, officially sanctioned faith.

But to return to Professor Brown's account: he suggests that the Anabaptists' baptism was a kind of civil disobedience, civil disobedience that "embodied their doctrine of the church, their stance toward society, their advocacy of religious freedom, and their doctrine of separation of church and state. The baptismal rite was a powerful political act and became highly sacramental . . . inasmuch as it participated in the divine commissioning of disciples and Christ's baptism of suffering."

I by no means intend to imply that the practice of baptism four or five centuries later carries exactly the same meanings as early Anabaptist baptism. But the historical case is instructive because it reminds us that when the church takes itself seriously as an alternative culture, baptism is politically charged. When we recognize that "the people of

God do not go to church; they are the church," baptism can quickly, easily and *accurately* be seen as an act of civil disobedience.[12]

Preaching and Language
If baptism rebirths or adopts us into a new culture, other acts of liturgy teach us a new language and grammar.

Modernity and emerging postmodernity have made us increasingly aware of how we are all shaped by culture. They have also made us aware of how much culture is linked to language. As the philosopher Ludwig Wittgenstein once put it, "The limits of language . . . mean the limits of my world."[13] Language provides us the categories with which we see the world.

One of the early and vivid examples of this realization came from the linguistic work of Benjamin Lee Whorf, who spent years in the American Southwest studying the language of the Hopi Indians. Whorf noticed that Indo-European languages such as English give us terminology that divides nature up into discrete, neatly separated entities such as "sky," "hills" and "swamp." These languages tend to segment nature, to break it up into manageable, somewhat static pieces. But the Hopi language, Whorf said, presents "means of expression . . . in which the separate terms are not as separate as in English but flow together into plastic synthetic creations."[14] So, put quite roughly and probably in a distorting fashion, the Hopi language and grammar caused these people to see not so much a hill beneath a sky as hill flowing into or merging with sky.

For an example closer to home, consider the current culture wars over homosexuality. Much of the perplexity comes from working with biblical and other ancient terms that make distinctions other than the late modern distinction between homosexual and heterosexual *orientation*. We argue over whether or not certain objects of sexual attraction or behavior are moral. Is it as right and good for, say, a man to have sex with another man as it is for a man to have sex with a woman? But as philosopher Martha Nussbaum has observed, for the ancient Greeks the gender of the sexual object was not morally problematic. In that setting, "boys and women are very often treated interchangeably as [legitimate] objects of [male] desire. What is socially important is to penetrate rather than be penetrated."[15] The Greek sexual universe, in other words, was not divided between homosexual and heterosexual, but between the active sexual and the passive sexual partner. And the Greek sexual universe was so understood because the Greek "grammar" of sexuality was organized around sex as subjugation, rather than (say) sex as orientation.

So it is that different cultures teach us different languages and grammars, which in turn cause us to see the world differently. Accordingly, the church as a culture teaches a language and grammar that causes Christians to see the world in a peculiar—namely a Christian—way. And the most significant place where we learn Christian language and how to use it is the liturgy.

In the liturgy we learn that certain of our inclinations and actions are to be called "sin," and that the grammatically proper thing to do with sin is to confess it. In the liturgy we learn to name God Father, Son and Holy Spirit, rather than, say, Moloch. In the liturgy we learn, quite literally, how to pronounce marriage vows.

In our learning and practicing of this language from week to week, surely one of the most important actors is the preacher. The preacher is the one who tells us the story of Christ and relates our lives to it. The preacher, the Christ-storyteller, has the crucial task of helping us articulate our lives—our weal and our woe—theologically, in relation to God.[16]

Such articulation, of course, extends from preaching to spiritual direction. For a more concrete notion of what I have in mind, let me offer this example from Methodist pastor William Willimon. Will writes of finding himself in a moment requiring spiritual direction for a woman named Jane, a woman whose alcoholic husband had just abandoned her and whose best friend had died only months before. Now Jane felt alone and overwhelmed.

As pastor Willimon sat and heard this woman tell her painful story, tell of her desperate sense that she was "going down for the third time," he suddenly realized how he could speak Christian grammar and help this woman see her situation in relation to God.

"Curious," I said, "when I listen to you use the image of drowning to describe your situation, I think of a story we both heard as children."

"Which one?" she asked.

"Well, you say you are afraid that you're 'going down for the third time.' Are you drowning? Are the waves rising faster than you can tread water? I'm thinking of a flood, the story of Noah and the ark."

"Yes, everybody knows that one," Jane said. "Am I on the ark or outside in the mud?" she asked with a slight laugh.

"Where do you think you are?"

"In the water! Yes, that's where I am, going down for the third time," she replied.

Jane picked up the story for herself and wondered if God was trying to drown her, just as the flood waters blotted life from the face of the earth. But her pastor and spiritual director reminded her that was hardly the whole story of Noah and the flood. Water not only drowns but also purifies and cleanses, "God not only judges but also renews, enables the human race to start over, re-creates, begins again. There is the rainbow, the promise."

Jane confessed she had never heard the story quite that way: "All I could think about was the destruction." That's understandable, her spiritual director replied, especially in her present circumstances. But now, he suggested, there may be new life coming: "I don't like what's happened to you. . . . But maybe, just maybe, all this is being destroyed so something much better can be born."

Jane was not sure. She began to hope a bit, realizing she hadn't drowned yet. But then she remembered tomorrow: Would she be able to get a job? Would she get married again? Her pastor was honest, and again he focused her predicament theologically: "I don't know the answers any more than you do, at this point. We'll have to wait. Like Noah. For 'forty days and forty nights' even. I don't see the rainbow yet."

Jane wished for a clearing of the clouds. But then she determinedly confessed, "I couldn't have made it without God, without the church and their support, I'll tell you that." Her pastor suggested then that maybe, just maybe, she was in the ark after all.[17]

I take this as an instance of particularly skillful spiritual direction. And it was skillful because it provided Jane with language and grammar that allowed her to see her predicament theologically, in relation to God.

Pastors in today's setting are severely tempted to substitute something else for their mother tongue or first language. Perhaps most notably in our context they are tempted to replace theological language with psychological language. Surely psychotherapeutic language has helped many people, Christians included. But it should be the church's second language, not replacing the first language of theology. Psychological culture would have us think "id," "ego" and "superego" are more concrete than "Father," "Son" and "Holy Spirit." They are not. If the gospel is true, Freudian divisions of the psyche are actually *more abstract,* less linked to objective referents, less fundamentally real, than the Christian designation of God as Trinity. Or, to take another example, *eschatology* is admittedly an awkward and Latinate term—but is it any less awkward and latinate than *dysfunctionality?* Is *redemption* really any less practical or down-to-earth than *self-esteem?*

The difference is not that psychological grammar is inherently more practical, more "real," more concrete than theological grammar. The difference is that there is a community ready to concretize and put into practice psychological grammar, while the church has accepted the marginalization of its language; it has concretized and practiced theological grammar less and less. Preachers and spiritual directors in particular can help us remember how to speak our first tongue. Worship, we might say, is where those who don't get paid for it learn and do theology.

Eucharist: You Are How You Eat

If baptism and proclamation give the church vast resources for the tasks of spiritual formation, we must say the same no less vigorously of the

Eucharist. I have emphasized baptism as resocialization, itself a practice of enculturation. I have emphasized proclamation in preaching and spiritual direction as the teaching of a primary language, and language is one of the most obvious and foundational aspects of any culture. With the Eucharist we turn to the preeminently social and cultural act of eating.

On its face eating may appear to be the most natural (and individual) of behaviors. Of course it is natural in the sense that every creature must do it or die. And it is individual in that it is inextricably linked to our separate physical bodies. But despite this, eating is one of the most densely and finely cultured acts we engage in.

Probably because it is so basic and elemental—eating is life itself—people always endow eating with all sorts of significance. Culture pervades our meals. It provides menus of the plants or animals we will and will not eat, times when we will eat, the sort of equipment we will eat with, ways in which we will decorate and present our food, the sequence in which we eat foods, and all kinds of dining manners. Classicist Margaret Visser observes that meals may in fact be at the base of many important human characteristics. Kinship systems evolved to answer questions about who belongs with whom; perhaps the larger part of those questions revolved around deciding who would eat with whom. Language may well have been forced to expand and spread so that people could discuss and plan for the acquisition and preparation of food and prevent or resolve disputes over food supplies. Surely technology arose and developed as people sought more sure and efficient ways to kill, cut, keep, carry and cook their food. Finally, we can imagine that some of the earliest and most important matters of morality were occasioned by food. What is a just distribution? Should we share our food or feel guilty if the people just over the hill are starving?[18]

Eating, then, necessitates our involvement with others. It is, willy-nilly, a social endeavor. There is for people really no such thing as "uncultured" or asocial eating. Even—maybe *especially*—cannibals have surrounded the preparation and consumption of their "food" with elaborate traditions and procedures. As Visser eloquently notes, eating is a "medium of social relationships: satisfaction of one of the most individual of needs becomes a means of creating community."[19] Exchanges of food inevitably link persons together in webs of mutuality and reciprocity. Eating symbolizes relationships and attitudes: we eat to celebrate birthdays and holidays, we gather and serve meals to mourning family and friends at a funeral. Eating mediates social status and power: so during the 1988 presidential election, in an attempt to link himself with the "common man," blue-blooded George Bush conspicuously snacked on pork rinds.[20]

Scripture has incorporated a recognition that the fundamental problems and hopes of the human community have to do with food. Thus, as Kavanagh writes, "Genesis says that we began in a swamp teeming with life, but that something went vastly wrong one evening at dinner. Apocalypse says that the difficulty was finally resolved into something called the Banquet of the Lamb."[21]

In this light, even if we might find the popular declaration "You are what you eat" a bit opaque, we can immediately and thoroughly affirm that "you are *how* you eat." If an anthropologist were allowed to study a culture but limited to observation of a single practice of the culture, that anthropologist would do well to choose to scrutinize mealtimes. And in fact an anthropologist could learn much about the church in particular times and places simply by observing its practice of the Eucharist. As I have suggested, one of the key questions attached to eating is "Who eats with whom?" In the antebellum South, white and black did not eat together at our Lord's table. Similarly, in 1857 the Dutch Reformed Church of South Africa, in deference to the "weakness of some," allowed the Lord's Supper to be celebrated in separate services for church members of different races. The ideology of apartheid—with its roots scandalously embedded in the church—grew steadily following this liturgical innovation.[22]

How we eat has consequences. I would suggest that the Eucharist serves at least four significant culture-forming and sustaining functions for the church.

1. The Eucharist discloses and forms us to be a people who are based on the common good of Christ's lordship. At the Lord's Supper we remember who we are by reflecting on his death and resurrection. We anticipate the consummation of the work he has begun by rehearsing the marriage banquet of the Lamb of God, as celebrant and people affirm together in the eucharistic prayer, "Christ has died, Christ is risen, Christ will come again." This is the past, present and future—the new history and hope—every member of the church has adopted. This history and hope, not that of a particular race, sex, nation or profession, provides the fundamental identity of every Christian. And the Eucharist is the special practice that enables us to see who we are. Like the disciples on the road to Emmaus, or like Paul in 1 Corinthians 11, we discern the body of Christ in our eating and drinking together—we see Christ and what it is to participate in Christ. In the Eucharist, as Dale Brown suggests, "the emphasis is not as much on eating bread as on breaking it. Bread already broken in many places constitutes a privatized symbol of chewing and swallowing, of individual possession. The breaking of bread signifies the intention to share it, to give it to others, thus portraying the character of Christ's body."[23]

2. The Eucharist discloses and forms us to be a people who are radically egalitarian. I have already emphasized that food is one of the ways people signify status and set themselves off from one another. We Christians are people whose Lord dined at an open table. As the Gospels indicate, this was to his contemporaries one of his most shocking and objectionable behaviors. They understood what it meant: it signaled acceptance, friendship and empowerment of the tax collector, the Gentile, the whore. Our word *companion* comes from a Latin word meaning literally "one with whom we share bread."[24] Certainly Jesus and the people of his time and place understood meals in that way. As one commentator puts it, in the Gospels meal-sharing is a test of social reconciliation.[25] And scholar John Dominic Crossan argues that the open table was "the heart of the original Jesus movement, a shared egalitarianism of spiritual and material resources."[26]

In the Eucharist we practice eating as Jesus ate, so that we might become and indeed be his people. Thus we must call to our table people of all races, all sexes, all social classes, all physical conditions. The shared table is a sign of—a practice of—our hospitality and support for all manner of people.

3. *The Eucharist discloses and forms us to be a people who have the resources to face conflict and admit failure.* It doesn't take long, in the face of talk like this about the high ideals of the church, for questions and objections to occur. "What's all this about the church being so special, so heroic? Look at all the horrible things that happen in the church, the abuse and the pettiness." A popular Constantinian response to such objections was to dismiss the church and attention from the church in order to point to an acultural, asocial savior, to be known by individuals in their isolation: "Don't look at the church, look at Jesus." But of course the argument of this book has been that this misconstrues the narrative logic of the Bible and the consistent political presence of a witnessing people that logic entails. God the Father and God the Son are not fundamentally known privately and ethereally. They are instead encountered through a holy people, a community set apart, a light to the world, a city on a hill, a tribe bearing promise to all other tribes. Christians are inescapably called to the corporate witnessing of the coming of God's kingdom in Jesus Christ. However beleaguered, however divided, however hateful we may sometimes be, still, as long as we remain the church in the slightest, that witness is our reason for being.

But there is something to be said about witness that is readily overlooked. Witness is not, at least not only, a matter of heroism. We can in fact witness to God's kingdom in Christ amid our conflict, through our failure. After all, as every newly married couple rapidly learns, there are distinctive ways to fight. My wife's parents were experts in the silent treatment; my parents preferred to shout it out—it took Sandy and me five years to work out our own constructive fighting style. And just as there are distinctive ways to fight, there are particular ways to fail. The ways in which people fight and fail vary from culture to culture.

Fighting and failure in the Christian culture are shaped by the resource of forgiveness.[27] Our regular practice of the Eucharist is a practice in accepting God's forgiveness and in forgiving one another. We should remember that not every culture has this resource. And without the possibility of forgiveness, it is impossible to admit failure or confess wrongdoing, since such admission or confession can only result in our being diminished—if not destroyed. Consider, for instance, the culture of the business corporation, in which admitting failure can only hinder a career. Forgiveness is a communal resource, perhaps the keystone of Christian politics, a resource and keystone that can enable us to face failure and conflict without destroying ourselves in the process. Because we have this resource, we should not cower before the prospect of failure or try to deny and hide our conflict. And being a people of forgiveness, we must aggressively redefine peace. Peace for Christians is not simply the absence of conflict. Instead, as Stanley Hauerwas writes, "peacemaking is that quality of life and practices engendered by a community that knows it lives as a forgiven people."[28] The Eucharist is our regular practice in accepting God's forgiveness and being reconciled with one another.

4. *The Eucharist discloses and forms us to be a people who are nonviolent.* At the Lord's Table we celebrate the death of the last scapegoat, Jesus Christ, removing any excuse for further violence. And at the Lord's Table, as I have just been saying, we celebrate forgiveness and practice peacemaking or reconciliation. In a warring world we are indeed a peculiar people, a people called to survive by worship rather than weapons. And, contrary to prevalent stereotypes, it is exactly because of our nonviolence that Christians must be the most political of all animals. This is so because, as Hauerwas writes, our "peacekeeping requires the development of the processes and institutions that make possible confrontation and resolution of differences" without resort to violence.[29]

Now if words of qualification were needed on Christian witness, they may be needed even more here, since most Christians do not accept a characterization of the Christian faith as pacifist. The debate between the pacifist and the just war traditions is profound, with significant differences. But it is still fair to insist that the vast majority of Christians are pacifist in an important sense: most Christians today and through history *presume against* violence. The just war theory as put forward by its leading interpreters places the burden of doubt on those who would resort to violence. It presents them with several hurdles to clear before war can be "justified." Ethicist Robin Gill gets at a crucial truth when he renames the just war tradition "selective" (as opposed to "thorough-going") pacifism.[30] Most Christians, whatever they label their position on war, are committed to a politics that makes possible confrontation and resolution of differences without killing people. Christians presume against violence.

But another qualification, almost as important, must quickly be added. Talk of war and peace makes nonviolence sound like a dramatic but only occasional concern. It is not. We do violence to one another in ways other than attacking one another's body. The violence we confront in the church on a regular basis is subtle but sometimes almost as hurtful as physical violence. The church is too often the place where people who have little power elsewhere can make their all-out power plays. So it is that even the most trivial matters are the occasions of some of the most violent church battles. I think of a friend who has been in the pastorate more than a decade and tells me the most horrible church fight he has endured revolved around allowing teenagers to wear ball caps in the sanctuary. Among other things, the Eucharist calls us to confront our violence, the violence that so easily pervades our lives, from the lethal violence provoked by Persian Gulf oil to the insidious violence provoked by baseball headgear.

Worship as the Real World

All these things are aspects of the Eucharist—and of baptism and preaching as well—that form and sustain the church as an alternative culture. Worship constitutes the church. Worship makes and keeps us Christians.

A minister in my home diocese of Chicago relates a telling tale from a pastorate he once held. One year new carpeting was installed in the church building. Apparently through some combination of the building's peculiar climatic dryness and the new carpet's own qualities, the rug built up a terrific charge of static electricity. On the first Sunday on the new rug, this pastor intoned the words of blessing, lifted the chalice to the lips of his senior warden—and saw the senior warden knocked flat on his back by a sudden electrical discharge. In fact, parishioners were so consistently shocked that it became customary to serve an acolyte first and let him or her absorb the initial and most charged jolt. The acolytes, in turn, would draw straws to assign this somewhat sobering duty.

The story is parabolic. It speaks of a church that learned, albeit by unusual means, to take the Eucharist quite seriously. Hearing it, we would find it hard not to think of Paul warning the Corinthians that some of them, in receiving the body and blood of Christ unworthily, "eat and drink judgment against themselves" (1 Cor 11:29). We do a serious thing when we eat and drink, when we baptize and preach. To cite Paul again, when we worship we "discern the body" (see 1 Cor 11:29). We see, we practice who and what we are as Christians.

That is why we must insist that liturgy, far from being an escape from the real world, *is* the real world. God is at work, of course, in all of reality, not merely in our fleeting hours of public worship. But humanity is a blinded race, and in worship we have a chance to look on the world as it truly is—the beloved and redeemed creation of God the Father, Son and Holy Spirit. For a brief definition of worship, I have seen few better than Abraham Joshua Heschel's: "Worship is a way of seeing the world in the light of God."[31]

Any culture lives and dies by the vitality of its rituals and symbols. As Kavanagh puts it, "Social rituals constitute the myriad ways in which any society enacts itself, gives itself distinctive form in space and time."[32] Try to imagine the United States remaining the United States without a national anthem, an Independence Day celebration, a State of the Union address by the president, without county fairs and Thanksgiving Day dinners. These rituals are when and how we remember what

America means and, quintessentially, experience what it is.

By Christian confession, our most fundamental identity is not that of Americans—it is that of Christ's disciples. So our most important culture is the church; our most important cultural activity is the liturgy. In the liturgy, day to day and week to week, we "do the world as God means it to be done."[33] This means that in worship we vigorously enflesh a restored and re-created world—a world returned to its genuine normality through holy abnormality—in a civic and cultural form, a public, powerful, visible, political form that challenges and stands in contrast to all other cultures. Worship is not simply world-changing. It is, indeed, world-making.

7

THE CHURCH
AS PARADE
The Politics of Liturgy

◨

hope by now it is abundantly clear that I am resisting the compartmentaliza-
tion of faith and worship. I reject the terms of those who think the
church at its worship is necessarily inwardly focused and removed
from the "public" world. I want Christians to stop thinking in the
essentially modern and liberal categories that cut up our lives as
"private" and "public," "inward" and "outward." The term *liturgy* comes
from two Greek words, *laos* and *ergon,* meaning "people" and "work."
So liturgy is the public work par excellence of the church—something
that, if omitted, would mean the church was no longer the church. Far
from being a retreat from the real world, worship enables Christians to
see what the real world is and equips them to live in it.

From Orgies Back to Liturgies
Liturgy also implies and enacts mission (the "outward" work of the

church). As I indicated earlier, students of the liturgy have noted that the word may mean not only work *of* the people but work *for* the people. In Roman society, "to build a bridge for a public road across a stream on one's private property would constitute a liturgy." Military service at personal expense was an act of liturgy. The wealthy sought favor by sponsoring lavish "liturgies"—huge dramas for the entertainment of the citizenry.[1]

It is once again worth emphasizing that had the first Christians wanted their worship and religious experience to be understood privatistically, they had at their disposal language that could have readily and precisely reflected that. The Greek word that more narrowly designated religious exercises—in the modern sense of private and focused on the nonphysical—was *orgia*. This is, of course, the root of our English word *orgy*, and it "connoted then as now ecstatic rites that were largely private and excessively indulgent."[2] I am concerned that the worship of the church leave off being orgies and return to being liturgies.

In worship as liturgy rather than orgy, the church builds bridges at its expense and welcomes the world's crossing. If nothing else, the church hopes its own drama, the weekly liturgy, will introduce those who don't already know God the Father, Son and Holy Spirit to that fundamental truth and reality.

So all liturgy is related to mission, to what happens in our world not just on Sunday but also on Monday through Saturday. The church exists for the sake of the world. When I speak of the Christian church as a distinctive culture, I am definitely not suggesting that the church shape and strengthen its identity so that it can withdraw into invulnerable isolation. Instead, worship teaches and forms us to live by the Jesus story so that others—the entire world, the church prays—will learn to live according to reality and wholeness. The people, the culture, that is now the church is joyful that God has already drawn it together, but it lives in hope of a greater joy, a joy that achieves fullness only with the kingdom's fullness.

To put it another way, I know that the immediate and strongest objection to all I am saying is that this is a proposal for the church to be "sectarian." And *sectarian* here is meant as synonymous with "insulated," "withdrawn" and "irresponsible." I am arguing that the church should be distinctive, that it should live by its own self-understanding as a community constituted and sustained by the lordship of Jesus Christ. And according to that very self-definition, the church does not exist for itself, but for its mission and witness to the world on behalf of the kingdom.

In this sense the church is not an institution like other institutions, concerned to preserve itself at all costs. In fact, the church is the one and only anti-institutional institution. It is not true to its own cultural identity unless it is constantly critical of itself and its shortcomings in the light of the kingdom. Its joy—*our* joy—is not merely that the kingdom will one day replace and renew the world, but that the kingdom will one day supersede the church as well. Christians hope and pray for the day when all nations and all of creation will recognize the lordship of Jesus Christ, so that there will no longer be any distinction between the church and the world.

So the church is the only institution that regularly celebrates the hope of its demise, the hope that it will not endure forever. What nation includes in its pledge of allegiance a plea for its end? What family opens its annual reunion with petitions for the day the family name will be forgotten?

In short, the liturgy itself demands that the world be brought into the church and that the church go out into the world. The Eastern Orthodox helpfully speak of mission as "liturgy after the liturgy."[3] To refer again to the language of the earliest Christians: *leitourgia* designated services in the temple, but equally designated the ongoing and daily life of the Christian community.[4] Mission is the "work of the people" Monday through Saturday, done after and formed by the "work of the people" on the first day, Sunday. Mission and witness is living every day according to the vision granted to us especially and most intensely when we gather for worship.

Later in this chapter I will compare the church's parade to American

Independence Day parades. But perhaps it is helpful to clarify what I mean at this point with reference to Independence Day celebrations. When my family and I attend a Fourth of July parade, we are certainly participating in American culture. But we continue to participate in American culture when, after the parade, we go to a friend's home for a picnic and fireworks. The Independence Day parade is a concentrated celebration of our Americanness, but we do not stop being and acting like Americans after the parade. We go home and do very American things like picnic on hot dogs and beer and toss a few firecrackers.

Similarly, if less trivially, Christians do not stop being Christians after they participate in the Sunday liturgy. They depart to live the liturgy, to celebrate God's goodness, to rely on the skill called forgiveness for the maintenance of truthful relationships, to practice hospitality to strangers in all their diversity.

Much of our difficulty in being Christians is due to awkwardness, a deficiency of skill in deploying our heartfelt dispositions—in more than one sense, a lack of gracefulness. We may feel the need to love, to be at peace with others, to express kindness or joy or gentleness, to be quietly faithful and patient, but we have not learned how to do it. And so our fumbling attempts at love come off as intrusive or maudlin. Our desire for peace becomes bland toleration or an overweening enforcement of our own will and way. We know and we are committed, body, mind and heart, to showing joy—but it is not natural to raise our hands, our singing voices, and we end up just being stiffly silly. Or our quiet fidelity and patience come off as aloofness and arrogant detachment.

How many times have we tried to say "I love you" to a friend or spouse or parent and only ended up embarrassing ourselves? How many times have our best intentions at gentleness, patience, kindness, at joy and fidelity, developed into halted roughness, curt inquiry of another's welfare or stupid moments of uncomfortable silence? So it is that oftentimes when we actually do love, are at peace with others or are disposed to gentleness, we cannot live it out. We lack gracefulness. We are ready to dance, but we are clumsy and step on our partner's toes.

In this chapter, to emphasize the public nature of Christian worship, I am referring to liturgy as parade. But it is more often designated as dance. And it is exactly because of our clumsiness, our gracelessness, that there is value in seeing the liturgy as dance. It is a rehearsal of the Christian story that takes us through the steps again and again. Doing the steps repeatedly—offering our gifts, tendering the kiss of peace and so forth—we learn the dance. We stop acting so self-consciously, and the dance becomes second nature. By reenacting the story—the patience and gentleness of Christ, willing to die on a cross; the fidelity of God leading Israel out of Egypt; the joy of Easter dawning—we gradually, if fitfully, are conformed to it. By dancing, we shed our awkwardness in the dance. We become graceful in hearing and living the story.

And just as dancing is inevitably social, so is liturgy. Worship is not private and disconnected from the world outside the walls of any holy building. It is in fact incomplete and distorted if it is removed from that outside surrounding. What is meant by the expression "liturgy after the liturgy" is captured by the final words of the old Roman mass, *Ite missa est,* meaning "Get out!" Until we have gotten out, the liturgy—the work of the church for the world—is not finished.

By alluding to New Testament Christians, Eastern Orthodoxy and the old Roman mass, I mean to remind us again that the church has not always understood the liturgy as something private and separated from the real or public world. If we are to recover a full and intentional sense of the liturgy as the church's cultural and political center, it may be worthwhile to give some attention to how it was rendered supposedly acultural and apolitical.

The Depoliticization of the Liturgy
Of course I have already hinted at this story in discussing the privatization of faith especially in the modern, industrial era. But historical periods are never so clear-cut, never so definite as we make them seem by naming them. In that sense the development of modernity and industrialism began centuries before the French Revolution or the invention of the cotton gin. So too the relegation of worship to the

private and purely spiritual world has historical roots that go much deeper than the topsoil of modernity.

By the time of the Renaissance and Reformation, Christian liturgy was getting what we would now call bad press.[5] Like a prolific ivy in a tropical climate, liturgy had grown and spread and complicated itself until it was strangling or smothering everything around it. There was too much liturgy, and it was too ornate and complex for all but the ecclesiastical experts. The church had created an atmosphere in which many Christians were ready for the Reformation's iconoclasm. The people could no longer see the blue sky for a net of tangled vines. They wanted some simplicity.

But another, and more important, development enabled the liturgy to literally get bad press. The printing press was invented. And in northern Europe, where the Reformation took off, literary humanism dominated. It was natural enough for followers of the Reformation, then, to fixate on the Bible as God's (printed) Word.

What we need to appreciate is that liturgy before the printing press was quite vigorously a communal and social affair. It was a corporate enactment and celebration of God's presence. Augustine writes that people talked excitedly during his sermons. John Chrysostom mentions that his auditors cheered or wept, pounding their breasts. Other early church writers tell of gatherings that got rowdy when a presbyter or deacon omitted a portion of the rite. In other words, people participated. And they did not imagine their liturgy confined to a "sanctuary," segregated from the surrounding public. Early Christians met liturgically in tenements, forums, shrines and cemeteries. Worship could raucously spill out of a cathedral into the streets of cities and suburbs.

As Aidan Kavanagh remarks, in this setting worship was theology—it was the eminent form of "knowing God." Primary theology was done not in the scholar's study but in the liturgy, the work of the people. Primary theology was not reflection *about* God but an encounter and engagement *with* God. Theology in such a setting was plebeian in that it was done by the common people and not by academic elites. It was communitarian in that it was done corporately rather than in the solitude of the study. And it was quotidian or everyday in that it was done regularly, in a daily, weekly and yearly round of public liturgical practice.[6]

Orthodoxy in the older and original Christian sense was "correct praise" or "right worship." The early church's stress was on faith "not so much as an intellectual assent to doctrinal propositions, but as a way of living in the graced commonality of an actual assembly at worship before the living God."[7]

All this decisively changed with the advent of the printing press. Formerly God's Word had been fundamentally experienced in the corporate act of worship. But as books and Bibles became abundant and widely available, even the illiterate could see God's words tightly regimented and contained on the printed page. Eventually God's Word was too easily understood not as a presence especially (though not at all solely) encountered in liturgy but as something set down in horizontal lines that could be isolated and studied by the solitary individual.

Soon church architecture yields places of worship arranged like a page of a book, the people situated in rows of pews aligned like so many typeset sentences. Soon those who attend the liturgy are invited not into a dance in which all participants have necessary steps, but into a performance by a single person who expounds the printed text. The atmosphere of liturgy is no longer that of a bustling, rowdy activity where much is happening; it is now a classroom in which the pastor/instructor must be granted exclusive attention. The focus shifts from what people do together to what happens "inside" each individual.[8] It shifts away from God's Word as a holy event to God's Word as a holy text. As Kavanagh observes, "The truth lies now exclusively in the text; no longer on the walls, or in the windows, or in the liturgical activity of those who occupy the churches."[9] Corporate worship recedes, is no longer seen as foundational and fundamental. Now Christians can imagine their private, individual acts of worship—devotions or quiet times or daily offices—as foundational and fundamental.

Liturgy, in short, has been depoliticized. In a rush to individualism and privatism, we have gotten things backwards. Important as our individual devotions surely are, it is not they that are constitutive of the church. It is the church's actual gathering or assembly. There, in the *ekklēsia,* we do the liturgy. The *ekklēsia* is the body gathered to attend to its common identity and welfare or—as we can just as well say—to its political affairs. The liturgy is the work of the people that makes us a people. We are constituted, granted identity and unity, by gathering around the Lord's Table to enact the Word, by hearing and responding to the Word in Scripture.

In our individualistic ethos we too easily neglect and forget all this. But the truth remains. Liturgy is formative. Liturgy is Christian culture, the cultivation of Christ's disciple community.

Two Parades

In all this I am not arguing that worship and the world (or faith and politics) need to be reconnected. I am saying something stronger: that the two are already profoundly connected, but the connection has been obscured. Perhaps a comparison of two parades will help make this point clearer.[10]

What I am asserting is in the end not at all arcane or esoteric. To be human is to worship, to adore, to admire and give our allegiance to powers greater than we, powers that grant our life meaning and purpose, substance and form. Worship presents the world as it is and as it is really supposed to be. It calls us to the imitation of heroes or gods whose ways would set the world right. At worship we consecrate our lives: what we worship or ultimately adore is what we live and die for. And at worship we celebrate our lives: what we worship is the source and sustainer of our existence. Thus worship shapes us, it forms us as a people.

And all good worship, or liturgy, includes a parade. Each Sunday morning, at the Episcopal church where I pray, the ministerial party processes into the midst of assembled Christians. The party is led by someone bearing a crucifix, held high so that we might all recall and adore the One we want to become like. At the end of the liturgy the ministerial party trails the cross-banner back through the assembly, implying that the newly reformed and rededicated Christians should now join the parade and follow their standard out into the world. In the beginning and ending of our service we adhere to ancient liturgical tradition, which means the church has long considered parades important enough to stage at least a couple every week.

Yet the church is ambivalent about parades. Parades are tricky, because fallen creatures tend to turn all celebrations into glorifications of themselves and their designs. The Christian story writes its ambivalence about parades right into the Gospel accounts, with Jesus' so-called triumphal entry. Jesus parades, but on a humble donkey rather than a proud warhorse. The people cheer and honor Jesus, but for what exactly? Days, mere hours later, they will publicly demand his execution.

Again at the church where I pray, the entire assembly literally joins the liturgical parade on one day of the year. That day is Palm Sunday. Even in April it is often chilly near Chicago. We don our coats and sweaters and march outside, carrying palms and cheering Jesus. But not long afterward we are back inside and read the Gospel in scripted parts, as if in a drama. Then we who were moments before honoring Jesus play the crowd at Pilate's court, shouting repeatedly, "Crucify him!"

This is a liturgical rehearsal of our human ambivalence, our inclination to desire saviors, but on our own terms and for our own purposes. By taking this ambivalence into our liturgy we mean to recognize and transform it. In fact, when we reenact the triumphal entry, there is an important difference between us and the original fickle, rabbling masses. Those original masses lived the triumphal entry before the crucifixion; we reenact it after the crucifixion. So we take note that the Savior rides an ass rather than a warhorse, and we realize he is about to submit himself to imperial violence rather than wreak revolutionary violence. Revolutionary violence would aim to put "our side" on top. It would provide us a leader and savior quite congenial to already existing hopes. Palm Sunday says Jesus will save us indeed, but his way of saving us will turn our dreams and desires inside out. This is not salvation on our terms. It is not celebration of ourselves simply as we are and, left alone, would have become.

Thus we transform the triumphal entry as we reenact it, and it transforms us. Palm Sunday is practice at proclaiming Jesus king and remembering whose subjects we are. Palm Sunday shows us that Jesus' kingship takes a distinctive shape, and that giving our allegiance to it makes us a distinctive people. In liturgical terms, it rehearses us in a parade by which we can judge all other parades.

And so the liturgical and the political inevitably meet. Or, better, the liturgical is political; it is practice in Christian politics calling us to judge all other politics by it. When we see liturgy and its parades in this light, we cannot, for instance, rush into uncritical participation at Independence Day parades. For then we will recognize those parades for what they are—the high liturgical occasions of a rival faith.

And at no time might this be clearer than shortly after a "successful" war. You will remember that the Persian Gulf War ended in February of 1991. Our own municipality, like many around the country, decided to celebrate victory and welcome homecoming soldiers at its annual Fourth of July parade. But being trained in the parades of a non-American King, I could only approach the Gulf War victory parade with suspicion.

I will not be coy. My own convictions are those of a Christian pacifist. I believe the way of the cross, rehearsed on Palm Sunday, calls for the renunciation of violence and the imaginative practice of peace. But, as I have said, that hardly limits such concern to professing pacifists. Palm Sunday *inclines* Christian pacifists and just war theorists alike toward nonviolence.[11]

A leading Protestant interpreter of the just war tradition, James Turner Johnson, declares forthrightly that Christian pacifism and just war theory have the same attitude about war: "both regard it with suspicion as something less than ideal to be reached in the kingdom of God."[12] They share a common first principle of opposition to war and violence. Their difference (and a significant one it is) comes in the principles that pacifists or just war theorists add to that common first principle.

Catholic just war theorist David Hollenbach writes in even stronger terms:

> Under *no* circumstances can war be considered a good. And for Christians, it is impossible to *presume* that the resort to lethal force is compatible with respect for the sacredness of human life or fidelity to the gospel of Christ. The original just war question implies that nonviolence is the Christian norm and that the use of force can only be moral by way of exception, if at all. Violent force should be *presumed* to be incompatible with a fundamental Christian moral orientation.[13]

If such is the attitude of Christians, then celebration of a military victory is a complicated matter. Of course there were, in the wake of the Gulf War, things worth celebrating. The day after Allied troops rolled into Kuwait City, a wire service published a moving photograph of a weathered old Kuwaiti. He stands beneath a low-hung American flag and is gently lifting its hem to his lips, kissing it. I can empathize with his jubilation and appreciate his gratefulness to the United States.

I sometimes work with a copy editor whose husband is a retired serviceman. Early in the war, she said she knew several of the Desert Storm field commanders. She worried over them. What's more, her son was in the Navy and stationed at a Great Lakes base. His responsibilities in the war would include visiting families with the grim news that a loved one had been killed. She worried over the strain her son would bear. But the war, as it turned out, ended with relatively small cost—at least to the United States. Very few American field commanders were killed; the copy editor's son was spared too many unenviable visits. The safe homecoming of soldiers is something to celebrate.

But Christians who march in Palm Sunday parades, and mean it, cannot simply celebrate "the war" or "the victory." We cannot celebrate violence, even "successful" violence. We cannot celebrate tens of thousands of Iraqi dead. We cannot celebrate the bombing of a nation's infrastructure back into the nineteenth century. We cannot celebrate starving Kurdish refugees or Persian Gulf oil spills.

There are appropriate and inappropriate celebrations. A friend dies after a long and painful illness. It is a time for gratitude that suffering has ended, but hardly a time for balloons and hoopla. Or neighbors bear a child with serious birth defects. There is new life. We appropriately go and welcome these new parents home, embrace their child and promise them assistance. But the circumstances are complicated. The occasion is too heavy for pink or blue ribbons and cardboard storks on the front lawn.

The problem with parades following the Gulf War was the problem of inappropriate celebration. These were parades heavily laden with bellicose flag-waving, gun salutes, tanks and jeeps. They idealized war. There perhaps could have been such a thing as a (Christianly) appropriate parade. It might have featured homecoming soldiers marching out of uniform, as well as visiting Kuwaitis or their Americanized relatives. Who knows, it might even have included, midway through, a marching band doing a New Orleans-style dirge, inviting appropriate silence as relatives of killed soldiers and Americanized Iraqis marched past. It would certainly have included, like Lincoln's Gettysburg and Second Inaugural addresses, a sense of the gravity and cost of war to both "sides."

But the Independence Day parades of 1991 (and most other years, for that matter) conveyed something else altogether. They conveyed triumphalism. They glorified "us" and "our way of life." They conveyed the notion that military might is the key to America's strength. They promoted the idea that violence is the best way to solve real problems. They taught our children that we can proudly and uncritically trust our nation to wage justifiable wars. These parades assumed, in short, that wars are to be unabashedly celebrated as long as "we" win them. (To get a true sense of the Gulf War parades, we can never forget there were no parades for soldiers returning from Vietnam.)

The summer following the Gulf War, the Fourth of July fell on a Thursday. Three days later millions of Americans, confessing Christians, were present at the weekly celebration of Jesus' resurrection. It was tragic that many didn't recognize the incongruity. Christians just didn't belong in both of those parades.

8

THE CHURCH
AS LISTENING
COMMUNITY
*The Performance
of Scripture*

◨

My *complaint thus far has been about the privatization, and thus* marginalization, of the church and its activities. I have argued that the church is a *polis,* a political body that promotes and sustains a distinctive way of living in the world, and that liturgy is a political activity. And I have tried to do all this biblically—under the auspices of the Bible's master story, frequently invoking one or another of its many particular stories. Now comes the time to look more closely and explicitly at the Bible itself. For in fact it is the Bible—or better said, a certain use of the Bible—that has contributed like nothing else to the privatization and depoliticization of the church.

The attentive reader may have picked this up in the last chapter, when I cited Aidan Kavanagh's concerns about the rise of print technology. Print, says Kavanagh, removed primary attention to God's Word from the context of corporate liturgy and replaced it in the primary context of the solitary reader's study. The Orthodox theologian Mary Ford echoes Kavanagh's concern when she writes that today "the crisis in biblical studies is largely the result of taking Scripture out of the context in which it was intended to be interpreted: the living Tradition of the Church, which includes the liturgical context, the context of the believing community, and especially the context of living spiritual experience."[1]

In short, the Bible was never meant, first and foremost, to be read alone. A fair portion of it (Psalms, hymns cited in the New Testament) comes right out of corporate worship. When the Persians let exiled Israelites return to their homeland, the Israelites did not retire to their homes each with his or her own scroll. Instead, the people assembled and heard Scripture read from dawn till noon.[2] Paul's letters are written to be read aloud to gathered Christians. So the salutation of each of his letters include a statement like "to the church of God that is in Corinth" (1 Cor 1:2). At places the Scripture explicitly discloses its intent to be read aloud and corporately, as in Revelation 1:3: "Blessed is the one who reads aloud the words of the prophecy, and blessed are those who hear and keep what is written in it." Even those books of Scripture written to individuals (such as the Gospel of Luke, addressed to Theophilus) were more widely distributed, and later made part of the biblical canon, exactly because they were found useful by a variety of Christian communities.

Not just in the biblical period, but in most of the sweep of Christian history, it is an anomaly to imagine the quiet time or the privately read daily office as the keystone of Christian spirituality. The invention of print was a major factor in the move toward privacy and privatized spirituality. As the philosopher Stephen Toulmin observes, "In the Middle Ages, the chief vehicle of medieval religious teaching was oral preaching. . . . Once the printed page supplemented or replaced the spoken word, lay scholars could read all the Scriptures and Commentaries *for themselves*."[3] It was printing that made it possible, even convenient, for a Bible to be put in each Christian's (and would-be heretic's!) hands. And it was with the age of print that Protestants began advocating private, individual interpretation of the Bible.

Beyond modernity, on the other side of the Enlightenment, it is understood that there is actually no such thing as private interpretation. Individuals are not autonomous isolates, but instead are socially constituted. The languages with which they read, their abilities to discern particular genres, the pretexts they presume to provide a text's "real meaning"—all these are socially created and communicated. Even something so basic as discerning a particular object as a "book" cannot be accomplished outside certain communities.

Imagine someone, such as a fifteenth-century Native American, who has never before seen or heard of a book. What is this object? It might be perceived as two pieces of bark with leaves bound between them. Is it, then, the fruit of an exotic tree? (Some disciples of ecological correctness, in fact, see the book as the disfigured corpse of a tree. Certainly I could say no better for at least some books.) Is this object a wonderfully decorated log, fit for fueling only holy fires? Is it some kind of brick, intended for construction? Perhaps the markings throughout the object are signs. But if so, who made them? And to what end? Along these lines the film *The Gods Must Be Crazy,* though a farce, makes a serious point: When a Coke bottle is dropped from an airplane onto the land of a remote African people, they have no choice but to make sense of the object in their context. Knowing nothing of soft drinks, of glassmaking and commercialism, they take the bottle as a sacred vessel, a gift from the gods.[4]

It is not hard to see how much more complex, and socially dependent, interpretation becomes once we move away from such "simple" objects as bottles to such complicated events as spoken or written texts. For instance, it is said that the seventeenth-century British monarch Charles II visited St. Paul's Cathedral on its completion and remarked that its architecture was "so awful and artificial." A twentieth-century English architect, hearing such an assessment, would be insulted. But Charles, in the idiom of his day, spoke approvingly—the cathedral evoked awe and was done with great art.

Or to take another case: Some years ago my wife and I visited

England for our first time. Having settled in at our bed and breakfast, we eagerly hit the streets in search of a pub where we might sample some English food and ale. But to our growing frustration, every pub we found in the area bore a sign on its door warning, "NO TRAVEL-LERS ALLOWED." It was only on returning to our bed and breakfast hostess, she well acquainted with the customs of the realm, that we learned "travellers" here referred to gypsies—not to hapless tourists such as ourselves.

But perhaps my favorite illustration of the necessity of knowing local practice in order to interpret comes from a friend who moved from an American northern state to Dallas in the late 1940s. After a day of unpacking and settling the apartment, she and her husband needed some clothes washed. She filled a basket and set out in search of a laundromat. Soon enough she found one, but to her consternation it was posted with a notice reading "WHITES ONLY." Dutifully she sorted her clothes and laundered only the whites. She departed grumbling about having her laundry less than half done, but as she drove back to the apartment via a different route she sighted another laundromat, this one fortuitously advertising "COLOREDS ONLY." Only days later, talking with locals, did she learn how foolish and troublesome the signs and the social practices behind them really were.

These relatively uncomplicated textual interpretive events demonstrate that interpretation (and misinterpretation) is socially based. How much more so when we consider not just a few words but entire books or songs or concerts or political rallies or barroom debates. Yet even if there is, strictly speaking, no such thing as private interpretation, the *illusion* of private interpretation leads to much mischief. It encourages individuals to forget that every text has an original, and so appropriate, context. To remove a refrigerator repair manual from its original context—the world of refrigerator selling and repair—is to render it useless. It hardly does for the conducting of a meeting to leave *Robert's Rules of Order* at home and bring along your refrigerator repair manual. Similarly, to understand the Bible as a private or individual manual is to remove it from its context as the charter of the church. It is a book for the *people* of God, not the *individuals* of God. Such honoring of private interpretation, and disrespect of communal interpretation, leads to our current state in which a new denomination is formed at the rate of one every week.[5] Its ultimate grotesquerie is the advent of what Robert Bellah and his colleagues famously described as "Sheliaism," after the woman who had decided she would live by her own private, individually tailored religion.[6] To read the Bible apart from community amounts to no less than each reader aspiring to his or her own religion.

But the Bible is not the charter of just any old community. It is the charter of a particular people, the people of Israel and the church. Thus true sense can be made of it only if attention is paid to the specific historical contexts of each of its parts. To understand Scripture adequately, contemporary Christians must hear it in the company of Moses and David and Nehemiah and Peter the apostle. We must know something about, and not merely ignore, such things as the psychology of ancient Hebrews and the economy of Roman-occupied Palestine. To the contrary, focus on private interpretation has often led to the practice of ignoring history—let me just see how this text speaks to "my heart" or "my experience," quite apart not only from other living Christians and the long tradition of the church but also from the understandings of its original writers and hearers.[7]

Scripture Alone?

Of course, both these interpretive misappropriations of the Bible have been fueled by the doctrine of *sola Scriptura*—relying on Scripture alone, in the company of nothing or no one. But I would argue that the turning of our interpretive backs on community and history has in fact been fueled by a distortion of *sola Scriptura*, a distortion sponsored by modern, extreme individualism.

There will be little argument that the Reformers wanted a historically grounded reading of Scriptures. Their elevation of a historico-grammatical reading of the Bible, and suppression of allegorical reading, is a legacy beyond doubt. What may be more surprising, and is certainly less often appreciated, is the Reformers' profound respect for the church—not the isolated individual—as the true and trustworthy interpretive home of the Bible. John Calvin is especially impressive on this point. He affirms,

> For those to whom [God] is Father the church may also be Mother.
> . . . For there is no other way to enter into life unless this mother conceive us in her womb, give us birth, nourish us at her breast, and lastly, unless she keep us under her care and guidance until, putting off mortal flesh, we become like angels [Matt. 22:30]. Our weakness does not allow us to be dismissed from her school until we have been pupils all our lives. Furthermore, away from her bosom one cannot hope for any forgiveness of sins or any salvation.[8]

For Calvin it is "of no small importance" that Scripture itself calls the church "the pillar and ground of the truth" and the "house of God" (1 Tim 3:15). He sees the church as the "faithful keeper of God's truth," the teaching or interpretive bulwark that stays the Word "pure" and prevents truth from perishing "in the world."[9] So it is clear that for Calvin no valid practice of *sola Scriptura* would mean the individual grasping his or her Bible and reading it apart from the rest of the church. That sort of *sola Scriptura* is a kind conceivable only after the development of modern individualism. For the Reformers, Scripture is power and truth not merely as ink marks on pages but as those words are enlivened by the Holy Spirit and heard and interpreted by the church in the illumination of the Spirit.[10]

It is in this sense that I think the contemporary Roman Catholic Catechism correctly protests that Christianity is not a "religion of the book." No book, simply as book, speaks for itself. (The pages in themselves, we might say, are not only bound but mute.) In this the Bible is like all other books: it must be read and interpreted. And the Christian confession is that it cannot be properly interpreted apart from the graceful intervention of the Holy Spirit. Indeed, as the Catechism insists, ours is a faith in the "Word" of God, and that "not a written and mute word, but incarnate and living."[11] Left alone, the ink marks on pages are simply "dead letters." They come alive in the context of the church, where they are obediently heard and enacted.

But—and here is something else the Reformers were concerned to get at—these words are obediently heard and enacted only when they belong to the whole church. They belong to the *whole* church in the sense that they are not heard and interpreted alone, but in the company of the saints, and also in the sense that they are not to be heard and interpreted by only a portion of the church—say the Magisterium of the Roman Catholic Church or the guild of biblical scholars.[12] They belong to the whole *church* in that they are for the hearing and interpretation of the church itself. In the heat and hurly-burly of revolutionary times, this last was too often swept aside by all but the most radical Reformers. Calvin, Luther and Zwingli all turned authoritative Bible reading (at least in part) over to city fathers or territorial princes.

But as I was at pains to remind earlier in this book, we no longer live in a world eager to have the sponsorship of the church. Nor do we live in a time when the church could, even if it wanted to, force the Christian laity to adopt specified practices and doctrines. Church participation is voluntary. Voluntary membership necessarily stands in contrast to "the coercive givenness of establishment." So we are freed, I think, to be faithful to the better insights of the radical Reformers and read Scripture as the church, for the church. Yet we are in no small confusion and danger of all the people doing only what is right (or desirable) in their own eyes.

What we need to complement this are the better insights of the Catholic Church and the magisterial Reformers. We need a vigorous, thriving sense of voluntary *community* that also stands in contrast to the "atomistic isolation of individualism." So it is that in our day as perhaps rarely before, "the alternative to arbitrary individualism is not established [coercive] authority but an authority in which the individual participates and to which he or she consents."[13]

How the Decline of Print May Be a Boon to the Church
As one who prays in a church (Episcopal) that hopes itself Catholic no

less than Protestant, I sometimes like to arouse my more thoroughly Protestant friends with comments along the following lines: "Listen to all this hubbub that the Christian faith is in trouble because of our electronic age. People may be reading less; some think illiteracy is on the rise. I'm a writer and an editor—I like the idea of people reading books. But it's a Protestant conceit that the welfare of the church depends on the welfare of print."

Having made such a rash statement largely for fun, but then being forced to defend it, I now find myself seriously believing it. There is much to decry in the descent of print and ascent of electronic media. But the electronic age may have opened a door that can allow the church to recover a more faithful, communal and participative reading of its Bible than it has known in centuries. To get at why this may be so, we need to reflect a bit more on the differences between oral and written communication.

In a way quite unavailable to oral communication, writing makes words endure. Without writing, words are "only" sound. Obviously, without writing we cannot see words. Once words are, via writing, made into something that can be seen, they can be captured, pinned on paper. So captured, the same words can be revisited, studied, dissected again and again. The words are in a sense killed so that they can be held still for study and dissection. Spoken words live in that they are occurrences borne on breath. Spoken words are events between speaker and hearer. They cannot be pinned down. There is nowhere to look for them after they have happened.

Consider it this way. One of the properties of the visual (and so the written) is that it can be captured, stopped, held still. So when I hit the pause button on my videocassette recorder, the movie holds a single frame on the screen—say, Butch Cassidy and the Sundance Kid frozen in midleap over the side of a cliff. But when I push the pause button on my audiocassette deck, there is nothing. The sound is not somehow prolonged. It does not stop in the sense of sitting still, making itself vulnerable to closer examination. It is simply done and gone.

So it is that oral communication is inherently dynamic or living. As

Walter Ong puts it, "Written words are residue. Oral tradition has no such residue or deposit. When an often-told oral story is not actually being told, all that exists of it is the potential in certain human beings to tell it."[14] This being the nature of spoken words, it is no accident that the Hebrew *dābār* means both "word" and "event."[15] For oral communication to exist at all it must occur—again and again and again. People must gather (in one way or another); they must speak and listen. So it is that oral communication never escapes, nor can pretend to escape, its context. It only happens, it only exists, in a particular setting, whether that be the setting of a business meeting or an auction or a card game.

The written word, on the other hand, can be abstracted or decontextualized. Words put on paper, made visual and "permanent," can be carried away from the business meeting in Jackson Hole to show up in a newspaper in Paris or a board meeting in Tokyo. And in those places the reader of those words may not know anything, personally, about their original speakers. Thus they can easily take what was said in jest as something spouted in anger. They can take as literally key to the meeting words actually spoken by someone that others who sat in the meeting—operating in context, having a history of interaction with the speaker—know to be an inveterate liar. In Paris or Japan they might even misconstrue the entire meeting, interpreting it not as business but as a comedy routine or (not such a leap, given American proclivities) an act of worship. As Ong puts it, "Writing fosters abstractions that disengage knowledge from the arena where human beings struggle with one another. It separates knower from the known." Writing establishes "context-free" language, words that cannot be directly questioned or contested because the writer is not immediately present.[16]

There is another key and relevant characteristic of writing, requiring little attention now because I have already made much of it in previous pages. And that is the potential for writing to individualize and privatize. As Ong observes, "Oral communication unites people into groups. Writing and reading are solitary activities that throw the psyche back on itself."[17] It was via writing, and especially the technology of print, that engagement with the Bible was rendered a solo act.

It is on these two grounds that I am at least provisionally heartened by the full blooming of the electronic age. The electronic media of telephones, television and radio have now dethroned the medium of print. We live in an age of what Ong calls "secondary orality"—not in a culture of primary orality, in which there is no knowledge of writing, but in a culture that knows (and still partly depends on) writing, yet has reinstated a profound respect for oral communication.[18] And with the renaissance of oral communication comes a new respect for reading in community, as well as a renewed awareness of the particularity, locality and time-specific quality of all communication.[19] Rather than imagine that the individual speaks from an abstracted, universal and timeless vantage point, we ask again what community one speaks out of, what its purposes and practices are, where it is located and what are the issues of its time. Thus the church is free to be the church, to be the people of an unabashedly particular God in specific times and places.

And a setting of secondary orality allows Christians to remember that we are a profoundly oral people. Ours is the God who did not *write* to create the world, but *spoke* it into being. Our God did not "inscribe" the Son but "uttered" him. The Son himself left nothing in writing. He spoke and acted, creating a community of discourse we now call the church. Only there, in life intimately shared, in the close proximity of hearing and touch, is the body of Christ or "Christianity" really known. Faith, said the apostle Paul, comes by hearing (Rom 10:17); the (written) letter kills, but the Spirit that enlivens the spoken word lives (2 Cor 3:6).

Jacques Ellul, like Walter Ong, knows that Christian life cannot depend on the written word removed from the spoken word and its organic, communal, ongoing context. As Ellul notes, a written word is a "word placed in space, a word by which no one any longer commits himself: a word that no longer involves dialogue." The word merely written is "diluted, weaker, and no longer backed up by a person's whole being." It "no longer has the sting of truth it had when said by another person. . . . No one is involved any longer. The truth is reduced to visual signs, which mean nothing in themselves."[20]

The church's oral center and basis draws it back to the communal, the present (both in time and space), the local and the concrete. And all this bespeaks the character of our God, who chose to communicate with and relate to us through the communal, the present, the local and the concrete.

In fact, the Gospel of John can be read as a sustained brief on behalf of just such communal, vital embodiment of God's Word. God's Word is not first and foremost abstract belief, propositionalized truth.[21] So it is that Jesus—a person, not a proposition—is presented as the supreme and unique embodiment of the Word (2:11; 20:30). And he is constantly about embodying the words of life. He speaks of the bread of life and miraculously feeds five thousand with edible, actual bread (chap. 6). He speaks of the light of the world and heals the blind (8:12; 9:1-11). He speaks of the resurrection and life and raises Lazarus from the dead (chap. 11). He speaks of servanthood and washes the disciples' feet (chap. 13). And John seems to expect that this speaking and its embodiment will continue, for Jesus says to his followers, "As the Father has sent me, so I send you" (20:21). To recognize the church as the body of Christ is to recognize that the church exists as a continual, ongoing embodiment of God's Word.[22]

So it is not for nothing that Christians continue to emphasize the importance of orality by reading the Bible aloud, and hearing it together, in our worship.[23] By such an act we not only communicate anew our story but indeed participate in that story by ways peculiar to us—peculiar to the people of a God who risks embodiment, who works through the timely and the local. By hearing the words read aloud we indicate in deed that the Word cannot show its power without our communal listening and obedience. It cannot live without being spoken and heard, always and again spoken to and heard by specific people, with their unique problems and dreams. When the church remembers it is an oral culture, it necessarily remembers that the message of the gospel is inseparable from the speakers and doers of the gospel. As Paul told the Thessalonians, "We are determined to share with you not only the gospel of God but also our own selves" (1 Thess 2:8).[24]

A secondarily oral culture, in short, may be one in which we rediscover God's Word as address, hearing God speak to us in our diversities and our varied situations and through the prophetic encouragement and challenge of those in the same situations with us. In this connection it is intriguing that "how-to" manuals exist only in cultures of writing and (especially) print. In oral cultures trades are learned through apprenticeship, through observation and practice with minimal verbalized instruction. The apprentice hunter hunts with experienced hunters. The beginning cobbler works on shoes with skilled cobblers. And what the apprentice learns is not so much abstracted rules or decontextualized generalities (the stuff of how-to manuals) as a vast range of particulars and a varied repertoire for responding to particulars.

Now I would suggest that Christian discipleship is better served by the model of apprenticeship than the model of the how-to manual. Christians best mature in the living of faith when they are apprenticed to wise Christians they can observe, question and work with in a range of concrete situations. Books on application, how to apply the Bible, flourish only because we have lost a sense of discipleship as apprenticeship. If we do not have a viable community to help us participate in the story where we are, we can only grasp at the inferior substitutes of application manuals—written as if from beyond time and place, for no particular time and place. My hope is that the development of ours as a secondarily oral culture will cause more and more Christians to see "how-to" and technique as inferior for Christian discipleship, and to turn with new earnestness from the application of Scripture to the performance of Scripture.[25]

Performing Scripture

The modern, print-based conception of application fit into a wider picture of biblical interpretation and authority, perhaps best represented by the Gideon Bible. The Gideons see the Bible primarily as a collection of acontextual rules or guidelines. As such, it has an authority like that of the repair manual, ready for consultation at any time by an individual with a problem or question. So it is that the lonely traveler can check into a hotel room anywhere in the country, open a drawer and find a Bible usefully indexed to address every difficulty. Feeling depressed? See these passages. Afraid? Consult these references. Have you failed? Turn here and here. In the modern, print-based picture, biblical interpretation has been fundamentally a solo and decontextualized activity.

But this is a distortion, and the postmodern, secondarily oral world may be one in which we can reaffirm that biblical interpretation is fundamentally the life, activity and politics of the believing community.[26] That is to say, the church does not so much apply Scripture as perform Scripture.

Consider Handel's *Messiah*. Is it most fully and genuinely interpreted when a musicologist sits down and reads through the score? Or is it not really interpreted when an orchestra and chorus perform it? Modern, solo interpretation of Scripture is akin to the musicologist's interpretation—useful, but devastatingly impoverishing if it is considered the height and fullness of interpretation. Isolated individuals can no more perform Scripture (that is, be the body of Christ in the world) than they can perform the *Messiah*.[27]

N. T. Wright helps us see scriptural interpretation and authority in just these terms, though he shifts from the metaphor of music to that of drama. Imagine that a formerly unknown play by William Shakespeare is unearthed. The entire theatrical world is aroused with excitement and anticipation. Then it is realized that only four of the original five acts have been recovered. What to do? Should someone study the play and write a new fifth act? But what individual playwright is the equal of Shakespeare?

Better than writing the concluding act once and for all, says Wright, would be to "give the key parts to highly trained, sensitive and experienced Shakespearian actors, who would immerse themselves in the first four acts, and in the language and culture of Shakespeare and his time, *and who then would be told to work out a fifth act for themselves.*"[28] In a real sense, authority resides in the first four acts of the play. They provide a wealth of characterization and make the overall direction of the play clear. The fifth act must be congruent and consistent with them. Yet for the play to be satisfactorily performed, it will not do for the actors to simply repeat earlier acts of the play. "It would require of the actors a free and responsible entering in to the story as it stood, in order first to understand how the threads could appropriately be drawn together and then put that understanding into effect by speaking and acting with innovation and consistency."[29]

It is hardly artificial, and not at all contrived, to see the Bible as four acts. Act One is creation. Act Two is the Fall. Act Three is Israel. And Act Four is Jesus. For Wright, the writing of the New Testament forms the first scene in Act Five, giving even more specific hints (Rom 8; 1 Cor 15; Revelation) of how the play should end. "The church would then live under the 'authority' of the extant story, being required to offer an improvisatory performance of the final act as it leads up to and anticipates the intended conclusion. The church is designed, according to this model, as a stage in the completion of the creator's work of art."[30]

So it is that Scripture is genuinely respected and obeyed only in community. And so it is that Scripture really has authority only when it is performed and not merely applied.

9

THE CHURCH
AS WORLD
On the Faithfulness
of Pagans

⬚

To speak of the church as itself a way of life, to refer often and unabashedly to the importance of its liturgy—these are noises that inevitably and repeatedly draw worries. To many schooled in the vestiges of the Constantinian ethos, such blatant ecclesiocentric (or church-centered) attitudes are sectarian and triumphalistic. They threaten to make Christianity irrelevant to the world, and Christians irresponsible. In even stronger terms, they promote a withdrawn Christian "tribalism."[1] These are severe worries indeed, not least so in the days of Bosnian and Rwandan "tribal" slaughter. So, though much I have said in earlier chapters is pertinent to these concerns, I want to devote this chapter to a sustained consideration of the church as a culture and its relation to neighboring cultures.

I begin by observing that we are all sectarians. If sectarians are those bound to a particular time and place, seeing and knowing the world through a limited perspective, influenced most profoundly by those closest to them in geography and affection, then there is no other option. Christians, Jews, Muslims, naturalists, Americans, Australians, scientists, modernists, shamans, males, females, heterosexuals, homosexuals—whatever we may consider the core of our identity, all of us learn that identity through the language and practices of one or another culture. This inescapability of human contingency is, it seems, more and more widely appreciated. But it has not always been so appreciated, and much of the persuasive power still freighted by criticisms of "sectarian" Christianity depends on the background assumption that truly rational people can shake the bonds of time and place.

Why *Sectarianism* Is Not As Threatening As It Sounds

This, after all, was one of the key aims of modern Western philosophy. Foundationalism is the "pervasive Western philosophical doctrine" that all rational belief must be built on the foundation of "a-cultural and universally compelling beliefs or realities, themselves in no need of support."[2] Foundationalism is that theory of knowledge usually chased back to the seventeenth-century French philosopher René Descartes. It is worth noting that Descartes was a man living in chaotic times. The Reformation, which occurred nearly a century before his prime, was now putting to bloom not only the flowers of truth but also the toxic weeds of dissension. Luther had insisted on the power of all Christians to discern right and wrong in matters of faith. Calvin had looked to the absolute certainty of inner persuasion. There came to pass in consequence a crisis in authority—or should we say of authori*ties?* There were in fact now more authorities than before, and potentially innumerably more authorities, since each individual conscience theoretically constituted its own separate pope. The result, as Jeffrey Stout writes, was that "for over a hundred years, beginning roughly at the end of the last session of the Council of Trent and continuing throughout most of the seventeenth century, Europe found itself embroiled in religious wars."[3]

This was the playing field of history onto which Descartes stepped.

He was not alone in his anxiety about the violent disagreement surrounding him. Nor, I should add, was the worry solely over religious chaos. As the historian Lorraine Daston observes,

> Seventeenth-century science was a battlefield where rivals and factions stopped at nothing to scientifically discredit and personally abuse (the two were seldom distinguished) one another. [To name only stars of the first magnitude,] Galileo relished blistering polemics and was a master of the *ad hominem* pamphlet title, and Newton crushed his adversaries by fair means and foul. . . . Newton nearly drove Robert Hooke out of the Royal Society over a priority dispute concerning the inverse square law of attraction; he not only stacked the Royal Society committee to which Leibniz had appealed for an impartial settlement of the priority dispute over the invention of calculus—he wrote its report, thus embittering relationships between British and Continental mathematicians for nearly a century. It comes as no surprise that the 1699 regulations of the Paris Academy of Sciences had to explicitly forbid its members to use "terms of contempt or bitterness against one another, both in their speech and writings."[4]

So situated, it is not hard to imagine how Descartes and others yearned for less partisanship and a more widely shared method for arriving at certainty. The presenting problems seemed clear. Time changes everything, including beliefs. And ideas or identities based in localities—whether cities, cantons or states—can be a veritable recipe for interminable fighting. But no longer are philosophers, scientists and politicians answerable to the church. And the church in any event is no longer a fairly unified, consolidated authority, the generally accepted conduit of truth eternal, truth from beyond time and place, for all times and places. Thus Descartes sought a secular, or nonecclesial, foundation of knowledge that rested on ground beyond time and place. This turned out to be his famous *cogito ergo sum*—"I think, therefore I am." The *cogito,* Descartes thought, provided knowledge at once indubitable and universally self-evident, unbeholden to any concrete and disputatious set of religious convictions. From this sure foundation one might reliably deduce the truth on any number of otherwise controvertible matters, across the range of human endeavor. Without recourse to the now discredited church, a singular and compelling authority was thereby regained. The wars—scientific and religious, figurative and literal—could cease.

With such aims, it's hardly a wonder that Descartes modeled his epistemology on mathematics. Stephen Toulmin has pointed out that the comprehensive term *logic* is confusing because it can be modeled on the rationalities of several different fields: his own preference of jurisprudence as well as the disciplines of psychology sociology, technology—or mathematics. Descartes, tapping into a deep and old well, chose the latter. As Toulmin puts it, the "history of philosophy [is] bound up with the history of mathematics." Plato directed a school of geometers and saw the geometrical proof as the ideal of all sciences. In similar cast of mind, Descartes invented a branch of mathematics known as "Cartesian geometry" and was attracted, says Toulmin, "by the idea of establishing in a quasi-geometrical manner all the fundamental truths of natural science and theology." Surely Descartes, Leibniz and others gravitated toward mathematical logic not least because pure mathematics is "possibly the only intellectual activity whose problems and solutions are 'above time' " and heedless of place.[5]

So "foundationalism" as I am now using the term is characterized by individualism, mathematical certainty and acontextualism.[6] That is, its truths aim to be indubitable and precise, along the lines of the geometric or scientific proof, and they are supposedly available to rationally able, well-intended individuals quite apart from any particular tradition or culture.

Now Cartesian foundationalism may appear non-Constantinian in that it is established in contrast to the church. But it is Constantinian exactly in that it depends on a God known apart from the particular, explicit witness of Israel and the church. Thus Descartes bolstered the axioms of Euclidean geometry as "clear and distinct" (that is, foundational) on the supposition that a benevolent God had implanted these ideas in all people in all times and places. But in point of fact, "even today, there exist cultures in which spatial relationships are handled in ways that diverge from the Euclidean ideal: the people involved even *perceive* spatial relations differently from the way they are perceived in modern industrial cultures, and are subject to [different] optical illusions."[7]

Foundationalism has consequently eroded because that singular, universal, supposedly nonparticular foundation could never for long or everywhere be agreed on. It was not just Descartes's *cogito* and related foundations that crumbled. Locke championed the senses, Hume the affections, Kant innate Reason; and these were only the first in what has now become veritable trains of cars emphatically not all gauged to run on the same tracks. The problem, as Toulmin describes it, involves the eventual recognition that

the exercise of rational judgment is itself an activity carried out in a particular context and essentially dependent on it: the arguments we encounter are set out at a given time and in a given situation, and when we come to assess them they have to be judged against this background. So the practical critic of arguments, as of morals, is in no position to adopt the mathematician's Olympian posture.[8]

Foundationalism, in short, demands a kind and degree of certainty and decontextualization that are simply not available to most, if any, substantial human endeavors.

Perhaps, tossed this way and that in furious culture wars, we are now most often and acutely aware of foundationalism's incredibility in the area of morality. The foundationalist C. S. Lewis argued that there is for all persons in all times and places a singular and innate sense of fairness. So, he said, when two people quarrel, one seldom says, " 'To hell with your standard.' Nearly always he tries to make out that what he has been doing does not really go against the standard, or that if it does there is some special excuse. . . . It looks, in fact, very much as if both parties had in mind some kind of Law or Rule of fair play or decent behaviour or morality or whatever you call it, about which they really agreed."[9] This, I allow, may have freighted cogency in Lewis's 1940s and

1950s England. But today our society is sufficiently pluralistic and candid that different standards are indeed seen to be at work. Thus the prochoicer's "decent behaviour" is the prolifer's "murder"; the Muslim fundamentalist's "fair play" is Salman Rushdie's unconscionable censorship; and the homosexual's "morality" is Jimmy Swaggart's "sodomy."[10]

Because foundationalism followed the mathematical model of rationality, it failed to see logical categories as contextual or "field-dependent." Its abstracted, idealized and impractically rigorous epistemological standards invalidated the undeniably field-dependent work and conclusions not just of theologians and scientific quacks. It also invalidated the work of astronomers, archaeologists, historians, ethicists and psychologists—not to mention car mechanics, bricklayers, plumbers, farmers or a few other people upon whose skill and knowledge the conduct of our daily lives really depends. Occupations simply require that those who would undertake them be initiated into certain terms, beliefs and practices. These they must follow and master before they are genuinely historians or astronomers or car mechanics. It is no different with a culture, or way of life. Ipso facto, those who do not know the appropriate terms and are not competent at the appropriate practices do not belong to a particular community.[11]

Every community—whether it be one of citizenship, of vocation or of religious commitment—is in this sense restrictive of its membership. Every community is marked by a particular language and by where it is in its history (to be a late-twentieth-century, post-Einsteinian physicist is not the same thing as being a nineteenth-century Newtonian physicist). Every community is in these regards sectarian.

But of course once the acontextual universalism of foundationalism is seen for the illusion it is, such "sectarianism" is hardly onerous. It is simply part of the human condition. Once the false alternative of acontextual foundationalism is seen through, it appears that the real alternatives, if we want to use nasty-sounding names, are between sectarianism and syncretism. That is, we are all marked by time, place and limited communities. The sectarian is one who strives to be marked by one predominant community. The syncretist, like the ancient Greek mystery religion adherents who invoked one god for fertility and another for success in business, is happy to belong to and serve a number of communities of more or less equal authority. The sectarian accordingly desires a more holistic, unified life, the syncretist a compartmentalized, unabashedly eclectic life. But neither, let it once more be noted, escapes history and limited perspective.

Sectarianism and Three "Chapters" of a Heritage

If the choice is in fact between sectarianism and syncretism, rather than between sectarianism and an illusory acontextual universalism, then it is likely that those who stand in the tradition of classical Christianity will be "sectarians." It has been observed that modern syncretism lives in the spirit of ancient paganism, with separate gods lording over separate aspects or spheres of life. Christians confess one God, one Lord who rules over all of life. Indeed, no less a charter than the first of the Ten Commandments insists on just this. Conceiving of ourselves (and others) as creatures of the one God, we can hardly cede spheres of our lives over to lesser gods. In this light, no serious and long-standing Christian tradition can be seen as syncretist. All are sectarian.

That said, it is true that some communities are narrower than others. Some really do try to insulate themselves from other communities, to make their claims unsusceptible to challenge or critique by outsiders. With their claims unchecked, they can become arbitrary. Such communities, "sects" in the worst sense of the word, are hence at least potentially dangerous, and all too often abusive of outsiders and insiders alike. But again, the option is not to step outside all communities onto some context-free place from which all may be summarily judged. Every judgment will be made from a community, from a context. The choice, when it comes to a choice, is *between* communities, and it is a choice executed *from* communities. So the question is not how the individual might somehow avoid or transcend community, but how the church can be a community open to and engaged by other communities.

On this count I believe the church has extraordinary resources. Its own defining narrative continually pushes the church outside its own borders.[12] The very purpose of the church—to witness to the kingdom of God come and coming in the world—propels it to seek out those in every corner of the earth. Of course, certain tellings of the Christian story have sent some believers into remote corners of the earth only to conquer. But, more carefully told, the church's narrative possesses vigorous internal checks against triumphalism or the insulation of the community. We can examine those internal checks under the chapter headings, if you will, of Election, Exodus and Diaspora.

Election reminds us that God's people are chosen not on merit but merely by virtue of God's grace. Moses often deflated Israel's triumphalism along just these lines. "It was not because you were more numerous than any other people that the LORD set his heart on you and chose you—for you were the fewest of all peoples," he said (Deut 7:7). He would not allow Israel to think that its own righteousness merited the vanquishing of the Promised Land (Deut 9:4). God chose Israel (and later the church) simply out of grace, and on behalf of the rest of the world. The only thing special about the people of God is that they are God's people. They are not necessarily more virtuous, numerous, intelligent or beautiful than any other people. They are unique only (but what an only!) because they have been engaged by the sovereign God of the universe.[13]

The name Israel itself means "God-wrestler" (Gen 32:28), and the church, in the tradition of Israel, may as often limp after its encounter with God as it leaps in triumphant joy. The Old Testament is almost alarmingly candid about how imperfect—how petty and brutal and faithless—God's chosen people can be. But like the angel holding on to Jacob at Peniel, God will not release his grip. God will on occasion fight against Israel, even become Israel's enemy (Jer 7; 21:3-7; Lam 2:5).[14] What God will not do is simply forget about Israel and about the power, truth and love of God's kingdom being shown to the world through God's relationship with Israel.

The church too has failed miserably and multitudinously. Yet Paul famously professed that God's strength is known in the weakness of God's people (2 Cor 11:16-30; 13:1-4). Judgment itself is expected to begin not with the distant wicked but with the household of God (1 Pet 4:17). The church's claim boils down to nothing more self-aggrandizing than that God will not let us (and ultimately all of creation) alone. Christians can claim moral transformation not at all in the sense that we have achieved perfection, but instead in the sense that we have been baptized into a life of struggle.[15]

Exodus, the next "chapter," reminds us that our heritage includes the outcast, the homeless refugee and the stranger. The original Hebrews were a ragtag collection of slaves in Egypt. As such, they were the dregs of the most powerful empire of their world. Once God led them from Egypt, they wandered homeless in the wilderness for three years. Notably, their later Scriptures called Israelites never to forget these aspects of their heritage—especially not to forget them when they faced the outcasts and strangers of their own day:

> When an alien resides with you in your land, you shall not oppress the alien. . . . You shall love the alien as yourself, for you were aliens in the land of Egypt. (Lev 19:33-34)
>
> For the LORD your God . . . loves the strangers, providing them food and clothing. You shall also love the stranger, for you were strangers in the land of Egypt. (Deut 10:17-19)

So influenced, Jesus invited strangers to his table, and the church is called to do the same. Far from being an insulated, elitist community, it is called especially to open its doors to those it might otherwise most readily ignore.

Finally, the "chapter" of *Diaspora* reminds us that God's people are sometimes dispossessed and spread throughout the world. Jerusalem and the temple are sacred places, but God is not left without witness when they are burned to the ground by invading barbarians. Now God's people will sing the Lord's song in a strange land (Ps 137). The kingdom may be proclaimed even—perhaps especially—in exile.

Exiles, of course, do not speak from a position of relative strength. They are not the governors of the land they inhabit. Yet they can point to God and, in their bolder moments, remind those who govern that they are not God.

The church in a post-Constantinian world finds itself in a kind of diaspora. It no longer governs or defines the lands in which it dwells. But the church's diaspora heritage lets it know that it need not govern or define. In diaspora it is in some ways freer to witness to God and God's way of life. In diaspora it has no reigning home to mistake for God's kingdom and is less likely to confuse the power of the sword with the power of the cross. In diaspora it cannot lean on the surrounding institutions to enculturate its children in the ways of God, but must take responsibility to be its own culture. And in diaspora it cannot ignore the outsider, for it lives inside the outsider's walls.[16]

The Fugitive Prophet: A Case Study in Engaging the Outsider

Several of these themes are distilled in the biblical story of Jonah. Jonah was the prophet called to "go at once to Nineveh, that great city" and speak out against its wickedness (Jon 1:2). Here is a prophet called to engage rather than ignore the outsider—and in this case an outsider of the most repulsive sort. Nineveh was, after all, the capital of Assyria, Israel's mortal enemy, which conquered Jerusalem in the eighth century B.C. and dispersed Israelites from their homeland. Furthermore, the Assyrians were known for their gross brutality. It is as if Hitler's Nazis won World War II and a British prophet were called to Berlin to beseech Germans to turn from their evil ways. "What?" this prophet might protest. "These are the ones who bombed London and tortured my countrymen. I can't begin to express the enormity of their crimes against humanity. I would rather hate them than forget them, and forget them than help them." So besides the risk at hand—Jonah may understandably fear that the Ninevites will want nothing of the truth he has to speak, and will respond with their characteristic violence— Israel's prophet has little reason to wish or hope Nineveh might turn from its evil.

Accordingly, he flees. He flees "from the presence of the LORD" (1:3), which, ironically, would have taken him toward the most evil and despicable city he could imagine. But Jonah is a bit ambivalent. He soon enough professes that his is the "God of heaven, who made the sea and the dry land"—in other words, the entire world (1:9). How can you flee a God who is to be found everywhere: not just in the anointed people's temple but in the capital city of their conquerors, not just in the church but in the whole wide world? It's futile to try to escape the presence of someone who will already be anyplace you go before you get there. Nonetheless, Jonah will try.

He hops a ship bound for Tarshish. Rather than the strenuous call of God, he seeks comfort. It may be no accident that the ship he chooses has Tarshish for its destination. Tarshish was reputedly a place where Israel's God was not known (Is 66:19) and was fabled to be a city of "luxury, desire and delight." But it lay at the ends of the earth, so it may paradoxically represent "a pleasant place of security that borders on nonexistence."[17] To go toward Tarshish means going toward atheistic and affluent apathy. Ultimately it is empty luxury and vain riches, for it is life without God. In the direction of Tarshish lies death, then, even if death in the lap of luxury. Still, Jonah hopes for some comfort, and the comfort of Tarshish will have to do. And Jonah will not only have comfort with his eventual arrival in Tarshish. He wants comfort immediately, so that he goes down into the hold of the ship and stretches out to sleep (1:5).

The fugitive prophet's slumber is interrupted by a sailor who informs him the ship is caught in a storm. Already desperate measures have been taken to keep the vessel afloat. But it appears tossing cargo overboard will not be sufficient: now everyone on board had better entreat his or her god. Jonah, who was running toward peace and comfort, is now dragged into the wind and rain pelting the ship's deck. Before he knows what is happening, the sailors cast lots to see whose guilt has brought this calamity on them (1:7). The lots, of course, fall on Jonah. Belatedly attaining some courage, our reluctant hero admits his actions have provoked the storm and suggests that he be thrown overboard to appease God's wrath and still the squall.

Here Jonah's story again pushes us toward sympathy with the pagans. For the sailors are pagans, and desperately frightened pagans at that. But rather than simply and immediately toss Jonah overboard, they row hard to bring the ship back to land (1:13). This, then, is a persistent theme of the story. The pagans are simply not necessarily and irrevocably wicked. It is a mistake for one of God's people to assume the pagans are beyond redemption.

(Sure enough, when Jonah later does arrive in Nineveh and calls for repentance, the wicked Ninevites quickly depart their evil ways and go into a fast. As it turns out, they are much more ready to desert their deathward ways than Jonah expects or would like. In fact, they less stubbornly head toward death than Jonah himself. So if the church lives in the spirit of Israel's stories—such as that of Jonah—and Israel's God, it cannot easily and finally write off the world. The faithfulness of pagans, we are reminded, will sometimes surprise us. It may even exceed our own.)

But God's people do not come by such recognitions lightly or easily. Jonah must suffer ordeal before he is ready to properly approach the pagans of Nineveh. Unable to row ashore, the sailors finally do throw him into the sea. "But the LORD provided a large fish to swallow up Jonah; and Jonah was in the belly of the fish three days and three nights" (1:17). There must be simpler ways to learn that God cares for the world than a weekend campout in the belly of a beast. But God's people persistently seem to be as stubborn as Jonah on this point. How much more appealing to simply think the worst of the pagans and forget about them.

The problem, once more, is the spirit of the story we live by. That story will not let us turn our backs on the pagans. In fact it repeatedly thrusts us into their presence and even allows that their faithfulness may challenge our faithfulness. Thus Jesus leaves Christians with the sign of Jonah: "For just as Jonah was three days and three nights in the belly of the sea monster, so for three days and three nights the Son of Man will be in the heart of the earth" (Mt 12:40). Jesus is a latter-day Jonah, descending into a tomb for three days and three nights. And even more than Jonah, Jesus will not let us forget the pagan Ninevites.

As Matthew reports Jesus' words, "The people of Nineveh will rise up at the judgment with this generation and condemn it, because they repented at the proclamation of Jonah, and see, something greater than Jonah is here!" (12:41). Jesus the latter-day Jonah proclaims God's truth to the chosen people, who fail to believe. And so God's chosen people stand in danger of being judged by the lowly Ninevites. But note well that the sign of Jonah is for the church no less than Israel. Every time the church recalls its Lord's death and resurrection—his three days and nights in the belly of the beast—it remembers that it may be liable to judgment by the Ninevites, that those it regards as rankest pagans are not beyond the grace and power of God.

But to return more directly to the story of Jonah: the fish vomits out the prophet, and at last he heeds God's call and heads for Nineveh. Arriving, he calls its citizens to repentance. They respond wholeheartedly. So wholeheartedly, in fact, that they cover animals as well as people with the sackcloth of remorse. The king decrees, "All shall turn from their evil ways and from the violence that is in their hands. Who knows? God may relent and change his mind; he may turn from his fierce anger, so that we do not perish" (3:8-9). And it is as the king hoped. Seeing their repentance, God relinquishes judgment on the Ninevites.

Only now do we find out why, in his own words, Jonah did not want to prophesy in the streets of Nineveh. Because he knew from the start that God is "gracious . . . and merciful, slow to anger, and abounding in steadfast love, and ready to relent from punishing" (4:2). Why does this threaten Jonah? Perhaps because it challenges the specialness, at least via merit, of him and his people. Perhaps because it deprives him of that most precious possession of those seeking unambiguous purpose and direction in life—the unqualifiedly evil enemy. Like nothing else, having clearly defined enemies gives us a brisk, clear identity and course of action. We become those who oppose this obvious evil, and what we must do with our lives is battle to squelch or eradicate it. What happens when these very enemies who have provided us the definition of our goodness are called into community alongside us? Our backs are against the wall. What can we do except make God and God's good the center of our lives? It is downright inconveniencing, even positively aggravating.

And so Jonah departs the city God is no longer angry at, himself filled with anger. Once more his stubbornness and yearning for comfort, security and peace show through. He builds some shade under which to rest, watch the city and nurse his anger.

It is apparently time for another object lesson, so God causes a bush to grow up over Jonah during the night. It is a most excellent bush, giving maximal shade and comfort. Jonah happily basks under it. But then the bush withers overnight. Jonah is again angry and depressed, enough so that he'd like to give up and die. The story closes with God's reply:

> You are concerned about the bush, for which you did not labor and which you did not grow; it came into being in a night and perished in a night. And should I not be concerned about Nineveh, that great city, in which there are more than a hundred and twenty thousand persons who do not know their right hand from their left, and also many animals? (4:10-11)

The story does not inform us whether the message finally got through to Jonah. It instead leaves us with God's question for ourselves. Whatever we think of this city, this corner of the world or that, it is not our creation, and its inhabitants often operate as much out of ignorance as out of wickedness. They (and their sackclothed animals!) are not beyond God's presence or concern or mercy. How, legitimately, can they be beyond ours?

As easily and naturally as we lapse into it, what the church is called to is not a spirit of superiority, insulation and triumphalism. Dostoyevsky, I think, better captures the spirit we are called to when he describes his famous monk Zosima and how he greeted the sinners that came to him for confession:

> Nearly everyone, who came to the elder for the first time for a private talk, would enter in fear and anxiety and almost always come out bright and joyful, and . . . the gloomiest face would be transformed into a happy one. . . . The monks used to say of [Zosima] that he

was attached in his soul precisely to those who were the more sinful, and that he who was most sinful the elder loved most of all.[18]

How to Eavesdrop Truthfully

All this can—all this *should*—be robustly and without qualification affirmed by members of the "sect" known as church. But it is important to note that Jonah's author and Zosima the monk discern whatever truth and faithfulness the pagans possess through the lenses of Israel's story. Nineveh's fidelity and redemption are not defined on Nineveh's own Assyrian and pagan terms. The city is saved because it heeds the very specific God of Israel. And Zosima's visitors, however they might want to define themselves, are on Zosima's Christian terms quite clearly "sinners."

When the church recognizes pagan faithfulness or truth, then, it is not abandoning or compromising its own criteria of faithfulness and truth. These pagan testimonies to faith and truth are accurately discerned only through the peculiarly Christian resources of Scripture and the church's tradition. They are then what Karl Barth calls "alien witnesses" to the God of Israel. And if they are genuine, they will not contradict the biblical witness but "illumine, accentuate or explain" it "in a particular time or situation."[19]

What they will point to is not purportedly universal conclusions of human reason or some vague cosmic force or the latest sentimental candidate for the bland deity that will give us whatever we've already decided we want. No. The Christian profession is that the cosmos was created and redeemed through Jesus the Christ. First and finally, if not always in the middle, the church must speak that name and refer to that story.

As Barth insists, there is "no secular sphere" abandoned and totally apart from God in "the world reconciled by God in Jesus Christ." But that is not because one or another secular sphere has somehow independently tapped into truth. There is finally no absolutely secular sphere precisely because the world has been reconciled by God in Christ. Because the world has been reconciled through Christ, no part of it is outside God's caring presence, "even where from the human standpoint it seems to approximate most dangerously to the pure and absolute form of utter godlessness"—such as Nineveh or, say, Saddam Hussein's Baghdad. Christians affirm this not out of any sense of goodness or truth innate to a community, vocation or way of life apart from the benevolent providence of the God of Jesus Christ, but by "thinking and speaking in the light of the resurrection of Jesus Christ."[20]

So doing, Christians can "eavesdrop" on the world at large with ears to hear the voice of the Good Shepherd even there, distinguishing it from other, competing voices.[21] Thus the aim of the church as itself a culture, a way of life, is not to simply withdraw from or uncritically embrace neighboring cultures. As theologian Joseph Kotva puts it, the "issue is not whether to participate" in other cultures, "but how and when" to participate. What Christians are called to is "discerning and selective engagement," engagement discerned and selected on Christian terms.[22]

Discerning engagement is dynamic and ongoing. The church in different times and places may respond differently to a worldly occupation or practice. In the third century, considering Roman drama's thoroughly religious (paganly so) nature, Christians rejected the theatrical occupations such as acting in toto.[23] In the substantially different world of the modern West, few would insist that Christians avoid all forms of acting. Likewise, the church for centuries uniformly rejected the practice of charging interest on loans; again, in the differing conditions of the modern West, few insist that Christians should avoid all occupations that have to do with the charging of interest. Acting and banking are now occupations Christians are invited to engage in with clean consciences. In such instances selectivity and discernment are not a matter of simply deciding for or against an entire occupation. They are a matter of what sort of actor or banker the Christian will be, which roles or banking practices the Christian will adopt.

Of course, in every time and place some worldly practices are of a sort that they are simply rejected as unfitting to any who would call themselves Christians. We may no longer reject acting and banking as occupations, but it is difficult, for instance, to imagine the church ever deciding that prostitution is an occupation some Christians might justly practice. Likewise, though torture and slavery were once (if "selectively") practiced by the church, they are now rejected outright and in their entirety.

The mere mention of such examples is a reminder how complicated the church's involvement with surrounding cultures is. Discernment never ends. As situations change, it often evolves in new and unpredicted directions. A fourth-century Roman Christian could probably never imagine Christians in theater; a seventeenth-century Christian slaveholder would have found incomprehensible the arguments that later decisively ended Christian slaveholding. There is no abstract, once-for-all formula to follow, then. And discernment is often a matter of protracted argument and conflict, even (if not especially) among Christians. Slavery, as we all know, did not end without a fight. Through the better part of its history, the church has disagreed over whether warmaking is a vocation Christians may sometimes pursue or should reject altogether.

The point, then—and contrary to the modern and technical spirit so widespread even in our churches—is not to arrive at a list of acultural dos and don'ts that resolve conflicts universally and finally. It is instead to see that God called the church into being as its own culture, as a witness within and through the vicissitudes of time and history. This was almost poetically expressed by first-generation Quakers in England, who beseeched, "We do not want you to copy or imitate us. We want to be like a ship that has crossed the ocean, leaving a wake of foam, which soon fades away. We want you to follow the Spirit, which we have sought to follow, but which must be sought anew in every generation."[24]

So wound into the contingencies of history, Christians cannot help but argue with the world and one another. We are different not because we can get beyond time and escape limited, creaturely perspective. We are different solely because we argue not only with the world and one another but with God as well. Like God-wrestling Israel, we have been engaged by the Creator and Redeemer of the universe. We are much too mortal and petty and confused, and too often our witness to this God is compromised or worse. But Israel's God has a grip on us and won't let go. In our better moments we hope to be marked and known by this engagement, albeit the mark is nothing more glamorous or heroic than the limp with which we walk away from the fight.

Yet even if our discernment of God's true presence and work in the world is often slow and faltering, we know we have resources. We look to Scripture, to church tradition, to the fruits that particular Christian practices bear.[25] Then we prayerfully eavesdrop on the world around us. For, as Barth asks,

> Has it not always been true that the community [of God's people] has always had cause and opportunity to hear in the nearer or more distant world around it words which are at least well worth testing, whether or not they are perhaps true words, and in which it will sooner or later recognise with joy something of its own most proper message, or perhaps be forced to recognise this with shame, because by them it is shown and made to realise the omissions and truncations of its own message?[26]

Only so, but most certainly so, may we regard the faithfulness of pagans.

10

THE CHURCH
AS MISSION &
MESSAGE
Evangelism
After Constantine

◨

Through much of its life, though by no means all of its life, the church has understood evangelism as one of its central tasks. Biblically, the importance of evangelism is undeniable. Jesus sends forth his apostles to spread the gospel. The book of Acts is an account of the nascent church's evangelistic work. And Paul's letters are, of course, missionary and evangelistic letters. Indeed, it seems fair enough to observe that the entire New Testament was written and handed down for evangelistic purposes: to testify that the "true light, which enlightens everyone," has come into the world (Jn 1:9).

And the church today largely recognizes evangelism as a crucial, if often neglected, undertaking. Those known in North America as evangelicals, of course, constantly emphasize the significance of evangelism. Recently mainline Protestant bodies, such as the Episcopal and the United Methodist churches, have shown new interest in the sub-

ject—as has worldwide Roman Catholicism. Even the Eastern Orthodox, comparatively ethnically bound, have devoted sustained attention
to evangelism.

I suspect the continued and renewed interest in evangelism has
much to do with the church's late-twentieth-century setting. As we
observed earlier, Christendom now wobbles clearly and undeniably on
its last legs. There can be no easy assumption that a local church or
denomination will maintain healthy membership rolls simply by virtue
of being situated in a "Christian" territory, since there are now fewer
and fewer nominally Christian territories. If churches are to continue
their existence, they will continue it by drawing people into their folds,
by making new Christians. In the world beyond Constantine, the
evangelistic mandate is stark and simple: evangelize or die.

Yet renewed attempts at evangelism are widely and deeply hindered
because most of them still rest on Constantinian assumptions. It is as
if the churches have realized they must evangelize, but only know how
to evangelize Constantinians. Thus they reach out with purposes and
methods that were developed to draw in a tribe once spread the world
over—yet this tribe is now on the verge of extinction. And the church's
methods are accordingly about as successful as missionaries trained
and immersed in the culture of Australian aborigines, then sent to do
their work in the suburbs of London.

Constantinian Evangelism and Its Legacy of Revivalism

Evangelism under Constantine, of course, has a long if not always
illustrious history. Once Christianity was made the official religion of
an empire, evangelism became as much a concern of the emperor as
of the church. The emperor, seen as "imitator of God," united in his
person both religious and political offices. As the missiologist David
Bosch has observed, "The objectives of the state coincided with the
objectives of the church and vice versa. . . . The practice of direct royal
involvement in the missionary enterprise would persist throughout the
Middle Ages and, in fact, into the modern era."[1]

Bosch sees the Western church of the Middle Ages as "always

compromised to the state."[2] Indeed, church and state were so completely identified that from 776 on, the annals of empire often cited Charlemagne's Saxon enemies as those who were fighting *adversus christianos*—"against the Christians."[3] But the Middle Ages are notoriously understood as the era of Christendom. What about modernity? Does state involvement persist even here?

If Columbus is understood as an early modern, the answer is unequivocally yes. The explorer saw Christianization of the New World as synonymous with the adoption of Spanish and European customs. He aimed that the Indians might "adopt our customs and our faith." Addressing the royalty, he expected that "Your Highnesses may have great joy in them [the Native Americans], for soon you will have made them into Christians and will have instructed them in the good manners of your kingdoms."[4] More ominously, he petitioned, "I hope in Our Lord that Your Highnesses will determine to send [priests] in great diligence in order to unite to the Church such great populations and to convert them, just as your Highnesses have destroyed those who were unwilling to confess the Father, the Son and the Holy Spirit."[5] Even slavery was anointed and partly justified in Christian terms, with Columbus averring in the New World, "From here one might send, in the name of the Holy Trinity, as many slaves as could be sold."[6]

Indeed, Columbus said of his exploration that "the beginning and end of this enterprise is the propagation and the glory of the Christian religion."[7] He lived and acted in a world in which most Europeans saw little incongruity between "converting" and destroying the inhabitants of the Americas. So on his second visit he was equipped by Ferdinand and Isabella with seventeen ships, more than one thousand men, and cannons, crossbows, guns, cavalry and attack dogs. Columbus's son later wrote of one encounter in the Caribbean in 1495, during which his father unleashed two hundred foot soldiers, twenty cavalry and twenty dogs on the Indians. "The soldiers mowed down dozens with point-blank volleys, loosed the dogs to rip open limbs and bellies, chased fleeing Indians into the bush to skewer them with sword and pike, and *with God's aid* soon gained a complete victory."[8]

Violently coercive Constantinian evangelization continued throughout the Spanish conquest of the Americas. The acceptability and normalcy of coercive evangelism are perhaps nowhere historically more salient than when government began to regulate the "settlement" (in European perspective) or "invasion" (in Native American perspective) of the New World. In the sixteenth century kings began to grant licenses for conquest.[9] The *Requerimiento,* dating from 1514, was the attempt of a Spanish jurist to legitimatize, control and moderate the activities of the conquistadors. It was a document required to be read to the inhabitants of a country before they were conquered, and behind it lay a decidedly Constantinian reading of human history. According to the *Requerimiento,* history culminated in Jesus Christ, "master of the human lineage," who in turn transmitted his power to St. Peter. Peter subsequently handed authority on to the succession of popes, and one of the most recent popes had bestowed the American continent on Spain.

So informed, the Indians who had heard thus far were faced with a choice. Those who accepted and submitted to this interpretation of history could not be taken as slaves. But those who resisted would be severely punished: "with the help of God," the Spaniards would "forcibly enter" the country, make war and "subject you to the yoke and obedience of the Church, and of their Highnesses." The conquistadors promised recalcitrant Indians that they would steal their goods, make their wives and children slaves, and "do all the harm and damage that we can."[10]

Except in its Anabaptist form, the Protestant Reformation did not break with the medieval understanding of church and state that animated Columbus and the conquistadors. So Bosch notes that the Reformers "could not conceive of a missionary outreach into countries in which there was no Protestant (Lutheran, Reformed, etc.) government." In fact there were only two missionary enterprises undertaken by "mainline" Protestants during the Reformation era, and both were sponsored by civil authorities.[11] Later Calvinist mission enterprises were "all undertaken within the framework of colonial expansion," with the evangelists envisioning a "perfect harmony between church and state."[12] So the famous Puritan Cotton Mather confidently advised, "The best thing we can do for our Indians is to Anglicize them."[13] Unabashed coercion was never far from hand in such Constantinian understandings and practices of evangelism. All too typically, as late as 1890, German chancellor von Caprivi could survey a German colony and suggest, "We should begin by establishing a few stations in the interior, from which both the merchant and the missionary can operate; gun and Bible should go hand in hand."[14]

Happily, eighteenth-century Pietism challenged such grossly coercive evangelistic and missionary methods. Unhappily, however, Pietists did not challenge the basically Constantinian compromise of the church to the state. Protestant orthodoxy had insisted on a structural link between church and state, declaring everyone in a given territory at least nominally Christian. Pietists broke with this custom, emphasizing personal, individual decision for (or against) Christ. But rather than see the church as itself a distinctive culture, an alternative *polis,* Pietists wrote the church off as a dead institution.[15]

With this move there is not even a church that might *potentially,* if not actually, confront the state. Instead there are only individual Christians at the mercy of the state and the surrounding culture. Privatized, depoliticized and disenculturated Christianity is not explicitly coercive on behalf of Constantinianism. It is instead itself subtly coerced by Constantinianism. For now Christians turn their cultural, political, economic and social lives over to the institutions of the surrounding nation-state, asking in exchange only that they may make what they want of their private, spiritual lives. Yet how much can they (or God) make of their spiritual lives when the rest of their existence is so decisively determined by non-Christian institutions and ways of being? In the last analysis, and right up to the present day of persistently privatized Christianity, the spirit of Constantine reigns no less surely than it did when a sixteenth-century conquistador could declare, "Who can deny that the use of gunpowder against pagans is the burning of incense to Our Lord."[16]

Thus the most prominent American evangelistic paradigm from the eighteenth century right into our day—revivalism—is a profoundly Constantinian approach to Christian mission. The very designation implies a Constantinian context. Revivalism aims to revive or revitalize the preexisting but now latent faith of birthright Christians. It presupposes a knowledge of the languages and practices of faith. It is an evangelistic strategy that "depended on the American population being Protestant."[17]

Revivalism as an evangelistic strategy made some sense as long as the nation was markedly influenced by Protestant Christianity. Then revivalistic evangelists could, with notable success, appeal to Protestant— and highly individualized—formulations of the faith. But revivalism makes little sense outside a Protestant individualistic setting, which the early revivalist George Whitefield implicitly recognized when he preached, "We do not love the pope, because we love to be popes ourselves, and set up our own experience as a standard to others."[18] Evangelism in the revivalistic cast was not (and is not) a call to become a part of a new people, a "holy nation," a contrasting community. It presumed not initiation into the transnational church but a reawakening of faith in the individual American—who, exactly as an American, was supposedly already something of a (Protestant) Christian. Revivalistic evangelism was not so much the presentation and unpacking of the faith to the uninitiated as it was an appeal to understandings and desires that supposedly already existed but were latent. To become Christians, people did not need to learn and participate in a new way of life embodied in a particular, visible community. They only needed to be individually aroused. They only needed to be reminded of what they already knew, it was assumed, simply by virtue of being human and an American citizen.

Thus to this day many evangelists emphasize the inwardness of faith, stressing what the individual believes in his or her heart, isolating and appealing directly to the individual ("every head bowed, every eye closed . . ."). Revivalism so concentrates on the moment of individual decision that those raised in revivalistic traditions are often puzzled about what to do once they have made the decision to "accept Christ." This, after all, is the epitome and apparently the goal of the Christian life. What now, what else? Just wait to die and go to heaven? No doubt this puzzlement contributes to the strange phenomenon of converts "walking the aisle" repeatedly during their lives and sometimes even undertaking multiple baptisms.

Privatizing and etherealizing faith, and altogether depending on the cultural formation of the surrounding society, revivalism inevitably "deteriorated into a technique for maintaining Christian America."[19] For revivalistic evangelists like D. L. Moody, separation from the world was more or less purely inward. As George Marsden writes, there was no appeal to "abandon most of the standards of the respectable American middle-class way of life. It was to these standards, in fact, that people were to be converted."[20] Or in the more pointed words of H. Richard Niebuhr, in revivalism "to be reconciled to God now meant to be reconciled to the established customs of a more or less Christianized society. As the Christian church became the protector of the social mores so its revivals tended to become instruments for enforcing the prevailing standards," which among other things meant enforcing the "codes of capitalist industry."[21]

The underlying attitudes of revivalism are still very much with us, which explains much about how many contemporary American Christians conceive of evangelism. Those who would retrench and reestablish a Christian America stand clearly and completely in the revivalistic tradition. But even others who would faint or flip at talk of a Christian America are often no less captive to the revivalistic imagination. This shows nowhere as much as in the widespread inclination to think of evangelism in terms of the market.

Today's evangelism is marketing, and today's pastor is expected to be a marketer. The marketer-pastor appeals to desires that already exist among the unevangelized. As usual in Constantinianism, their Christianity is already present, if latent now in the form of "felt needs." Notably, the Constantinian God is always tamed, always domesticated. When evangelism is marketing, God is nothing more than the guarantor (yes, the sponsor) of whatever the market has already determined is good and valuable.[22] Accordingly, adopting marketing conceptuality and methodology turns the church into an instrument for enforcing prevailing American standards—or, in an increasingly pluralistic America, adopting one or another group's perception of what should be prevailing American standards.

But as I have argued earlier, America is not the issue. In terms of evangelism, then, revivalism is not the route to follow. Better, more hopeful paths lead outside the territory, beyond the dreamscape, of Constantinianism.

Evangelism Before Constantine

We are helped in imagining non-Constantinian evangelism by remembering that the earliest church evangelized before Constantine. The Bible knows nothing of preoccupation with the isolated, acultural individual and his or her inwardness. It instead shows a keen and abiding concern with time and place, with unfolding history, human societies and physical creation. The goal or proper end of human life, according to the Old Testament, is not the individual soul's flight from the constraints of time and body. It is instead the enjoyment of wholeness in communion with God and God's people, amid a healed and no longer strife-driven creation. In this enduring Jewish tradition, the New Testament looks ahead to the communal resurrection of those redeemed in Christ (1 Cor 15) and longs for the healing of the "whole creation" (Rom 8:18-30).

For the earliest church, then, evangelism was not a matter of inviting individuals to recall what they somehow already knew. It was rather a matter of inviting them to become part of nothing less than a new humanity, reborn of the last Adam who was Jesus the Nazarene. It was a call to life "in Christ," and as Ben Meyer puts it, "to be 'in Christ' is not to be alone but to be with others who are in him, to constitute with them an organic unity and, with them, to transcend division, conflicts, bondages."[23] So it is that Paul famously argued, "As many of you as were baptized into Christ have clothed yourselves with Christ. There is no longer Jew or Greek, there is no longer slave or free, there is no longer male and female; for all of you are one in Christ Jesus" (Gal 3:27-28; see also 1 Cor 12:13). However we might cut up the world, whatever we might see as the most significant categories that define people, each and all are subsumed by baptism into the body of Christ.[24]

There was no more profound way, in Paul's day and cultures, to cut up and define the world than by Jew and Greek, slave and free, male and female. Some of these categories no longer occur to us as the most significant markers of people. But Paul's message stands: no matter how the world is divided—East and West, black and white, conservative and liberal, gay and straight, developed and developing, communist and free, democratic and nondemocratic—none of these categories are more basic to identity or formative of the self than belonging to God and one another in Christ.

Accordingly, evangelism in the earliest church involved attracting and inviting people into a new culture, what was widely regarded as nothing less than a third race. Christians constituted a third race in their own eyes by virtue of being chosen as a people by the God of Abraham, Isaac and Jacob. They constituted a third race in the eyes of the surrounding world by virtue of their distinctive way of life.[25] As Bosch puts it, "Of far greater significance than the mission of the peripatetic preacher . . . was the *conduct* of early Christians, the 'language of love' on their lips and in their lives. . . . In the final analysis it was not the miracles of itinerant evangelists . . . that impressed the populace—miracle workers were a familiar phenomenon in the ancient world—but the exemplary lives of ordinary Christians."[26]

In the light of Christianity as a new culture we can properly hear and understand Jesus' Great Commission. These are actually not words that comport at all with Constantinian and revivalistic approaches to evangelism. What Jesus calls for is not a simple conveyance of information, not a mere inward acknowledgment, but a making of disciples from all nations and a teaching of them "to obey everything that I have commanded you" (Mt 28:18-20). In our terms, he calls for the induction of people into a different way of life—and so a departure, in one fashion and then another, from old ways of life that formerly defined them and made them what they were.

Evangelism After Constantine

As Constantinianism wanes, Christians are once again able to conceive of evangelism in non-Constantinian terms. But make no mistake about it, the changes of mind, attitude, behavior and method required are significant.

Evangelism in a non-Constantinian setting requires that *evangelism be understood not simply as declaring a message to someone but as initiation into the world-changing kingdom of God.* It is not enough to think of evangelism as proclamation. We must understand it once again as the earliest Christians did, as "the persuading of people to become Christians and take their place as responsible members of the body of Christ."[27] Not everything the church does is evangelism, but everything the church does—and is—relates to evangelism. Evangelism per se becomes not merely the activity of proclamation or adding another name to the church roll. It is rather a set of activities including proclamation, catechism, community service and even potlucks—each and all evangelistic when they at least partly aim to draw and admit persons "into a society, a set of principles, a body of knowledge, a way of living."[28]

Evangelism in a non-Constantinian setting then requires that *the convert understand that he or she is becoming the member of a new race, humanity or family.* Such evangelism must make it clear from beginning to end that there is no genuine Christian formation and life apart from the body of Christ. It makes no more sense to think of Christian faith as primarily private and hidden than it does to imagine national citizenship as something first and finally invisible to observers. Just as my full participation in the goods of American citizenship (voting, eligibility to run for office, receiving social security benefits and so forth) demands public acknowledgment of my citizenship, so vital involvement in the life of Christ demands public confession and practice of my faith.

Relatedly, evangelism in a non-Constantinian setting requires that

Christians understand witness as corporate and not only or even primarily individual. The words and behavior of one person do not a culture make. Non-Constantinian nonbelievers will attend Christian claims when they catch glimpses of a way of life that somehow challenges the ways of life they already know and find to be lacking in one manner or another. The aim of such contextualized, full-orbed evangelism, then, is not to answer "felt needs" as they already exist, but to present Christian concepts, language and practices in such a way that we might alter the meaning of people's experience as they have understood it and introduce a new set of felt needs into their already existing felt needs.[29] Altering the meaning of experience occurs, for instance, when the woman who has just lost her husband and her job learns to see her life not as a nihilistic wash but as a hopeful struggle against the powers of sin and death in a broken world. Felt needs (or better, desires) are changed when, for example, the executive who formerly wanted nothing more than to gain control of one more company learns that he is more deeply and lastingly gratified in faithful relationships with fellow Christians—including his once neglected wife and children.

The point is that when we understand evangelistic witness as corporate, as organic, ongoing and flowing naturally from a Christian way of life, then we are prepared to participate in and recognize conversion in its hundreds and thousands of manifestations. The fact is, very few if any people are argued into the faith or commit themselves to follow Christ merely because they've heard an evangelistic message. Conversion occurs in all kinds of ways and for all kinds of reasons. Augustine heard at random a Bible verse being read by a child. Paul fell off his horse on the road to Damascus. People convert to Christianity after getting sick or meeting the love of their life or spotting their first gray hair or getting sucked into the ravages of war or having a baby or quitting drugs. And their acts of conversion do not occur in isolation. Augustine did not convert merely because he heard a Bible verse, and Paul moved from persecuting Christians to becoming one of them not just because he took a spill. Years of experiences, of encounters with Christians (to say nothing of the Holy Spirit), played into these conversions—and have played into all since.

People make judgments and change their lives cumulatively or episodically, over periods of time, through series of events. Conversion occurs when a new friend or economic collapse or something else raises an issue, "when real life pressures [are] felt by men and women who must make decisions. . . . Then, in the course of discussion or by virtue of the introduction of a new and arresting vocabulary, or by the pronouncements of a particularly revered figure, or by a thousand other contingent interventions, some of us might come to see the situation and its components in new and different ways."[30]

To assist such conversion, and especially conversion in a world less and less marked by quasi-Christian understandings, Christians must remember that our message is not a "message which could be separated from the embodied message that the church always is."[31]

Evangelism in a non-Constantinian setting, given that it is a calling of people to a new way of life, also requires that *Christians not assume common understandings between themselves and those more determinatively shaped by other cultures.* Actions and words carry the meanings they carry only as they are woven into the fabric of a culture. Raising a hand means one thing in the culture of the classroom, another thing in the culture of worship, and yet another in the culture of an auction. Constantinian evangelism too easily and quickly assumed common understandings and interpretations. Thus European Christians who came to the Americas rarely appreciated how alien they and their ways were to the Native Americans. (For instance, they were appalled by the Aztec custom of cutting out and burning human hearts, but could not comprehend that Aztecs were at least equally appalled by the European custom of burning offenders alive from the feet up.[32]) Constantinian evangelism too often assumed that words, behaviors and attitudes might be correctly understood apart from a wider web of beliefs and practices. Thus Spanish conquistadors might through their words call on Indians to take Jesus Christ as their Savior. But through their actions the conquistadors routinely lied to the Indians, so that when Indians were asked if they were Christians, they quite seriously replied, "Yes, sir, I am a bit

Christian because I have learned to lie a bit; another day I will lie big, and I will be a big Christian."[33]

In this light I agree with George Lindbeck that Christian affirmations (such as evangelistic claims) are true or false only in full Christian context, a

> total pattern of speaking, thinking, feeling and acting. They are false when their use in any given instance is inconsistent with what the pattern as a whole affirms of God's being and will. The crusader's battle cry *"Christus est Dominus,"* for example, is false when used to authorize cleaving the skull of the infidel (even when the same words in other contexts may be a true utterance). When thus employed, it contradicts the Christian understanding of Lordship as embodying, for example, suffering servanthood.[34]

This really need not be an overly controversial proposal. Conservative evangelicals often use it to complain of liberal Christians that they employ the same religious language but have different (unorthodox) meanings for it. All sorts of affirmations change their meanings when they are moved into different contexts, employed in different cultures, uttered by different persons. Two entirely distinct things are intended, after all, when Francis of Assisi and Don Juan say to a woman, "I love you." Similarly, a right use of Christian language "cannot be detached from a particular way of behaving."[35] Faithful and effective Christian evangelism can occur only as part and parcel of Christian culture.

But if non-Constantinian evangelism means recognizing the differences of others, it also requires that Christians *understand and practice evangelism as proposing rather than imposing Christ.* Constantinian evangelism, as we have noted, was often coercive or manipulative. Christianity was forced on non-Christians. Yet we Christians now dwell in a world we do not control. We are no longer in a position to impose our faith on others. Even more important, we are in a position to recover the understanding that it is wrong to impose faith on others. We are truer to faith in the Suffering Servant we call Lord when we propose rather than impose. The God of Israel and Jesus Christ makes himself known by entering into vulnerable relationship with his creatures. This

God—preeminently in the life of Christ—does not force people to faith but attempts to persuade them to faith.[36]

Genuinely proposing means that evangelism is honest persuasion, a matter of fully informing others and allowing them to choose as they will.[37] It means that the church must renounce any attempt to make or manipulate others into wearing Christian shoes, accepting the Christian way of life. Christians are required instead to affirm our willingness to suffer the consequences of opposition to Christian culture. This approach alone both certifies the seriousness of our convictions *and* proves our willingness to let others have their say. And so it opens the door to relationship and dialogue at the very moment it faithfully presses forward the aims of evangelism.[38]

Here we must make no mistake about the matter: genuinely proposing the faith usually entails an ongoing relationship, continuing conversation, with those now outside the faith. It definitely entails dialogue rather than monologue, that the Christian evangelist not only speak but also listen to learn how words and actions are being interpreted. And it entails, yet again, that the evangelist be part of and be able to point to a community worthy of attention and respect, a way of life that prompts curiosity, questioning and a new searching. After Constantine, blessedly bereft of powers of imposition, the church must indeed be the message it wishes a watchful world to hear and embrace.

11

THE CHURCH
AS A WAY OF LIFE
*Liturgy After
the Liturgy*

◻

A*friend of mine grew up in Missouri and, for much of his life, despised* country music. Maybe he especially despised it because he was from Missouri. Originating from Oklahoma, I know how it is when the boy from the boonies tries to make good in Chicago, or New York or Los Angeles. Settled residents of the "big city" have about them an air of confident knowingness, a sophistication and jadedness. So the last thing a rural newcomer wants to admit is that he enjoys something as unsophisticated and naive as country music.

It was at a big-city newspaper that my friend changed his mind. He was talking to a settled and confident resident at the office. She had nothing to prove, and when she learned he was from the hinterlands, she enthusiastically inquired if he listened to country music. Of course not, he said. She only smiled, and the next day she brought him two or three albums by country singer Emmylou Harris.

What he heard changed his conception and indeed his entire perception of country music. He heard a lilting, sweetly aching, angelic voice. He heard harmonies so pure and perfect that they could only have been recorded in the Garden of Eden. He heard the honest and wry lyrics of men and women steeped in the bountiful gifts of an oral storytelling people. Through Emmylou he heard country music anew—maybe he really heard it for the first time—and now (like me, very often with me) he listens not just to her but also to George Jones and Merle Haggard and Patsy Cline. That's hard country, nasally tones and steel guitars and self-pity. It's country straight.

I realize that many, perhaps most, readers of this book face a similar challenge when it comes to conceiving of Christianity as a culture. Just like a country boy with country music, we think we know what church is and what it is all about. It is about the sacred, the eternal, the Good and the True and the Beautiful beyond time and space. We may have decided we like church that way, or we may have written it off exactly because of all that. But now to be told church is about the profane no less than the sacred, the timely no less than the timeless, about place no less than grace—to be told true Christianity is not so much beyond culture as itself a culture—there is a stretch.

Of course a book, like a recommendation to listen to a record album, can accomplish only so much. I have worked as hard as I can to elucidate and make attractive a fresh (and I hope faithful) reconception of Christianity and the Christian life. The response certainly depends on the quality of my argument, but it also depends on the reader's willingness to work at hearing the argument and to "try it on." What remains, then, is some final attempts to clarify what is meant (and what is not meant) by reference to the faith as a culture and (in my final chapter) some suggestions about trying it on.

On Facing Cultures Rather Than Culture

The church is culture in the sense that culture is a "signifying system," a collection of language and other signs that make sense of the otherwise chaotic and unrelated events of our lives.[1] Culture in this regard includes "formal and conscious beliefs"—the narratives and doctrines of the Christian church—but also rituals, folkways and practices, as well as feelings, attitudes and assumptions.[2] Thus worship (*leitourgia*, liturgy, the "work of the people") is at the center of Christian life both theologically and culturally. It is theologically at the center because Christians believe themselves and all else created, ultimately, to praise God the Holy Trinity. It is culturally at the center because Sunday worship rehearses the "formal and conscious beliefs" (in creed and sermon) and the feelings, attitudes and assumptions (in baptism and Eucharist) of a decidedly peculiar people who cannot ignore the Jews and venerate a first-century Galilean peasant agitator. But worship is also culturally at the center of Christian existence because worship is itself a way of life. This is the sense in which, borrowing from the Eastern Orthodox, it is helpful to think of life beyond the walls of the church building as "liturgy after the liturgy."[3] Church is the "work of the people" not just on the first but on every day of the week. Church is who Christians are and what they do not just on Sunday but on Monday through Saturday.

So church as culture is not merely a building, not merely what happens on Sunday morning. Nor is it as immediately or easily separated from other cultures as some (particularly those prone to worry about sectarianism) may imagine. That is the case for reasons (such as the church's own theological convictions) I have already discussed, but also for some reasons I have not.

A key unrehearsed reason that church as culture need not mean irresponsible withdrawal from the "world" is that the world itself is divided.[4] In these pluralistic, postmodern times, it makes less sense than ever to think of culture as monolithic, Culture with a capital *C*, as if culture were a single entity to be accepted or rejected as a block. H. Richard Niebuhr's *Christ and Culture*, profound as it certainly is, assumes just that. Recall again the various typologies: Christ over culture, Christ against culture, Christ transforming culture and so forth. On the one hand, Christ. On the other, the singular (as opposed to plural) Culture—culture as a block, a monolith to be accepted, rejected or transformed in its entirety.

I mentioned our pluralistic and postmodern times. These times have made us keenly aware that we live not amid a single, capital-*C* Culture but among many small-*c* cultures. Women, men, gays, straights, Muslims, Jews, Christians, Buddhists, traditionalists, progressives, Asians, African-Americans, Anglos, Latinos—all these categories and many, many more enrich or intrude on us nearly every day of our lives.

Consider the following scenario, from a not-at-all unusual day for me—nor, I am safe to assume, for many of my readers: I awaken to a radio alarm clock, fresh with news from South Africa, California and Bosnia. After my shower (departing from the earlier European habit of bathing as infrequently as possible), I appreciate Jewish culture by having a bagel for breakfast. Driving to work, I listen to reggae music, encountering a bit of African-Caribbean culture. At the office my morning is occupied by a meeting with a book publisher visiting from England and conversation allowing me to indulge my taste in British culture. For lunch I and my English visitor head to a Mexican restaurant. After lunch I spend my afternoon editing a manuscript by a Canadian author. Driving home, I listen to country music, with its roots in Scottish and Irish cultures. My wife and I quickly dine on leftover Chinese food, then meet some friends (the wife in the couple is Vietnamese) and go downtown to take in a French film. Back home, I choose for my reading nightcap a section of Karl Barth, a Swiss theologian who wrote in the German language.

Such days incline me to recognize that there are all kinds of cultures, not a single, monolithic Culture. This recognition can be extended to a deeper level, to see that the church responds to different manifestations of different cultures differently. Or, as James McClendon has put it, "The world (or 'culture') has appeared for us not as one smooth global unity, but as an indefinite congeries of powerful practices, spread over time and space, so that any number of these practices may impinge upon believers in a variety of ways, while our witness to them will necessarily take a corresponding variety of forms."[5]

Some elements or manifestations of culture the church rejects entirely. For instance, though it is not too much of a leap to imagine a Christian rock musician, we could not accept the endeavor to be a Christian prostitute or Christian mafioso—even if such endeavors were made with guarantees to "Christianize" these practices by never over-charging a trick or by praying for a competing mobster before shooting him. Pornography, cultic idolatry, tyranny and torture are all cultural practices the church categorically or entirely rejects.[6]

There are other cultural practices the church accepts within limits. Consider economic systems. The church in different times and places has been able to accept, variously, socialism and capitalism. But at its best the church in whatever country has always recognized that socialism or capitalism or any other economic system known to humanity could become oppressive and unjust, and has put limits on what Christians should accept of any such system.

There are yet other aspects or kinds of culture that the church has embraced but has given new purpose and meaning on its own terms. The family is a premier example. The church sees family life as a great good. But the Christian family does not live, as some families in some cultures have, to perpetuate a name or preserve a nation-state by providing taxpayers and soldiers. The Christian family is defined by its action as an agent of the church to witness to the truth of the kingdom of God.[7]

Finally, there are yet other cultural practices and institutions the church has created—such as the hospital. And through time the hospital has drifted away from its Christian cultural moorings, so that now the church must ask serious questions about such hospital-sponsored endeavors as abortion on demand and bureaucratized medicine. Thus what began as one of the church's cultural endeavors now stands in considerable tension to it.

The point, in sum, is that the church's engagement with culture—or, better, cultures—is complex. We simply cannot decide once for all to be for or against or over or under or in paradox with culture. The engagement with cultures is better understood as something under-taken on a case-by-case basis. Some manifestations of culture we can embrace, others we must reject, some we will approve with changes, and yet others we will accept with qualifications.

It helps when we think of the church itself as a culture. Then we can more readily appreciate the complexity of confronting a multicultural world, of which we as a church are a part. A Chinese-American friend comes to mind. His family, now three generations in the United States, is deeply devoted to this country. And yet his family staunchly maintains aspects of its Chinese heritage that run against the deepest grain of some of the American ethos. For instance, though my friend is in his mid-twenties—past the age when typical American children are supposed to be independent of their parents' wishes—he is attending law school not because he wants a career in law but because his father insists on it. Obedience to parents, even in adulthood, is an aspect of Chinese cultural identity that family will not abandon, even though it can be called nothing less than patriotically American.

Analogously, the church as a culture will approach any particular host nation (or cultural practice) with discrimination. It need not indiscriminately reject, and it cannot indiscriminately accept, any and all aspects of a particular culture. From the perspective I am arguing, Christians are not haters or lovers of culture, any more than fish could be said to hate or love water. Culture is simply an inescapable medium. The question is not choosing for or against it; the question is *what kind of culture is at hand?*

The church is itself a culture, changing and ideally growing, sometimes correcting itself, sometimes finding itself corrected by others, but never pretending that it can or should want to withdraw from history and society and public affairs. Christians operate out of our own culture, which provides our own root goods, symbols and meanings, and out of our culture we are constantly and diversely interacting with aspects of other cultures. We sail our own ark, in other words, but in shipping lanes shared by hundreds of other vessels, with a willingness to learn from the shipbuilding and seafaring skills of others, eager to trade at ports Christian or not, never satisfied merely to stay afloat, since we bear a cargo we believe to be of infinite value to all other sailors.

Christians amid the Tournament of Narratives

The simple fact of the matter is that no culture develops or maintains itself in a vacuum. Consider again the "settling" of the Americas, so often read as a monocultural European accomplishment. It is well known that Columbus was inspired and instructed by the exploits of Henry the Navigator, of Portugal, who sailed to Madeira and the Azores and sent out ships to circumnavigate Africa. What is not so well known is that Henry relied on Muslims who preserved Greek knowledge and enhanced it with ideas from China, India and Africa, then passed it to Europe via Spain. Columbus's adventures, in turn, had all sorts of cultural inputs and ramifications. Nearly half the crops now grown throughout the world—including corn and potatoes—originated in the cultures of American Indians. More than two hundred medicines come from plants whose therapeutic potentials were first exploited by American Indians. It is at least arguable that the American traditions of public meetings, free speech and democracy were learned from such Native Americans as those in the Iroquois League. More concretely, cultural interaction accounts for soul food's being partly Indian (consider cornbread, grits and hush puppies) and for American cowboys' speaking Spanish (as in "rodeo" and "lariat").[8]

Much of the worrying about cultural insulation or isolation is done, actually, by those looking at the world from a Constantinian position—from the vantage point of empire, which has willfully suppressed or simply failed to remember the contributions of other cultures to its own culture. When we look at the world from the viewpoint of the peasant rather than the prince, it is clear that cultural borders are permeable, that they are constantly passed and trespassed. Cultural borders are accordingly constantly shifting, taking new twists and windings, like the paths of rivers that mark so many geographical borders. Cultural creativity (what the anthropologists fittingly call efflorescence) is largely due to engagement with other or "alien" cultures. On these counts, as well as the important theological considerations set out in chapter nine, Christianity as culture need not at all be incorrigible, which is to say immune to correction or change prompted from "outside."[9]

Indeed, Christians are members of more than one culture (the church) at any given time. Besides the obvious differences of nationality, individual Christians may participate in and be influenced by professional, artistic, political and other cultures. Many arguments within the church arise for exactly that reason. If no one were both a homosexual and a Christian, the church *might* (it would not have to) avoid the societal debate over the status of gays. If no one were both a feminist and a Christian, the church might have continued merrily along its patriarchal way. And if no one were both a conservative Republican and a Christian, the church might not as strenuously debate whether or not there should be a "Christian America." In these and manifold other areas, it is clear that Christians live and move among a "tournament of narratives" or "multiplicity of codes."[10]

It is exactly because life is lived and understood through specific narratives or codes that so many of our most intense disagreements are matters of wildly different interpretations. Those Ronald Reagan called "freedom fighters" were, to many Nicaraguans, rank terrorists. And is America, as in Lincoln's vision, the "last great hope" of the earth, or is it, as in the eyes of Iranian Muslims, the "Great Satan"? As literary critic Robert Scholes writes, "Most acts that justify the term 'interpretation' at all involve the use of several [sometimes contradictory] codes, and most interpretive disputes can usefully be seen as disputes over the proper hierarchy of codes: whether a particular code is relevant at all, whether one code is more or less relevant than another, and so on."[11] Reagan and Nicaraguans, Lincoln and Iranians, dispute in each case a proper hierarchy of codes. They operate out of opposed construals of history and even varied understandings of the right, good and true aims of human beings.

Non-Constantinian Christians have no vested interest in undermining the tournament of narratives or stifling the multiplicity of codes. We confess a God we understand as Creator of the cosmos, so the fount of all creativity, and as vulnerable Savior, so granting creatures freedom and risking their rejection in order to win their unqualified love. What we strive to do is to check all other stories by the story of Israel and Jesus Christ, to live by a hierarchy of codes that always sees the Christian code as most relevant and, indeed, as uniquely and finally true.

Culture and Truth

The question of truth in fact represents one of the most serious challenges to considering Christianity as culture. After all, in many cultural matters we are accustomed to regarding one culture's goods as no better than another culture's. Earlier I wrote about a day in which I enjoyed both Mexican and Chinese food. It would seem misguided to insist that one cuisine is somehow superior to the other. I might *prefer* one kind to the other, but how would I go about demonstrating that such should be the judgment arrived at by everyone? Likewise with the varieties of music I enjoy. Classical music is certainly in some ways more complicated than country music, but who says complication is the premier aesthetic criterion? Economy and straightforwardness have also been regarded as aesthetic qualities, and here some country music might take an edge. Things are even more difficult when we move to the realm of morality and truth. Is Chinese food morally superior to Mexican food? Is classical music somehow truer than country music? Arguments could be made, and in fact we are often at least vaguely motivated by intuitions of just these sorts. But we tend to relegate these matters of culture largely to the area of taste and personal preference.

So the concern about considering Christianity as culture becomes obvious. Is it in the end then reduced to someone's personal preference? Christianity may be better, truer, preferable to me, just as I prefer Mexican to Greek food; but then there is nothing I can say to those who find Buddhism better, truer and more preferable to them, just as I have little to say by way of persuasion to those who like Greek food more than Mexican. If all this is the case, then considering Christianity (or any other faith) as culture ultimately trivializes it. People have died for this faith; few would die for the advancement of Greek cuisine—or even an extraordinary enchilada molé.

The problem with this objection is that it slides whole-hog back into the terms of modernity and liberalism. Culture and the cultural are in these terms confined to the private, and so a matter of personal taste. These terms, as we have seen, themselves reduce and trivialize Christianity. Since it is patently not universally self-evident and refers to as well as grows out of a particular history, Christianity is itself assigned to the modernist-liberal's private realm.

So what I have here endeavored to do is to reject the modernist-liberal conceptuality and work instead with Christianity robust and undiluted—that is, as a quite particular way of life, or culture. In the process I have freely poached on the work of social and literary theorists who understand culture in a broader, more profound sense than do the modernist-liberals. Culture in this broader, deeper sense reminds us that not all discussions of such things as food and music are as frivolous or negligible as, on liberal-modernist terms, we might first think. For instance, if certain Hindus are right and persons really are reincarnate in the flesh of animals, some cuisines emphatically are morally superior to others. Accordingly, some vegetarians would argue *on moral grounds* that a bean burrito is better than filet mignon.

Thus the cultural perspective does not exclude serious commitments nor the desire that those commitments might be held universally. What it does is reveal that there is no acultural or acontextual position to argue from. Again, as I sail on one or another of the arks in the fleet called church, I engage sailors on other ships. I seek to persuade them to take on the cargo my ship bears, believing it indeed to be the most valuable cargo there is or can be. Occasionally I may be at sea and spring a leak. I may borrow planks from a passing ship, then saw and fit those planks to my vessel and its immediate needs. Where this analogy breaks down, from a cultural perspective, is that I cannot take my ship into dry dock and examine it fore to aft for dry rot. The ship Christianity is the ground I stand on. There is no neutral ground I can escape to from which to judge it neutrally and disinterestedly. I *can* make judgments and criticisms of Christianity—but only from the perspectives I learn from other ships.[12]

Put more literally, I cannot judge Christianity simply as a human being; I am always a particular human being, made the human being I am by specific attitudes, practices, feelings, beliefs and "signifying systems." Exactly as a Christian human being, I strive to make the Christian narrative the root narrative or code of my life. If I ever reject Christianity as my root narrative, it will be because I have learned enough of another narrative or code to find Christianity wanting. But as long as there is any direction and coherence to my life, I will not be without one or another narrative or collection of narratives.

At this stage it is important to emphasize that the cultural perspective does not put Christianity in a disadvantageous position, as compared with other religions or philosophies. Those who hold to and live by other religions or philosophies have, and are possessed by, their own cultural perspectives, which is to say at the least that they make sense of the world and construct their experience through specific signifying systems.[13] Sometimes those with very old or very large boats—or perhaps those whose boats are equipped with gunnery—will try to convince us that they speak entirely objectively, with no specific interests, for all times and places. But no matter how old or large or intimidating, a boat is still a boat. Non-Constantinian Christians who understand faith as a way of life may then confidently set sail.

Whither Evangelism and Apologetics?

So let us admit that we are, in the best and adventurous sense of word, afloat. On what account do we then present our God and ourselves to non-Christians? What, in cultural perspective, is the basis for Christian evangelism and apologetics? True to Christian numerology, I have seven steps or points in mind.

The first step is not something that can be isolated and tested in itself, but it must be true for all else to follow, and is *in that sense* foundational. Nothing else, even if supposedly "universally" available and self-evident, can be more basic than this: For Christianity to be true, there must be a God who engages people in their history. There must be truth in something like the Christian trust in prevenient grace and the illuminating power of the Holy Spirit. More specifically, who or what we call God must first of all have reached out to Israel and, through Christ, to the people known as church. And this God must, through the Spirit, provide guidance in discerning and interpreting God's acts—else no one would believe in *Israel's or Jesus'* God even if this God existed and acted in history. Without such illumination and guidance, God's acts could be construed (or misconstrued) in all kinds of ways. They could be interpreted nontheistically (as "nature" is read in atheistic evolutionary schemes) and certainly non-Yahwehistically. In short, we can know the God of Israel and Jesus only through that God's revelation of himself to or through Israel and Jesus. Were this not true and real, nothing else would follow. Certainly our arguments or logical posturing, however impeccable, would not make it true and real.

The second step is then related to the first. For faith to occur, for it to be passed on to those who do not already walk in the way of Christ, there must be a faith community. And this faith community will be sustained (by those inside it) or considered relevant and interesting (by those outside it) only if it is the kind of community that suggests the gospel to be true in practice and so in reality. No one will come to know Christianity's particular God, or will want to know that God, without the vital and promising life-witness of the community called church. For if we expect the Christian story to bear any persuasive potency, then "at the very least, that story must have the power to take hold of our life and sustain it and even possibly transform it. . . . And if those who espouse a particular master story nevertheless show themselves unwilling or unable to follow it . . . with fidelity, why should anybody else take their story seriously?"[14]

So it is that only at the third step can we begin to approach the evangelistic and apologetical task in a more traditionally modern, rationalistic or intellectual manner. Here we can say that a faith narrative (Christianity or otherwise) is potentially compelling if it is coherent on its own terms. Does it hold together? Are its various parts consistent with the whole?

We can also, at a fourth step, ask how widely translatable a specific faith narrative is. It has more potential to compellingly persuade if it has successfully spread and been adaptable to a variety of cultures, if it has thrived in different times and places.[15]

At a related fifth step, a faith narrative is more worthy of our consent if it is able to encompass a variety of life experiences, and need not deny experiences that persistently present themselves. So it is that Christian Science is threatened to survive little more than a century, not least because it has great difficulty dealing with the pervasive experiences of illness and death.

At yet another related, and sixth, step, a faith narrative has more potential to persuade if it is able to hear representatives of other faiths honestly and fully, then (a) "absorb" or account for challenges raised by these "competing" faiths and (b) cogently interpret aspects of its own faith narrative to allow for discoveries, insights or understandings previously not conscious to it.

Finally, and in a different vein, we may from a cultural perspective say that a faith has more potential to persuade if it is enacted and presented to others nonviolently. That is to say, we are entitled to suspicion of any faith narrative that resorts to brute, coercive power to "convince" others of its truth. Then we may legitimately suspect that a faith narrative has nothing truer to offer than the bullet or the whip. Truths can stand on their own. It is lies and illusions that require deception and violence for their maintenance.

Participating in Rather Than Objectifying Truth

In sum, I am arguing that interpreting Christianity as culture (rather than as philosophical system or even worldview) allows Christianity to be more fully itself. What God has created in Israel and the church is not a tribunal that dispenses propositions mirroring or corresponding to some static, finally decided truth in another and ahistorical spatial realm (such as "heaven" utterly uncoupled from the earth, or some other version of the Platonic forms). What the book of Hebrews shows instead is that the real has come to humanity "in the historical life and death of Jesus of Nazareth" (see, for instance, Heb 7:27, 9:12, 10:10).

Certain Greek and other rationalists have envisaged the difference between perfection and imperfection in the categories of *space*—and so between a heavenly, perfect world and an earthly, imperfect world. The early Christians, living in the light of the apocalypse of Messiah's coming, considered perfection versus imperfection under the categories of *time*. The Jewish and Christian hope is not for the flight of the soul, at death, to an invisible world of eternal reality. It is instead eschatological, looking not so much "above" in space as "ahead" in time, when God's new heaven *and* new earth will be realized in their fullness.[16]

Until then, it is the Christian confession and expectation that men and women—indeed, entire cultures—are free to ignore or only very selectively hear the Word of God. Only on the last day will every knee bow and every tongue confess Jesus as the Lord whom Christians already see and consider him to be (Phil 2:5-11). For now, we all see darkly as through a murky glass (1 Cor 13).

So what God has created in the church is a dynamic, ongoing form of life, a way of being human, which is to say an arena of social interaction that uniquely dwells in relationship with the one and true God and witnesses to a day when all creation will be in proper, fitting and true relation with that same God. To quote John Milbank again, in its beliefs, practices, attitudes and projects the church can claim nothing less than "to exhibit the exemplary form of human community." For it is the case that the very logic of Christianity "involves the claim that the 'interruption' of history by Christ and his bride, the Church, is the most fundamental of events, interpreting all other events. And it is *most especially* a social event, able to interpret other social formations [other cultures], because it compares them with its own new social practice."[17]

Accordingly, Christians do not find truth "out there," detached from their lives, so much as they "live in it and so declare it in everything they do."[18] It is time and past time for all Christians to relive the experience of Mary Magdalene, who three days after the crucifixion went looking for Christ the object (an inert corpse) but instead was herself found and comprehended by Christ the living subject, raised from the dead. Christians rightly do not possess or simply recite truth so much as we *participate* in truth.

Reclaiming Christianity as culture enables us to move from decontextualized propositions to traditioned, storied, *inhabitable* truths; from absolute certainty to humble confidence; from austere mathematical purity to the rich if less predictable world of relational trust; from control of the data to respect of the other in all its created variety; from individualist knowing to communal knowing and being known; and from once-for-all rational justification to the ongoing pilgrimage of testimony.

In this spirit, I do not deny that there are important philosophical and intellectualized questions that can be put to Christianity and to the church. But I think the first and more important questions are ones such as these: Does Christian worship enable or disenable us, encourage or discourage us, to spot, confront and work against the political, social and economic horrors of our time? Does it remake our everyday lives, shaping and equipping us to both admit and resist tragedy, and to celebrate and cultivate God-given goodness and joy? Do our week-in and week-out praise and prayer and study as the church open our eyes, or do they not? Do we feel at all times, exactly *as Christians,* involved in the real thing, or are we continually choking down suspicions that what we do, and where we are, is not the real world?[19]

If our conceptions of church and the Christian life so disarm us, that in itself is proof that we have abandoned the faith—the culture, the way of life—of Abraham, Isaac, Jacob and Jesus.

12

THE CHURCH AS A COMMUNITY OF FRIENDS
*About Beginning
Where We Already Are*

□

I *f, then, Christianity is a culture rather than a philosophy or a worldview,* where do we begin? So much would surely change if the church regarded itself as a way of life and not simply a spiritual retreat or the promoting society of a belief system. In fact, I have argued that Christian worship, evangelism, use of the Bible and politics would all look considerably different from the way they do now. Given such a radical vision, what possible first step might we take?

William Faulkner was once asked how he would counsel those who had read *The Sound and the Fury* once or twice but still didn't get it. "Read it three times," he said. My previous chapters have already suggested much by way of an answer to the question of where to go from here. But I am, of course, nowhere near Faulkner's authorial and authoritative status, and I am also so appreciative of any readers who have made it this far, that I am obligated to work harder with such a question. So my reply is that we begin where we already are.

I mean this in more than one sense. It is crucial that we no longer look for general, technical, once-for-all answers to challenges set in the way of Christian endeavor. The faith is cultural and timely, not acultural and atemporal. It is important for the church in each time and place to embody and communicate the life of Christ exactly where it is. Christianity is not about compartmentalization or withdrawal: it is radically and relentlessly life-encompassing. Christianity understood as culture is about a living tradition, a continuing argument, a still-unfolding history. It is about being engaged by a God who is not through wooing, harassing, changing and redeeming an estranged creation. So there is no escape to abstract and settled formulas about how to make things right. Things will be made right, but only after a wonderful and horrible story not yet at its end has run its course. Christians are called to live the story, not restate it in the form of universalized propositions.

But beginning where we are also means that we are already, in at least some ways, on the path we should be treading. If Christianity is culture, it would be self-defeating to say that the church as a way of life does not already exist. Christianity is not an ideology to be recovered or a philosophical system to be remembered. There are Christian traditions that do embody, to a real degree, non-Constantinian Christianity. However imperfectly, there are saints who perform Scripture and local churches that not only speak but actually are the gospel. To the extent that any of us are currently confessing Christians, we are in touch with such saints and churches—we *are* such saints and churches.

In fact, we are like the little girl who went to the river to look for a hippopotamus, but really wasn't sure what to look for. She stood on a big gray rock in the middle of the water for a better view, then went home disappointed. If she had known what to look for, she would have known that the rock was a hippo, that she was standing on top of what she was searching for the entire time. What she needed was not a new reality but a better way to see the reality already at hand. Likewise, what we need is not a new path but better language and sharpened imaginations to discern the path we are already following.

Accordingly, what I can offer in conclusion is not another program or a newly fabricated blueprint. It is, instead, a word about the locale many of us dwell in and about strengthening the Christian community that already gives us life.

The World As We Know It

There can be no mistake that the church today faces considerable obstacles to its being a distinctively Christian culture or way of life. Many of those obstacles, as we have seen, are internal to the church; they are fostered by its unwillingness to give up Constantinian habits. But other obstacles are more external. Those of us who live in North American and European countries—and indeed those who live in much of the rest of the world today—face a formidable challenge. For good and for ill, we live amid a pervasive, infinitely insinuating social, political and economic ethos. It is something that in biblical terms might be called a principality or power, a vast and captivating structure that both holds our world together and threatens to destroy it.[1] There are four key elements to this principality, so that we might comprehensively (if awkwardly) call it mass-techno-liberal capitalism.

It is *mass* in that it is built and operated on a large, highly centralized basis. This includes communications media (television, radio, telephones, computers), transportation, energy and disposal systems. Most of the world—certainly all of the "developed" world—collects news and entertainment from mass media. We rely on mass transportation, not only riding buses and trains but also flying on multinational airlines. Our homes are fueled and powered by gas and electricity companies providing such services for millions of customers. Our trash is collected, our sewage eliminated, by corporations and municipalities. Most of these systems exceed the reach of local governments. Accordingly, centralized, bureaucratized government has grown in importance and power.

This pervasive principality is *techno* in that it is technologically complicated and intensive. Entire societies are markedly dependent on technology for communication, transportation and the rest. A fire at a single telephone switching station can interrupt service for thousands of businesses and residences. An electrical failure can jeopardize dozens of planes and hundreds of passengers at an airport. Technology thus supports all the systems listed under "mass" above. But it also includes the concentration on technique and machinery in most other spheres of our lives: the professionalization and mechanization of medicine, the popularity of marketing and managerial procedures in religion, the passage of publishing from cottage industry to corporate conglomeration, and so forth. Like the emphasis on mass, the emphasis on technological pulls away from the local toward the centralized, away from particular communities toward the abstract "global community."

The predominant world system is also *liberal* in that it is philosophically guided by classical liberalism. It focuses not on community but on the individual, interpreted as a maximizer of self-interest. Thus it assumes there is not and cannot be a common substantive good. Whatever good or goal someone lives for is accordingly a "private" and never a "public" matter.

Finally, the ideal economic system to accompany this political system is *capitalism*. Capitalism is intended to regulate the activities of self-interested, liberal individuals by putting them to competition in the free market. Now arrived at the stage of advanced capitalism, markets are themselves massive, technologized and centralized. As anyone who has bought a home mortgage knows, we live in a world of extensive commercial as well as governmental bureaucracy.

Again, one of the most salient characteristics of mass-techno-liberal capitalism is its sheer pervasiveness. We are always bumping against—if not being run over by—one or another of its manifestations. With every meal, every flick of the computer switch, every drive in the car, we encounter this inescapable system. Its values relentlessly bear down on us. We may not mind being "consumers" of food and movies, but we are also made "consumers" of health and religion. Centralization and technology seem all to the good when we can turn the tap and draw fresh water that will not make us sick. But the same centralization and technologization have also eroded community, if we think of a community as persons commonly inhabiting a place, sharing common interests or goods, and depending on a local culture and economy.[2] Downtowns die as franchise supermarkets and department stores move into outlying malls. Any sense of belonging to and caring for a true neighborhood dwindles as people sleep in one 'hood, work in another, shop for groceries in a third, play golf in a fourth and worship in a fifth. Suburban dwellers are much more likely to be capable of naming the president of the United States, or the prime minister of Great Britain, than the mayor of their own town.

Professionalized, specialized, federalized and capitalized, the modern world system "simply cannot register the wisdom inherent in any indigenous culture."[3] Herbal healing, no matter how much pharmaceutics continues to depend on the properties of plants, is dismissed and forgotten as superstition. Family businesses fail because they cannot afford to satisfy the expensive and irrelevant regulations devised by a government three thousand miles away. Universities grant religious studies doctorates and tenure only to those who learn not to take a religion on the terms of those who seriously try to live it, but to recast it in supposedly more fundamental social, psychological or economic terms. Native American pottery and weaving, once key to an entire way of life, is commodified and reduced to the "Santa Fe style." Breast-feeding is displaced as "primitive," only to be revalidated once its instruction is safely in the hands of physicians and out of the hands of grandmothers. The amateur musicmaking of families and friends fades and passes, sounding hopelessly second-rate next to polished, mass-produced and easily accessible performances of professionals. Even the most sublime or costly moral stands are absorbed by the system and trivialized to the status of mere commodity—hence Malcolm X two decades after his murder means nothing more to many teenagers than a "cool" cap.

With our sense and actual experience of authentic community replaced by helpless enmeshment in a mass, impersonal "public," and with our most urgent hopes privatized and commodified, we are prone to wake up in the middle of the night and wonder, dreadfully, about the hollowness of our days. "Ironically," Robert Inchausti caustically observes, "this very longing for a more profound existence makes [us] prey to salesmen and commercial visionaries who sell [us] dreams without inspiring [us] to the discipline necessary for authentic transcendence." Hence weight loss without exercise and with "fat-free" dessert, or spiritual growth without fasting and prayer. We are made into consumers of the worst, most demeaning sort: "systematically miseducated, under-estimated, financially pampered, and morally exploited." In the end we are ceaselessly pressured toward becoming "nonpersons who are celebrated by the media as existentially free but whose history, ethnicity," moral character and religious commitment "have been marginalized, if not entirely debunked, by a world socio-economic order that runs according to its own impersonal rules and agenda."[4]

But again, however destructive this world order or principality and power may be, there is no escaping it. For one thing, Christians have strong theological grounds to respect as well as criticize the principalities and powers. Culture is a part of God's good but now fallen creation; its manifestations are usually not something to be monolithically rejected or accepted. Nor are Christians called simply to save ourselves. Surrounding cultures—the world—demand instead a more strenuous but more faithful selective engagement. For another thing, and to repeat, this world system is not all to the bad. In some regards, it surely has created new wealth and contributed to a less brutish existence. Finally, we must note again the sheer pervasiveness of the system. If so minded, Christians of two centuries ago might have been able to relatively separate themselves from surrounding cultures. But it is the very nature of mass-techno-liberal capitalism that it encircles the globe and invades every nook and cranny of our lives. Even the hermit hears the planes pass overhead and drinks from a stream that is polluted by the city upriver. The extremes Christians would have to go to in order to even attempt avoiding this nearly omnipresent world system would mark and determine us by the system as much as wholeheartedly and uncritically living by it.

Incidentally, the very potency and tenacity of this world order are yet another reason for Christians to abandon the Constantinian posture. This is a world order remarkable, in some respects, for its disorder. The multiplicity of options—commercially, religiously, politically and otherwise—is overwhelming in this transient, pluralized and commodified ethos. Those who would retrench and retake "Christian America" face a much more daunting task than they would have in 1776 or 1855. There are simply too many Jewish, Muslim, Buddhist, Hindu, atheist, agnostic and other Americans who would not willingly accept even the mildest version of "Christian America." What to do? Disqualify them from political office? Shut down their newspapers and magazines? Deport them? No even remotely serious spokesperson of the religious right would countenance as much. The level and kinds of coercion necessary, even should such Christians gain the governmental power they desire, would likely be considered, in actual prospect, too draconian by their own standards.

On purely pragmatic grounds, then, as well as the more important theological considerations advanced throughout this book, a Constantinian, meet-worldly-power-on-its-own-terms approach makes little sense. Christians who abandon the Constantinian posture recognize that they are no longer in control, and doubt both the wisdom and feasibility of reasserting imperial control. A non-Constantinian engagement of surrounding culture as we now know it, then, would not make a frontal attack on the "world" and would instead seek to propose the gospel (good news!) rather than impose the law of God. At the level of implementation, such an approach would involve at least two necessities: the rebuilding of distinctive Christian community and the relearning of what might be called sanctified subversion.

Rebuilding Christian Community

Strengthening distinctive Christian community is at once one of the most essential and the most formidable challenges the church faces in our world. As we have noted, mass-techno-liberal capitalism is a principality and power that ceaselessly breaks down and inhibits real community. Not just faith groups but also nation-states, political parties, towns and cities, businesses, media, and ethnic segments are sucked into a vortex that drains them away from locality, respect for place, stability and a sense of any enduring transcendence. This is a world system that rewards and promotes novelty over the familiar, reservation of options over commitment, an "open" future over an accepted past, functional over substantive relationships, what works over doctrine, independence over interdependence and quantitative measures of worth over qualitative measures of worth. None of this bodes well for community. Yet Christians who desire stronger Christian community—groups of persons dedicated to one another for the purpose of serving the kingdom of God initiated in Jesus—are by no means totally at a loss.

Beginning where we already are, we can first of all *recognize that we are inescapably communal creatures*. We really can't—contra the modern myth—create ourselves. We are made in the image of a trinitarian, communal God. We depend on others to be born, to survive, to be buried and remembered. We live and have our being in community, however attenuated it may become.

As Christians, we can recognize and claim what our modern stories and conceptualities can cause us to overlook. For instance, I have realized that my own discounting of Christian community owed something to an illegitimate separation of church and friendship. But it was through shared church—worship, work, fellowship—that I learned to love and came to be loved by many of my closest friends. These are the people who have encouraged me in heart's endeavors, seen me through the deaths of parents and parents-in-law, given me money and time, spoken hard truth to me when I needed to hear it, partied with me, loaned me pickup trucks and saws and lawn mowers, godparented my daughter—and on and on. They are people I would not know or continue to know outside a common commitment to following the Christ.

Community may be jostled, deprived, squeezed, but it is as persistent and hard to kill as a rattlesnake. We want it too much; it is too much, without remainder, what life worth living just is. Part of strengthening Christian community, then, is simply recognizing, acknowledging and building on the community that already exists, but that we have been trained to ignore or deny.

Beginning where we are also means *recognizing the power of the church's regular gathering and worship.* Robust Christian community obviously requires more than merely "going to church" every Sunday, but even that level of commitment should not be taken for granted or ridiculed. In an increasingly secularized culture, Sunday morning is more and more the one day of the week to sleep in or the last remaining available slot for park district sports. Without any more effort than simply getting out of bed and driving to a place of worship, Christians simply are distinctive. And that is to say nothing about the stubborn, profoundly formative power of worship itself. However feebly and distractedly we participate, we are acknowledging a reality outside ourselves and the world as it is otherwise known. We are confessing at least the possibility of being accountable to something (to someone) other than our individual desires and "needs."

Even something so apparently mundane as singing together sets Christians apart and influences character. Where else in our society do people sing together, harmonizing and making art in common cause? A friend remembers that just decades ago, when his father first worked for IBM, the employees each morning sang together the corporate song. The day of company loyalty is past; now even the thought of a "company song" seems ludicrous. Yet shared song is a profound way of remembering, solidifying and celebrating our commonality. It is something we do at worship naturally, something we could not fail to do every time we worship. If in nothing more than our continuing acts of worship, then, we have community and the basis for building stronger community.

Beginning where we are can in addition lead us to a third already existing resource: we can build Christian community by *reclaiming and giving more deliberate attention to Christian language.* Language is not the whole of reality, but it plays an indispensable role in making things and relationships real.[5] *Racism* and *sexism* were not invented as terms until the twentieth century. Only with such terms could we develop a widespread recognition of the interests of or injustices done to minority races and to women as women. Or consider the language of codependency and addiction—with it people see that they can be "addicted" not only to drugs but to also people and relationships. Only with such language and its widespread adoption could there have been the grassfire proliferation of twelve-step groups and the development of a new niche in publishing.

To reclaim and cultivate Christian language will naturally, if often surprisingly, check and challenge all manner of practices promoted by the predominant world system. Trinitarian and ecclesial language challenges the adequacy of the grammar of atomistic individualism. Christian categories such as losing the self to gain it throw conceptual monkey wrenches in the works of commodification. As Inchausti notes in reference to the nun of Calcutta, "Anyone who attempts to interpret Mother Teresa confronts the fact that today's common secular idiom simply lacks the requisite symbolism and moral sensitivity necessary to express adequately the meaning of Christian service."[6] Interpreting everyday life—as well as world events—in Christian language will inevitably enliven imaginations and open up formerly undreamed-of options.

And that in turn suggests we can rebuild Christian community by *honoring and taking the small step, trusting that God is always bigger than our imaginations.* Further possibilities and ways of acting will present themselves as we reform our language and imagination. Creatively naming a problem or gaining a new way of seeing things immediately opens a variety of ways of being and acting. Out of Marx's language and imagination came the disasters of Stalinism, but also the category of "class" now embraced and used by conservatives as readily as revolutionaries. No one could have predicted all the ramifications of the internal combustion engine on the day it was invented. Once we accept that managerial control and comprehensive prediction are illusions of modern and Constantinian mentalities, we can more appropriately honor small, immediate steps. Living out of control, we can properly respect and strengthen the ties we already have, even in a limiting and frustratingly anticommunal setting.[7] Sticking with a failing church, preparing meals for the homeless, "adopting" a refugee family, turning down a job offer that requires a cross-country move—all these may seem little things, but who knows to what greater things they may lead? And even if they do not, they can be in themselves the stuff of truly richer and fuller life.

The possibility of authentically rich and full life is a resounding advantage the church (and other genuine communities) profoundly holds against mass-techno-liberal capitalism. As John McKnight writes, real and vital communities are based on care and consent. "Care cannot be produced, provided, managed, organized, administered, or commodified. Care is the only thing a system cannot produce. Every institutional effort to replace the real thing is counterfeit" and is inevitably recognized as such. I can never escape the nagging suspicion that my therapist might not give me so much time and attention if I was not paying him. The store clerk smiles not so much because she is glad to see me as because she wants my business. The cancer specialist can stay only five minutes in my father's hospital room, then she must rush ahead to tell several other patients the results of their CAT scans. All these are honorable enough endeavors, of course, but not really practices of deep and abiding care. We can care and be cared for only in genuine community.

People who belong to such a community want to belong to it—they cannot imagine worthwhile life without it. Such a caring and consensual community is a place, a collocation of relationships, where "interdependence creates wholistic environments, people of all capacities and fallibilities are incorporated, quick responses are possible, creativity is multiplied rather than channeled, individualized responses are characteristic, care is able to replace [professionalized] service," and active citizenship rather than passive clienthood is made possible.[8]

The predominant world system would indeed have us entirely dependent on its centralized services and products. It would have us imagine that the only politics that matter and can make a difference are national or international politics. It is powerful, awesomely powerful, but it cannot provide care and it does not elicit consent.

It is through the genuine community of church that Christians can tell their stories, celebrate their life and their hope, and acknowledge their tragedies.[9] Admitting that we are out of control, that we cannot determine our destiny, we are freed to admit that we sometimes suffer and most definitely will die. Partly through accepting our death, we are empowered to take back our life and put back together the pieces the world system has broken it into.

Composer James MacMillan so Christianizes, empowers and reintegrates life in one of his *Cantos Sagrados* ("Sacred Songs").[10] In a shocking and revelatory choral work, MacMillan superimposes on the words of the Latin Creed a poem about the unjust execution of a South American political prisoner. The piece begins with one group of singers soothingly remembering that God became incarnate in Christ. But then other singers break in with whispering, ominous tones about a prisoner being placed against a wall. The creed continues its steady, undergirding march beneath a narrative of a soldier tying the prisoner's hands. Then the soldier touches the prisoner and gently says, "Forgive me, compañero." The separate choruses swirl and rush together. The prisoner hears the echoes of the soldier's repenting plea, so that his body fills with intensifying light and he "almost" doesn't hear the report of the rifles fired on him. At the very moment the prisoner is shot, the creedal chorus answers with the exclamation "crucifixus etiam pro nobis"—"for our sake he was crucified." Christ dies for (and in a sense with) the prisoner. Thus the sacred and the profane are rejoined. A system that would, in good liberal fashion, confine the sacred to the private is thwarted. The sacred is seen through the profane act of a military execution, the profane through the sacred act of Jesus' holy death.

We might wish that the soldier had been heroic and refused to participate in the execution. Perhaps MacMillan means to protest such indifference and injustice by starkly juxtaposing Christ's execution to this execution. After all, Christ was the victim who sought forgiveness on behalf of or *for* his executioners, while in this case one of the executioners seeks forgiveness *from* the victim. Yet even if the soldier fails to exploit it as dramatically as he might and ideally should, he clearly sees a chink in the armor of the system. He participates, but he knows what is being done is wrong. His merest gentleness and repentance, meager as they are, manifest to that degree a Christian community that a demonic and totalitarian system could not crush or exclude. The community of soldier and prisoner is surely reduced and distorted, but it is not eliminated, for the soldier chooses to call the prisoner and not his coexecutioners "companion." He seeks reconciliation and so solidarity with the victim, even as he is complicit with the victimizers.

Likewise, and usually in much less urgent circumstances, we are all complicit in a system that depersonalizes, that sometimes degrades and too often does violence. And whatever we do, the injustices of the system will not end tomorrow. As with the soldier and his dilemma, who can say when the smaller, quieter act is less a failure of courage than it is a victory of prudence? At the least, might not a tiny act of courage today lead to greater acts of courage later? MacMillan would have us know that even in their feeblest manifestations, decent Christian care, the Christian language of the creed and the Christian practice of forgiveness make a strike against any principality and power that would dishonor community and destroy wholeness, preventing life as God gave it and calls it to be.

Sanctified Subversion

Thus it is misleading and finally counterproductive for us to fixate on the dramatic act, the quick fix, the heroic stand. Church as a way of life is incremental obedience, passion subdued but sustained over years. It is discipleship for the long haul, over a road that is inevitably bumpy and includes detours, switchbacks and delays. It is the persistent if not perfect unlearning of the world system's established separation of the practical and the theoretical, the profane and the sacred, the political and the spiritual, the theological and the sociological.

Church is a way of life lived not with the expectation that Christians can, through managerial arts or sudden heroism, make the world right. It is instead a way of life lived in the confidence that God has, in the kingdom of Christ, begun to set the world right—and that someday Christ will bring his kingdom to its fulfillment. Only then will wars cease, will the lion lie down with the lamb, will death itself die, will children frolic at the mouth of the viper's den. In the meantime, Christians are about surviving and alleviating the worst effects of a world bent on self-destruction, about reminding that world of its true nature as fallen and redeemed creature, about demonstrating to some real degree that there is and can be communal solidarity on God's good earth. Accordingly, worship and the spiritual disciplines of prayer, fasting and Bible study are ways we gracefully fail to absorb the distorted ethic of the world system.[11] Non-Constantinian Christians are in no position to overthrow that system. What we can hope to do, most often and over the long haul, is survive it and subvert it to its own good. What we are about might then be called sanctified subversion.

It would be a travesty of profounder suffering to equate the powerlessness of Christians living in contemporary, Western democratic settings with that of the disenfranchised and sometimes persecuted Christians of the pre-Constantinian period. Yet I think Christians living in a post-Constantinian world have much to learn from our forebears, and indeed from plebeians who throughout the ages have had to struggle and die under conditions that their kind did not create and could not control. The common people have always lived in a world shaped by and in the interests of the ruling classes. They have always operated out of weakness, at least weakness in terms of brute and immediate power. Yet as the late French priest and social theorist Michel de Certeau observed, ordinary people have endlessly devised ways to "use the system" to their own ends.

For instance, the ambiguity that subverted from within the Spanish colonizers' "success" in imposing their own culture on the indigenous Indians [of what is now called Central and South America] is well known. Submissive, and even consenting to their subjection, the Indians nevertheless often *made of* the rituals, representations, and laws imposed on them something quite different from what their conquerors had in mind; they subverted them not [necessarily] by rejecting them, . . . but *by using them with respect to ends and references foreign to the system they had no choice but to accept.* . . . Their use of the dominant social order deflected its power, which they lacked the means to challenge; they escaped it without leaving it.[12] Perhaps even more familiar to North Americans is Southern U.S. slaveholders' justified fear that slaves might get their own Christianity. Slaveholders suppressed separate and unsupervised worship by their African-American charges because they realized, intuitively if not explicitly, that the slaves might interpret Christianity in a fashion that subverted the institution of slavery. And indeed when slaves did worship behind power's back, they developed a faith and church that have been a mainstay and base of empowerment for black culture ever since.

Rulers have consistently interpreted the apparent submissiveness and the feigned incomprehension of commoners in denigrating terms (such as *docility, stupidity* and *laziness*). But as political scientist James Scott notes, such practices are actually "the weapons of the weak . . . the tenacity of self-preservation—in ridicule, in truculence, in irony, in petty acts of noncompliance . . . in resistant mutuality, in the disbelief of elite homilies, in the steady grinding efforts to hold one's own against overwhelming odds—a spirit and practice that prevents the worst and promises something better."[13]

Christians ready to put aside the dream of ruling the world in Jesus' name will have to adapt similar tactics. As I have already observed, we cannot in any event leave or even take a vacation from mass-techno-liberal capitalism. That is a system that, for the foreseeable future at least, we have no choice but to acknowledge. What we can do is appropriate and reappropriate aspects of the system to Christian ends. We need not (vainly) seek to get outside the system so much as change it from the inside out. The church may be at times a kind of benevolent parasite, creating for its host cultures new and unanticipated necessities—necessities the host would never have chosen on its own, but eventually comes to know as healing necessities nevertheless.

Actually, once we stop reading the Bible from a Constantinian, imperial perspective and begin reading it from a plebeian perspective, its pages explode with examples of sanctified subversion. From a position of slavery and imprisonment, Joseph redirects the Egyptian empire. Esther the lowly concubine works behind the scenes on behalf of her subjugated people. Nathan, calling King David to account for grievous crimes, resorts to the indirect and plebeian tactic of the parable to slip beneath the king's superior defenses and convict him with his own words.

The entire book of Daniel can be fairly and profitably read as a case study in sanctified subversion. Exiled and drawn into the service of a series of Babylonian kings, Daniel and his Hebrew companions do not mount a frontal rebellion. But they judiciously and discreetly resist Babylonian ways. For instance, they politely and carefully reject the royal diet in favor of the food that defines them as Israelites (Dan 1:3-5). Such small but significant habits prepare and strengthen them for greater acts of resistance, so that they are later able to refuse worship of Babylonian kings and their gods (3:16-18; 6:10-16). Walter Brueggemann is surely right to assert:

> The rhetoric and imagery of these narratives [Daniel and other apocalyptic stories] refuses to abide by the rationality of dominant society; refuses to live in the understandable world of common sense or of common experience. The rhetoric of the narrative invites the listener out beyond the world of predictability into another world of thought and risk and gift, a world in which the unexpected happens, in which connections surprise us, and in which new life is miraculously given.

Daniel and his companions exemplify the canny, plebeian Israelite understanding that "individual persons are able to withstand the pressure of persecution and its depersonalization because they have an identity that is beyond the reach of the persecutor. In the case of Israel, that liberating identity is given by God, so that persons of faith need not believe or accept the identity that their persecutors want to give them."[14]

In the light of such sanctified subversion, Jesus' whole life, work and death take on new meaning. Like his father, Jesus was identified as a carpenter (Mk 6:3), a term that in the Roman world of the day was snobbishly used to denote plebeian origins.[15] A number of Jesus' parables and other sayings hint at a subversive plebeian mentality and spirit, maybe nowhere so concisely as Matthew 10:16, "See, I am sending you out like sheep [apparently docile and uncomprehending] into the midst of wolves; so be wise as serpents and innocent as doves." New Testament scholar Walter Wink intriguingly reads the Sermon on the Mount—which has long struck Constantinian Christians as unrealistic, impractical and even masochistic—as something of a plebeian political resistance guide.

For instance, Jesus counsels, "If anyone wants to sue you and take your coat, give your cloak as well" (Mt 5:40). Wink reminds us that Jesus' original hearers are without many possessions and certainly without much power. They are caught up in a system that "subjects them to humiliation by stripping them of their lands, their goods, finally even their outer garments." What we must also realize is that one who has been robbed of a coat, then stripped off his or her "cloak," would stand naked before the court. And public nudity was a taboo, with the shame falling less on the naked person than on the person viewing or causing the nakedness (as in the case of drunken, slumbering Noah and his hapless sons [Gen 9:20-27]). Thus the creditor who sues a debtor for the coat off his or her back is craftily exposed and shamed—perhaps unto repentance and a change of ways. For make no mistake, "the Powers That Be literally stand on their dignity. Nothing depotentiates them faster than deft lampooning. By refusing to be awed by their power, the powerless are emboldened to seize the initiative, even where structural change is not immediately possible."[16]

We may finally, and most importantly, notice that in his atoning death Jesus submits to the brutal methods of the powers and is executed in a humiliating fashion reserved for slaves and peasant revolutionaries. It is exactly by the subversion of their own means that he "disarm[s] the rulers and authorities," publicly reveals their true bankruptcy, and triumphs over them (Col 2:15; see also Heb 12:1-2). In Christian perspective, it is perhaps the supreme example of plebeian tactical maneuvering that through the cross Satan, the Prince of the powers, deceives himself through his own deceit, that the system knocks the struts out from under itself exactly with the blow it thinks is its coup de grace against a pesky resister, that violence violates itself and death tramples down death.[17] Are we not justified, then, in respectfully regarding the One we follow as the Holy Subversive, and ourselves when we are true to him as sanctified subversives?

Friendship: A Case Study in Sanctified Subversion

These would be, I hope and believe, strong enough concluding words. Yet I remain concerned that we be made ready to begin where we are, that we not be overwhelmed or finally unmoved by examples we think too grand or culturally distant and so irrelevantly exotic. It would not do to have us inspired but in the last analysis still marooned in the middle of the vague impression that Christianity as a way of life does not quite connect with our everyday and "real" world. Thus I will instead conclude by returning to a crucial but very much down-to-earth subject earlier mentioned. I mean the Christian practice of friendship.

As I have said and we can all readily attest, mass-techno-liberal capitalism as a world system does not normally cultivate genuine community of any sort, let alone Christian community. Surely ingredient to genuine community—people gathered consensually and carefully of one another—is the practice of friendship. I want to argue that such Christian cultural resources as biblical language, the performance of Scripture and the Eucharist can enable the church to embody a kind of friendship not otherwise available.

In the United States, to focus on the instance I know best, a majority of people live in "bedroom communities," sorry imitations of villages with no defined downtown areas and no sense of neighborhoods. Such suburbs, even if they possess some sort of downtown, rarely have sidewalks more than a few blocks long. So suburbanites glide through their "community" in automobiles, armored and glassed off from "neighbors." True to the character of the world system I earlier noted, we work in one suburb (or the city), go to church in another suburb, shop in a third, join health clubs in a fourth. Our children attend schools in separate neighborhoods or even separate municipalities.

Largely because they are so fragmented and impersonalized, our lives are organized to the hilt, and frenetic. Our children, for instance, no longer spontaneously create sandlot baseball teams. Instead they must join the (centralized and professionally managed) park-district little leagues, burdening their parents' schedules with trips to practices and games.

And, of course, the parents hardly need more demands on their time. In many of our households, both spouses work outside the home. The status prized in our ethos is centered on work advancement and the steady accumulation of wealth. Our jobs demand most of our time and energy. Frequently they demand that we move to another state. So even if we had time and energy for friendships, the pain of friendships lost in our transience does not encourage us to form new ones.

In short, the social and economic demands of suburbia create space for material attainment and status seeking but destroy space for the practice of friendship. So it is not necessarily overinflated rhetoric to say that friendship has become a subversive practice. If such is the case, the church in suburbia may have a surprising new mission: to establish a cultural space for the birth and supported practice of friendship.

Here it may help to outline "practice" a bit more precisely. I have in mind Alasdair MacIntyre's rather complicated definition.[18] MacIntyre says a practice is a socially established activity. Friendship is obviously a socially established and cooperative activity. MacIntyre says that the end (the goal or aim) of a practice is internal to the practice. The goal of friendship is certainly internal; anyone making "friends" to gain social or financial advantage does not really understand or appreciate friendship—and in fact is likely to end up without any friends. MacIntyre says a practice is something that, when undertaken, extends and prospers the goods internal to it. As James McClendon notes, "friendship is a practice for which standards of excellence both exist and may be extended, with the development enhancing those virtues of friendship such as patience, sympathy, and fidelity."[19]

Friendship has become a difficult, even subversive practice because of transience, mechanization, centralization and various other factors inherent to the world system we now inhabit. But the church may perhaps best begin the rehabilitation of friendship by examining the effects of what MacIntyre considers the dominant language and culture of this world system—that of the bureaucratic manager. Certainly that is the language and way of thinking that dominates suburbia, so much shaped and sustained by corporate America. Consider three distinctives of the bureaucratic manager, as MacIntyre interprets this "character."[20]

(1) The manager sees other people as means, not ends. Work relationships are to be manipulated in service of greater production, profit and the "bottom line."

(2) For the manager, a utilitarian ethic reigns undisputed and unqualified. Cost and benefit analyses are applied to every decision or activity. Rationality is a matter of "matching means to ends economically and efficiently." Significantly, the focus is not on internal but on external goods (e.g., profits). Thus the manager will self-consciously calculate, say, the number of lives "acceptably" lost if a car is designed less safely but more cheaply and so more profitably.

(3) The manager believes he or she acts with moral neutrality and cannot determine ends—they are "given." Thus he or she is pre-eminently concerned with technique, with effectiveness in transforming raw material into products, unskilled labor into skilled labor, and investments into profits.

I am not prepared to say these assumptions have absolutely no place in the marketplace, though I do not doubt that a much more humane marketplace could and will perhaps someday be developed. My immediate concern is that managerial language is so appropriate to and expressive of the contemporary world system (not least suburbia) that it has invaded all realms of life. As MacIntyre, Robert Bellah and others worry, perhaps the exclusively contractual structure of the economic and bureaucratic world is becoming the model for all of life, including the practice of friendship. The danger is that now we can see and unironically talk about even our friends only in the way managers see and talk about employers.

Thus "time demands" weigh on couples seeking friends, just as they do the manager. Friendships have "agendas" and are "maintained" until they no longer serve a purpose and are "terminated." Given the chaotic busyness of our lives, visits with friends are a matter of "organization" and "arrangement." We can regard the advantages of friendship in managerial terms, namely that it provides "accountability." And friendships are viewed from the vantage point of "productivity," so that we "invest" in a friend. I have been struck recently by how much I and other suburbanites worry about keeping "ledgers" in our friendships. Have we been negligent and not invited Shelly and Kenneth over for too long? Willis and Lisa have now asked us to baby-sit their kids three times to our one—maybe it would be better if they just hired sitters and we stopped trading off. Should I borrow Frank's tools again, or have I done so little for him lately that I'm in danger of sponging?

I am suggesting that managerial language and culture constantly distort friendship. They maximize its work and burden while they minimize its spontaneity. They incline their users toward manipulation and calculation rather than free appreciation. They make inappropriate external demands on friendship while denying or at least ignoring its abundant internal rewards. I suspect Stanley Hauerwas has these kinds of effects in mind when he writes, "Contemporary political and ethical theory seems to ignore entirely the nature and social significance of friendship and other special relations such as family. As a result we are left devoid of any language that can help articulate the significance of friendship and family for our personal and political existence."[21] So what might be a Christian subversive response?

Most fundamentally, the church can proclaim the gospel's attitude toward friendship and celebrate it in the Eucharist. Consider a scriptural passage that concisely, if not exhaustively, defines Christian friendship. John reports Jesus to say (Jn 15:12-17),

> This is my commandment, that you love one another as I have loved you. No one has greater love than this, to lay down one's life for one's friends. You are my friends if you do what I command you. I do not call you servants any longer, because the servant does not know what the master is doing; but I have called you friends, because I have made known to you everything that I have heard from my Father. You did not choose me but I chose you. And I appointed you to go and bear fruit, fruit that will last, so that the Father will give you whatever you ask him in my name. I am giving you these commands so that you may love one another.

The basic statement of the gospel in relation to friendship is that we are (or can be) friends to one another because Christ chose us, making us his friends by laying his life down for us and revealing to us his Father's intentions. Christian friendship, then, is a matter of what God accomplishes rather than what we do. It is not best addressed in the managerial terms of technique, nor is it primarily yet another assignment to be squeezed onto a packed agenda. The good news is that friendship is a gift, an opportunity provided by God in Christ. By first of all making us his friends, Jesus frees us to be friends to one another.

Friendship as the gospel here has it is also consensual—it is Christian community built through invitation, a way of life proposed rather than imposed. As we have noted, truly proposing involves first fully informing the other we seek to persuade or win over. Accordingly, Jesus transforms his servants into friends by making known to them "everything that I have heard from my Father."

Christ's mandate to be friends is revolutionary in our [managerial, bureaucratized] serving society. Here we are, a nation of professionalized servers, following Christ's mandate to serve. And here He is, at the final moment, getting it backwards once again. The final message is not to serve. Rather, He directs us to be friends.

Why friends rather than servants? Perhaps it is because He knew that servants could always become lords but that friends could not. Servants are people who *know the mysteries* that can control those they give "help." Friends are people who *know each other.* They are free to give *and* receive help.[22]

But how does the gospel have it that we are Christ's friends? By obeying his command, which is to love one another as he loved us. Such friendship (or love) is cruciform, since Jesus ultimately loved us by dying on a cross. We are Christian friends by living cruciformly, by giving ourselves rather than imposing ourselves. Christian friendship is not a matter of managing or controlling others, but of genuinely accepting their differentness and standing open to surprises—surprises that, whether joyful or demanding, extend our powers to achieve greater excellence in the practice of friendship epitomized on the cross.

At the cross Jesus denies all means of coercion and manipulation, and to the cross he calls his disciples. The Christian can emphatically agree with philosopher Iris Murdoch that genuine love (including friendship) is nothing less than "nonviolent apprehension of differences."[23] Truly, as Rowan Williams puts it, "to let the other *be* strange and yet not reject him or her, to give and be given attentive, contemplative regard—this is all part of our encounter with a risen Lord."[24] Friendship so conceived clearly possesses internal goods, and each friend is unique rather than being an interchangeable cog in a machine designed to increase my productivity at work or improve my mental health (goods external to friendship).

So in John's Gospel we have a new language of friendship, a language of participation instead of management. Cruciform and subversive friendship, as opposed to managerial friendship, is attentive rather than manipulative, organic rather than technical, relational rather than rational, open-ended rather than calculating. The New Testament language and enculturation of friendship is more that of abiding than that of profiting. Its most likely metaphors for friendship are organic and agricultural rather than economic or managerial: the disciple does not "invest" in friendship so much as he or she is "grafted" onto the vine or participates in the body where friendship flourishes.

In this light, the church's immediate and extended task on behalf of friendship is the freeing task of proclaiming and embodying the gospel and, in so doing, teaching and cultivating an alternative language, a contrast culture, for friendship—a language and culture that support friendship as a full-fledged social, political practice and enable it to realize more of its rich potential.

To take it a step further, the church's joyful task is the eucharistic task of celebration. For if the church proclaims a different language and lives a different culture for the practice of friendship, it also rehearses them in the Eucharist. There we are called to the same table, to seal friendship in the Lord so that we might live "in unity, constancy, and peace."[25] The Eucharist itself bolsters the credibility of the cruciform language of friendship, for there we are given vision to "discern the body," to see ourselves as an organic, mutually supportive whole (see 1 Cor 11:23-32).

And it is there, like the disciples on the Emmaus road, that with the breaking of bread we see Jesus for who he is, in all his compelling significance (Lk 24:31). Moreover, Eucharist moves us toward being a forgiving people, for we are ill-advised to approach the table if there is a tablemate whom we have not forgiven. Forgiveness, in turn, emboldens us to practice a friendship that will sometimes faithfully wound and not settle for sentimentality. Indeed, a world speaking only the managerial language of friendship is especially prone to sentimentality about friendship, since it can conceive of friendship only as functional and finally superficial. Ironically, it finds friendship simultaneously more burdensome and more frivolous, more trivial. Having instrumentalized friendship, it has no use for friendships that no longer provide a steady supply of warm fuzzies. By contrast, the centrality of forgiveness to the cruciform culture of friendship reveals sentimental friendship for the counterfeit it is. The promise of Christian friendship is not that it will always be easy or enjoyable but that it will never be less than friendship.

So here is how the church can engender and support the community-building, subversive practice of friendship: by speaking its own language of friendship and celebrating its own culture of friendship. What harried suburbanites and other moderns need is not one more program in which to exert their already overextended will, but a language that reorients vision on an object more compelling than that which managerial argot can reveal or contain. Genuine friendship will become a more viable practice not by virtue of plying more techniques but as we see and live, however fitfully, a reality that lures us beyond ourselves and our plans and efforts, by allowing us to dare believe that reality as it is known by the bureaucratic manager is not the only reality we can live.

It is not the shot heard round the world. It is not the occupation of the White House or the redirection of Parliament. But it is a vital performance of Christian culture; it is its own wild and wonderful politics; it is one of many, many fruits of church as a way of life.

Notes

Chapter 1: The Church as Unchurch

[1] Henri J. M. Nouwen, *The Wounded Healer* (Garden City, N.Y.: Image/Doubleday, 1979), pp. 86-87.

[2] Strictly speaking, it was Theodosius I (in the year 380) who declared Christianity the state religion. But Constantine de facto made Christianity such. In 312 he issued the Edict of Milan, making Christianity a legal religion for the first time. He went on to pass a series of laws that in effect made Christianity the religious sponsor of the Empire and that laid the groundwork for the Christian Europe of later centuries.

[3] For example, in the United States, from 1968 to 1984 the United Methodist Church saw its total membership decline by 1,687,000. In 1970, 1 of every 90 Americans was Episcopal; by 1980, 1 in every 124 was. And the United Church of Christ saw its membership peak at 2.2 million in 1960; by 1985 membership had declined to 1.7 million. See Charles H. Lippy and Peter W. Williams, eds., *Encyclopedia of the American Religious Experience* (New York: Carles Scribner's Sons, 1988), 1:552, 417, 496.

[4] See John Spong's *Rescuing the Bible from Fundamentalism* (San Francisco: HarperCollins, 1991), pp. 35-36. Emphasis added in my quotation.

[5] See Sonia L. Nazario, "Crusader Vows to Put God Back into Schools Using Local Elections," *The Wall Street Journal,* July 15, 1992, pp. A1, A5.

[6] A direct-mail solicitation of the Christian Coalition, received September 1993.

[7] D. James Kennedy, "Flex the Muscle," *Leadership,* Spring 1993, pp. 24-26.

[8] Michael Warren, "Imitating Jesus in a Time of Imitation," in *Schooling Christians,* ed. Stanley Hauerwas and John H. Westerhoff (Grand Rapids, Mich.: Eerdmans, 1992), p. 254.

[9] Stanley Hauerwas, *Vision and Virtue* (Notre Dame, Ind.: University of Notre Dame Press, 1981), p. 101.

[10] Alasdair MacIntyre, *The Religious Significance of Atheism* (New York: Columbia University Press, 1969), p. 24; quoted in Hauerwas, *Vision and Virtue,* p. 113.

[11] I adapt Alasdair MacIntyre's remark: "The creed of the English is that there is no God, and that it is wise to pray to him from time to time." From *Against the Self Images of the Age* (London: Duckworth, 1971), p. 26; quoted in Kenneth

Leech, *The Social God* (London: Sheldon, 1981), p. 34.

Here allow an admission of my ongoing nervousness about the use of gender-specific (usually masculine) language to designate God. The debate between those who would introduce feminine-gender language to designate God and those who will have none of it vacillates between being exceedingly complex and hopelessly polarized. I cannot say that I am finally decided on the matter. I am certain, however, that the God of Israel and Jesus Christ is narratively (and so quite specifically) identified, so that the unsurpassable and irreplaceable name of the Christian God is Father, Son and Holy Spirit. How this may or may not be *supplemented* remains a matter of debate, but there can be no doubt that we *primarily* name God by unavoidably masculine terms that include *Father* and *Son*. Given all this, in these pages I never shy away from trinitarian language for God, and occasionally use the masculine personal pronoun for God—particularly where, as here, simply repeating the term *God* would be forced and awkward. On the narrative identification of God, see the excellent discussion of Robert W. Jenson, *The Triune Identity* (Philadelphia: Fortress, 1982), and on masculine language particularly, pp. 13-16.

[12]George Lindbeck has commented, "Constantinian Christendom seems to be definitively ending, and reshapings of ecclesial thought and practice greater than those of the Reformation and comparable, perhaps, to the fourth century may well be unavoidable." See his "Scripture, Consensus and Community," *This World* 23 (Fall 1988): 16-17.

[13]Charles Norris Cochrane, *Christianity and Classical Culture* (London: Oxford University Press, 1944), p. 12. It is now in fact debated whether Constantine was genuinely a Christian. Some suggest he simply used Christianity as an ideological support for a regime that was in many ways anti-Christian. For a summary of this debate see Philip LeMasters, *The Import of Eschatology in John Howard Yoder's Critique of Constantinianism* (San Francisco: Mellen Research University Press, 1992), pp. 102-7.

[14]John Howard Yoder, "The Otherness of the Church," *Mennonite Quarterly Review* 35 (October 1961): 212. This seminal essay of Yoder's is now happily more accessibly found in his *The Royal Priesthood*, ed. Michael G. Cartwright (Grand Rapids, Mich.: Eerdmans, 1994), pp. 53-64. Much of the account to follow leans heavily on Yoder. For another, basically congruent account, see David J. Bosch, *Transforming Mission: Paradigm Shifts in Theology of Mission* (Maryknoll, N.Y.: Orbis, 1991). Besides providing historical detail throughout, Bosch observes that "the Roman Catholic (or Western) Church was always compromised to the state. The same was true of the Byzantine Church, only more so" (p. 205). He also notes that the Reformers (excepting Anabaptists) did not break with the medieval understanding of church and state: "Since Constantine the idea of a 'Christian' state . . . was simply taken for granted" (p. 240).

[15]Cochrane, *Christianity and Classical Culture*, p. 211.

[16] *The Book of Common Prayer* (New York: Church Hymnal Corporation/Seabury, 1979), p. 302.

[17] John Howard Yoder, *The Original Revolution* (Scottdale, Penn.: Herald, 1977), pp. 72-73.

[18] Yoder, "Otherness," p. 288.

[19] Cochrane's statement is qualified; he calls Constantine "architect (to a very great extent) of the Middle Ages" (Cochrane, *Christianity and Classical Culture,* p. 211).

[20] John Howard Yoder, *The Priestly Kingdom* (Notre Dame, Ind.: University of Notre Dame Press, 1984), p. 136.

[21] Yoder, "Otherness," p. 289.

[22] Ibid.

[23] Yoder, *Priestly Kingdom,* p. 138.

[24] John Milbank begins his magisterial *Theology and Social Theory* (Oxford: Basil Blackwell, 1990) with the words "Once, there was no 'secular' " (p. 9). He then uses much of his first chapter to provide an account of how the church in fact created the conceptuality and institutions of secularism, with more sympathy for the synthesis of Christendom than Yoder's account allows. But Milbank sees changes that, by the time of the late medieval and then Reformation periods, issued in the sorts of developments Yoder deplores. Thus Milbank laments the "self-understanding of Christianity arrived at in late-medieval nominalism, the protestant reformation and seventeenth-century Augustinianism, which completely privatized, spiritualized and transcendentalized the sacred, and concurrently reimagined nature, human action and society as a sphere of autonomous, sheerly formal power" (p. 9).

[25] Yoder, "Otherness," p. 290.

[26] Ibid.

[27] Ibid. H. Richard Niebuhr, writing of the revolutionary implications of the Reformation, confirms: "While the religious leaders affirmed the power of God against all human powers, the secular movements identified their own power with the divine. They seemed to believe that since the exercise of absolute power by the papal church was wrong its exercise by the opponents of the papacy was right. If the church had no claim to the supreme political power, did this not mean that kings had the right to claim this power? If the church was in error in maintaining complete rulership over the economic life, did not this show that the economic man was entitled to rule himself? In place of the absolute claims of one relative institution or person other relative institutions and individuals were to be made absolutes" (*The Kingdom of God in America* [New York: Harper Torchbooks, 1937], p. 29).

[28] For a very illuminating article confirming this point, see William T. Cavanaugh, " 'A Fire Strong Enough to Consume the House': The Wars of Religion and the Rise of the State," *Modern Theology* 11 (October 1995): 397-420. I am grateful to Stanley Hauerwas for drawing this essay to my attention.

[29]Yoder, "Otherness," p. 292.

[30]Ibid.

[31]Ibid.

[32]See note 24 above.

[33]James Davison Hunter, *Culture Wars: The Struggle to Define America* (New York: BasicBooks, 1991), p. 69. I am indebted to Hunter's book for the account of American Protestant disestablishment that follows.

[34]Quoted in ibid., p. 71.

[35]Robert D. Linder and Richard V. Pierard, *Twilight of the Saints* (Downers Grove, Ill.: InterVarsity Press, 1978), p. 74.

[36]Yoder, *Priestly Kingdom,* p. 141.

[37]Ibid., p. 138.

[38]See Richard John Neuhaus, "While We're at It," *First Things,* August/September 1992, p. 73.

[39]See note 34.

[40]Martin Marty, "Rapid Growth of Islam in Iowa," *Context,* July 15, 1992, p. 4. The figure on the number of U.S. mosques currently comes from Hunter, *Culture Wars,* p. 73.

[41]Hunter, *Culture Wars,* p. 76.

[42]I provide a more developed account of postmodernity in the initial chapter (and its notes) of my *Families at the Crossroads* (Downers Grove, Ill.: InterVarsity Press, 1993), pp. 9-26, 171-79.

Chapter 2: The Church as Private Club

[1]John Howard Yoder, *The Priestly Kingdom* (Notre Dame, Ind.: University of Notre Dame Press, 1984), p. 141.

[2]Philip J. Lee, *Against the Protestant Gnostics* (New York: Oxford University Press, 1987), pp. 9-10.

[3]Harold Bloom, *The American Religion* (New York: Simon & Schuster, 1992), pp. 32, 64, 65.

[4]N. T. Wright, *The New Testament and the People of God* (Minneapolis: Fortress, 1992), p. 22.

[5]Ralph Waldo Emerson, *Emerson's Essays* (New York: Harper Colophon Books, 1926), pp. 56, 35, 36, 41, 46, 48 (emphasis mine).

[6]Bloom, *American Religion,* p. 43. Note that Bloom writes sympathetically as a self-identified "Jewish gnostic." For an analysis that reaches similar conclusions about Emerson and the American situation, but from an antignostic Christian standpoint, see Roger Lundin, *The Culture of Interpretation* (Grand Rapids, Mich.: Eerdmans, 1993), pp. 76-136. For connections between the privatization of faith and gnosticism, see David F. Wells, *No Place for Truth* (Grand Rapids, Mich.: Eerdmans, 1993), pp. 130-31, 154-56.

[7]My intent is not to condemn psychology in toto. I have myself been the beneficiary of psychotherapy. Yet I think we have been entirely too uncritical of

many forms of psychology and psychotherapy, particularly those that exalt the modern, isolated and reified individual self. I find more promise for genuinely Christian psychotherapy in those approaches that recognize the social constitution of the self, such as object relations theory or family systems therapy. In other words, I reject the popular contemporary notion that culture is a composite projection of individual psychologies. On the contrary, I understand the individual's psychology as a retrojection of culture(s).

[8]I discuss these developments at more length in my *Families at the Crossroads* (Downers Grove, Ill.: InterVarsity Press, 1993), pp. 48-66.

[9]Donald Meyer, *The Positive Thinkers* (Middletown, Conn.: Wesleyan University Press, 1988), p. 59.

[10]Ibid., p. 103. L. Gregory Jones helpfully notes that the "bifurcation of spirituality and politics is one of the reasons that contemporary spirituality can be consumed as a luxury consumer good, primarily designed for middle- and upper-class folks. One will not be confronted by massive suffering around the world, or even around the corner from where one lives. Nor will [one] be confronted with Amos's stinging prophetic indictments and Jesus's call to costly discipleship. Rather, [one] is invited to an increasingly inward journey that leaves the world largely as it already is.

"The presumption created by these sorts of intellectual grids and habits of thought and 'practice' is that the sacred has little if anything to do with morality, social institutions, or political power. What really matters are the inner experiences of isolated individuals, cultivated and evaluated largely by those same individuals. Yet such a presumption both distorts our readings of the patterns and practices of many spritiual figures and communities within the history of Christianity and masks the social values and commitments entailed in much of contemporary spirituality." See his "A Thirst for God or Consumer Spirituality?" *Modern Theology*, forthcoming. The essay will also appear in *Spirituality and Social Embodiment*, ed. L. Gregory Jones and James J. Buckley (London: Basil Blackwell, 1997).

[11]From Richard Sibbes, "The Soul's Conflict with Itself," in *Works of Richard Sibbes*, ed. Alexander B. Grosart (Edinburgh: Banner of Truth Trust, 1973), 1:170 (emphasis deleted).

[12]Meyer, *Positive Thinkers*, p. 31.

[13]Ibid., p. 155.

[14]Ibid., p. 157.

[15]Ibid., p. 230. For a congruent account, focusing in more detail on the rise of consumerism and the concordant corruption of Christianity, see William Leach, *Land of Desire: Merchants, Power and the Rise of a New American Culture* (New York: Vintage, 1993), pp. 191-260.

[16]Howard Thurman, *Jesus and the Disinherited* (Nashville: Abingdon, 1949), pp. 11-12.

[17]Meyer, *Positive Thinkers*, p. 244.

[18]Ibid., p. 289.

[19]Ibid., p. 313. This enfeeblement has come to full effect in the modern service economy. Particularly in the late modern economy, psychological, medical and social services are business—and indeed constitute a substantial part of the entire economy. Thus our economy requires "consumers" who construe their needs as deficiencies that might be rectified by professional service providers. As John McKnight writes, "A need could be understood as a condition, a want, a right, an obligation to another, an illusion, or an unresolvable problem. Professional practice consistently defines a need as an unfortunate absence or emptiness" *in* the individual. In effect, "the politico-economic issues of service are hidden behind the mask of love," behind the genuinely well-meaning professional's complicity in interpreting and treating all needs as individual deficiencies. See McKnight's *The Careless Society: Community and Its Counterfeits* (New York: BasicBooks, 1995), pp. 39-46 (quotes from pp. 43 and 39). See also the revealing essay "The Cultural Consequences of Deficit Discourse," in Kenneth J. Gergen, *Realities and Relationships: Soundings in Social Construction* (Cambridge, Mass.: Harvard University Press, 1994), pp. 143-64.

[20]Meyer, *Positive Thinkers*, p. 314. Social critic Robert Inchausti pithily summarizes the case here made at length. Inchausti observes that in late modernity "private therapies replaced common culture as the means for self-perfection and ethical accomplishment." See his *The Ignorant Perfection of Ordinary People* (Albany: State University of New York Press, 1991), p. 9.

[21]Lundin, *Culture of Interpretation*, p. 111. Lundin disapprovingly quotes Ralph Waldo Emerson, "Historic Notes of Life and Letters in New England," in *The Transcendentalists: An Anthology*, ed. Perry Miller (Cambridge, Mass.: Harvard University Press, 1950), p. 496. In Bloom's account, "What the American self has found, since about 1800, is its own freedom—from the world, from time, for other selves. But this freedom is a very expensive torso, because of what it is obliged to leave out: society, temporality, the other. What remains, for it, is solitude and the abyss" (*American Religion*, p. 37).

[22]I discuss all this at more length, mischievously using a certain famous bear as the foil, in "The Sin of Winnie-the-Pooh," *Christianity Today*, November 9, 1992, pp. 29-32.

[23]Lee, *Against the Protestant Gnostics*, p. 27.

[24]Anthony Giddens, *The Consequences of Modernity* (Stanford, Calif.: Stanford University Press, 1990), p. 139.

[25]Nicholas Lash, *Easter in Ordinary* (Notre Dame, Ind.: University of Notre Dame Press, 1988), p. 85. Lash's book is a brilliant argument that the knowledge and "experience" of God is not fundamentally private but social and cultural. Thus it is extremely helpful and pertinent to the themes of this book, particularly of the church as itself a culture.

[26]Ibid., p. 86.

Chapter 3: The Church as Nation-State

[1]These quotes come from Richard Rorty, "Religion as Conversation-Stopper," *Common Knowledge* 3, no. 1 (Spring 1994): 1, 5. Rorty is more or less a classical liberal, except that he affirms liberalism from a postmodern antifoundationalist base rather than a modern rationalistic foundationalist base. That is, Rorty freely admits that liberalism cannot appeal to universally self-evident truths for its justification. But like a good liberal, he is quite pleased that religion in public matters is as insignificant as other "private" matters, such as hobbies and hair color. He endorses the "Jeffersonian compromise"—privatize your religion and you can believe whatever you want. So Rorty can accept religion as, "at its best, Whitehead's 'what we do with our solitude,' rather than something people do together in churches" (p. 2). But my argument is the exact opposite and *in that sense* profoundly antiliberal: Christianity at its best is something people do together in (or as) churches. For more on Rorty's embrace of liberalism, see his *Contingency, Irony and Solidarity* (Cambridge: Cambridge University Press, 1989), a book dedicated "in memory of six liberals." I am grateful to David Wright for drawing my attention to the *Common Knowledge* article.

[2]Certainly the Germans, French, Russians, British and Dutch—all of whom at one time or another considered theirs a chosen Christian people—have no marked tendencies to do so today. Yet many Americans, particularly those on the religious right I will refer to shortly, still see America as God's chosen nation. They stand in a long and intense tradition. As historian Sidney Mead said, throughout much of American history the churches have "found themselves as completely identified with nationalism and their country's political and economic systems as ever had been known in Christendom" (*The Lively Experiment* [New York: Harper & Row, 1963, 1975], pp. 88, 157; quoted in Robert Booth Fowler, *Unconventional Partners: Religion and Liberal Culture in the United States* [Grand Rapids, Mich.: Eerdmans, 1989], p. 78).

[3]Actually, the categories "conservative" and "liberal" are problematic because they hide from challenge the true political identity of these "conservatives." Liberalism is that political system which makes the individual, rather than the community, the primary political unit. It also assumes that truth is ahistorical and acultural and so must be freed of tradition. And largely because it cuts itself off from *churchly* community and tradition, liberalism features an "implicit state worship" (Fowler, *Unconventional Partners*, p. 10). In his authoritative history of American fundamentalism, George M. Marsden comments frequently on fundamentalist individualism and its penchant for Scottish Common Sense Realism, which taught that "any sane and unbiased person of common sense could and must perceive the same things," that "basic truths are much the same for all persons in all times and places." Add to this the "conservative" religionist longing for a Christian America, which Marsden also documents. A key reason, then, that fundamentalists and

conservative evangelicals have had so little success combating liberalism is that they themselves are actually liberals. (See Marsden, *Fundamentalism and American Culture* [New York: Oxford University Press, 1980], quotes from p. 111.)

[4]Stanley Hauerwas, *Dispatches from the Front: Theological Engagements with the Secular* (Durham, N.C.: Duke University Press, 1994), p. 11. See also his *Against the Nations: War and Survival in a Liberal Society* (Minneapolis: Winston, 1985), pp. 23-50.

[5]Though there is no doubt America's founding Puritans blurred church and state in Constantinian fashion (they declared themselves to have pioneered not only "for the Glory of God" but also for the "Honour of King and Country"), it is worthwhile to note that in other ways their conception and practice of church were actually much closer to the ecclesiology advanced in this book. Crucially, the church for Puritans was a cultural and political body, and accordingly Christian faith had vital corporate dimensions. Thus, for example, the Mayflower Compact opens by declaring that the pilgrims "Covenant and Combine ourselves together into a Civil Body Politic." (See for both quotes William Bradford, *Of Plymouth Plantation: 1620-1647*, ed. Samuel Eliot Morison [New York: Modern Library, 1952], p. 76.)

In addition, Puritan triumphalism was checked (if not eliminated) by several factors. As Darrell Jodock writes, the Puritan interpretation of their colonies as a light to the nations "gave a band of immigrants, camped precariously on the edge of an unfamiliar continent, a bold sense of mission and purpose, an incentive to create a humane, just, and free society." The deeper problems arose as America moved toward coalescence into a nation-state, and this nation-state was flatly and tragically identified with the "church estate" of the original Puritans. Jodock helpfully continues, "The Puritans' interpretation is frequently repeated today, as if it still applies to the United States. But does it? A comparison of settings indicates that it does not. The Puritans were powerless; the contemporary United States possess enormous power and influence. The Puritans saw themselves beginning anew; a two-hundred-year-old nation is hardly beginning anew. The Puritans shared a single religious outlook; contemporary citizens do not. Though not exactly equal, the Puritans were all of poor to middling means; enormous inequities now characterize our society, making it in this regard more like the one the Puritans left behind. If the Puritans were to describe the contemporary United States, might they not find it more like the Egypt of the pharaohs than the Israel of the exodus? The original and contemporary settings are now too dissimilar to make the interpretation begun by the Puritans a plausible recontextualizing of the biblical text." (See *The Church's Bible* [Minneapolis: Fortress, 1989], p. 136.)

[6]See H. Richard Niebuhr, *The Kingdom of God in America* (New York: Harper Torchbooks, 1937), p. 179.

[7]Michael J. Shapiro, *The Politics of Representation* (Madison: University of Wisconsin Press, 1988), pp. 93-94. (He cites Donald K. Emmerson, " 'Southeast Asia': What's in a Name?" *Journal of Southeast Asia Studies* 15 (March 1984): 1-21.) In what follows I am much indebted to Shapiro's brilliant chapter (written with Alfred Fortin) "The Constitution of the Central American Other: The Case of 'Guatemala,' " pp. 89-123.

[8]John Fiske, *Power Plays, Power Works* (New York: Verso, 1993), pp. 156-57.

[9]Ibid., pp. 157-58.

[10]I have said nothing about maps other than political maps—say, topographical maps or geological maps or weather maps. But these too are constructed by particular persons for particular uses. No map, in other words, escapes being an interpretation. As the geographer Carl Sauer warns, even nature is not as "natural" (that is, permanent and neutrally observed) as we often suppose: "A postulate tends to displace reality. Climatic regions are cartographic abstractions, useful as elementary teaching devices to give some first notions of weather contrasts over the earth. 'Final or stable' communities are quite exceptional in nature: weather, soils, and surfaces are continually changing; new organisms are immigrating or forming, old ones may be giving way. Change is the order of nature." See Carl O. Sauer, *Seeds, Spades, Hearths and Herds: The Domestication of Animals and Foodstuffs* (Cambridge, Mass.: MIT Press, 1969), p. 15; cited in Renato Rosaldo, *Culture and Truth: The Remaking of Social Analysis* (Boston: Beacon, 1989), p. 103.

[11]Harry E. Chrisman, *Lost Trails of the Cimarron* (Athens, Ohio: Swallow, 1964), p. 38. I already owed much to my Grandma Lila Clapp. Now, in addition to unfailing love and uncounted slices of the world's best devil's food chocolate cake, I thank her for discovering and loaning me this book.

[12]Ibid., pp. 46-47.

[13]*The Kansas City Star,* April 1913; quoted in Chrisman, *Lost Trails,* pp. 47-48.

[14]"Citizenship and Armed Civic Virtue: Some Critical Questions on the Commitment to Public Life," in *Community in America: The Challenge of Habits of the Heart,* ed. Charles H. Reynolds and Ralph V. Norman (Berkeley: University of California Press, 1988), p. 51. The "*national* identity that we assume, or yearn for, is historically inseparable from war. The nation-state, including our own, rests on mounds of bodies," Elshtain writes. Her essay is cited in Stanley Hauerwas, "The Difference of Virtue and the Difference It Makes: Courage Exemplified," *Modern Theology* 9, no. 3 (July 1993): 247-64 (Elshtain quote p. 250).

It could, of course, be said that I am "deconstructing" America. And to the extent the likes of Derrida and Foucault teach us to pay close attention always to history and context, I am not afraid to be labeled a deconstructionist or postmodernist. But for those who would consider it damning to be designated Derridean or Foucauldian even to a degree, I would protest that what I am doing here is Micheneresque. Novelist James Michener has become spectacularly famous and wealthy, and is regarded as an American icon to boot, by writing novels that trace the long, complicated and conflicted histories of places such as Hawaii, Texas, Alaska and the Chesapeake Bay. But Michener (and here I admit tongue is a bit in cheek) is even more radical than Foucault. After all, Foucault goes only so far as to recover historical origins—Michener digs beyond these all the way to the geological.

[15]David M. Potter, *History and American Society: Essays of David M. Potter*, ed. Don E. Fehrenbacher (New York: Oxford University Press, 1973), p. 229.

[16]See James W. Loewen, *Lies My Teacher Told Me* (New York: New Press, 1995), p. 117.

[17]Howard Mumford Jones, *O Strange New World: American Culture—the Formative Years* (New York: Viking, 1964), p. 331. Some, including lexicographer Noah Webster, feared that if British English was used, Americans would be influenced by corrupt British ideals, such as the monarchy. So Webster, for example, removed the British *u* from words like *honour* and *colour* (pp. 331-32).

[18]Ibid., p. 345.

[19]Robert Hughes, "The Fraying of America," *Time*, February 3, 1992, pp. 44-45. The gist of Hughes's article argues against so-called political correctness and concerns over what is often labeled Eurocentrism.

[20]Potter, *History and American Society*, p. 230.

[21]Richard John Neuhaus, *The Naked Public Square* (Grand Rapids, Mich.: Eerdmans, 1984), pp. 72-73. Neuhaus does not use the language of "true American" but declares that "the affirmation of loyalty to a community is the ticket that grants admission to the critical debate about the meaning of that community" (p. 73) and clearly intends his proposition as a heuristic indication of whether or not one actually affirms loyalty to the United States. I take it that the true American is one who holds a ticket to enter the debate about America's meaning.

[22]Indeed, I think there is more than a little truth to Shapiro's judgment: "In evoking the idea of the 'United States,' . . . we could refer not to an administrative unit controlled by the federal government but rather to the process by which white Europeans have been consolidating control over the continental domain (now recognized as the United States) in a war with several indigenous ('Indian') nations. This grammar, within which we could have the 'United States' in a different way—as violent process rather than static, naturalized reality—would lead us to note that while the armed hostilities have all but ceased, there remains a system of economic exclusion, which has the effect of maintaining a steady attrition rate among native Americans. The war goes on by other means, and the one-sidedness of the battle is still in evidence. For example, in the state of Utah, the life expectancy of the native American is only half that of the European descendant." See *Politics of Representation*, p. 95.

[23]Quoted in Potter, *History and American Society*, p. 283.

[24]Potter, *History and American Society*, pp. 222, 191.

[25]John Milbank, *Theology and Social Theory* (Oxford: Basil Blackwell, 1990), p. 96.

[26]Bruce D. Marshall, "The Disunity of the Church and the Credibility of the Gospel," *Theology Today* 50, no. 1 (April 1993): 81-82.

[27]Ibid., p. 83.

Chapter 4: The Church as Type

[1]Paul Ramsey's back cover endorsement on H. Richard Niebuhr, *Christ and Culture* (New York: Harper Torchbooks, 1951).

[2]In Stanley Hauerwas and William Willimon, *Resident Aliens* (Nashville: Abingdon, 1989), p. 40.

[3]In an address at the Wheaton Theology Conference, Wheaton College, Wheaton, Ill., April 21, 1994.

[4]In Raymond Williams, *Keywords: A Vocabulary of Culture and Society* (New York: Oxford University Press, 1976), pp. 76-77.

[5]For this paragraph, see the helpful discussion of D. Stephen Long, *Living the Discipline* (Grand Rapids, Mich.: Eerdmans, 1993), pp. 5-11. See also Raymond Williams, *The Sociology of Culture* (1981; reprint Chicago: University of Chicago Press, 1995), pp. 10-11.

[6]Chris Jenks, *Culture* (London: Routledge, 1993), p. 7.

[7]Jay Clayton, *The Pleasures of Babel: Contemporary American Literature and Theory* (New York: Oxford University Press, 1993), p. 29.

[8]Ibid., p. 6.

[9]Jenks, *Culture*, pp. 9, 19-20.

[10]Roger Lundin, *The Culture of Interpretation* (Grand Rapids, Mich.: Eerdmans, 1993), p. 33.

[11]See the notes by editor R. H. Super in Matthew Arnold, *Culture and Anarchy: An Essay in Political and Social Criticism* (Ann Arbor: University of Michigan Press, 1965), p. 413.

[12]For a penetrating examination of how the high-low culture split has sabotaged Christian understandings of American popular culture, see William D. Romanowski, *Pop Culture Wars: Religion and the Role of Entertainment in American Life* (Downers Grove, Ill.: InterVarsity Press, 1996).

[13]Arnold, *Culture and Anarchy*, pp. 94, 95, 108, 226. Emphasis in original.

[14]Clayton, *Pleasures of Babel*, p. 28.

[15]"It is a liberal model in which the private individual is transformed by 'his' encounter with art, and this transformation is allowed to carry over into public life. The model depends on a conception of the autonomous self and of a public realm controlled by the decisions of 'great men,' whether they be leaders of government or commerce. It relies on a strict division between the realm of culture and the rest of society" (Clayton, *Pleasures of Babel*, p. 6; on

the liberal fact and value division within this view of culture, see Jenks, *Culture*, p. 9).

[16]Quoted in Lundin, *Culture of Interpretation*, p. 61. Arnold's universalism and related formalism also led him to grossly blur cultural and religious particularities. So in his well-known contrast of the Greek and the Jewish, Arnold could see the two ultimately fused and indistinguishable: "The final aim of both Hellenism and Hebraism, as of all great spiritual disciplines, is no doubt the same: man's perfection or salvation." Quoting Scripture with no apparent concern for precise (or even loose) contextual or theological meaning, he insists the final end all aim for is "that we might be partakers of the divine nature" (*Culture and Anarchy*, p. 164).

[17]John F. Kennedy, "From the Address of President John F. Kennedy at the Dedication of the Robert Frost Library, Amherst College, October 26, 1963," in *Of Poetry and Power*, ed. Erwin Gilkes and Paul Schwaber (New York: Basic Books, 1964), pp. 135-36; quoted in Clayton, *Pleasures of Babel*, pp. 6-7.

[18]Arnold, *Culture and Anarchy*, p. 94 (emphasis in original). The scriptural quotation is Luke 17:21. For theological reasons that will be most fully evident in chapter five, I consider "within you" a faulty translation. For now, I only note that most translations render the Greek *en* here in a social, external sense. "Among you," for example, is adopted by the New Jerusalem Bible, the New Revised Standard Version and the New English Bible; the New American Standard Bible renders it "in your midst." Among contemporary translations, the New International Version is conspicuous in going with the individualistic, internal sense "within you."

[19]Niebuhr, *Christ and Culture*, p. xii.

[20]Troeltsch also refers to the "mystical" but considers this an entirely individual, noninstitutional manifestation and so as something marginal to the social questions explored in his book.

For his characterization of the church-type as "institutional" and the sect-type as "voluntary," see *The Social Teaching of the Christian Churches*, trans. Olive Wyon (New York: Macmillan, 1931), 1:340.

[21]Ibid., 1:32.

[22]Ibid.

[23]Ibid., 1:331, 334. Troeltsch's preference for the church-type is made explicit in ibid., 2:1006-13.

[24]Ibid., quoting respectively, 1:39, 40, 52, 55, 56; 2:1007; 1:55.

[25]Niebuhr, *Christ and Culture*, pp. 2-3.

[26]Ibid., p. 32.

[27]Ibid. (emphasis deleted).

[28]Donald A. Luidens, Dean R. Hoge, and Benton Johnson, "The Emergence of Lay Liberalism," *Theology Today* 51, no. 2 (July 1994) 249-55.

[29]Survey respondents, randomly selected from the rolls of twenty-three (mainline) Presbyterian churches, were those having made confessions of faith in

the 1960s. Twenty-nine percent of the respondents were still Presbyterian. Others were active in different mainline churches (the mainline including, besides the Presbyterian Church U.S.A., the United Church of Christ, the United Methodist Church, the Episcopal Church and the Reformed Church in America). Smaller numbers were fundamentalist, Baptist, Catholic and other Christians. A full 48 percent attended church not at all or fewer than six times a year, and by that criterion were considered "unchurched." See ibid., pp. 249-50.

[30]Ibid., p. 252.

[31]Richard Rorty, "Religion as Conversation-Stopper," *Common Knowledge* 3, no. 1 (Spring 1994): 2.

[32]Luidens, Hoge and Johnson, "Emergence of Lay Liberalism," p. 253.

[33]Nicholas Lash, "Hoping Against Hope, or Abraham's Dilemma," *Modern Theology* 10, no. 3 (July 1994): 233.

[34]Luidens, Hoge and Johnson, "Emergence of Lay Liberalism," p. 254.

[35]Ibid. Luidens, Hoge and Johnson define lay liberalism as "liberal" "in its stress on acceptance of differences, its tolerance of uncertainty, its strong commitment to individualism, and its generally liberal position on social and moral issues" (p. 253).

[36]See Charles Colson with Ellen Santilli Vaughn, *The Body* (Dallas: Word, 1992), and Paul Brand and Philip Yancey, *Fearfully and Wonderfully Made* (Grand Rapids, Mich.: Zondervan, 1980) and *In His Image* (Grand Rapids, Mich.: Zondervan, 1984).

[37]Charles Colson, "Crime, Morality and the Media Elites," *Christianity Today*, August 16, 1993, pp. 29-32, quote from p. 31.

[38]Ibid., p. 32.

[39]Aristotle, *Nicomachean Ethics*, trans. Terence Irwin (Indianapolis: Hackett, 1985), bk. 1, chap. 7, par. 4.

[40]Ronald Beiner, *What's the Matter with Liberalism?* (Berkeley: University of California Press, 1992), p. 22. By contrast, "the great mistake of liberalism is to pretend that modernity forces us to regard private morality as reigning supreme and public morality as limited to the business of negotiating 'successful accommodation' between ourselves as rational individuals" (p. 34).

[41]Philip Yancey, "Holocaust and Ethnic Cleansing," *Christianity Today*, August 16, 1993, pp. 24-28, quote from p. 28. Other concerns aside, such a construction avails nothing of the New Testament's teaching about the principalities and powers for understanding, and confronting, social evil. Such teaching is valuable for that purpose even if the powers are viewed as personal superhuman entities, as many evangelicals would interpret them. See John Howard Yoder, *The Politics of Jesus,* 2nd ed. (Grand Rapids, Mich.: Eerdmans, 1994), pp. 158-61.

[42]Philip Yancey, "The Riddle of Bill Clinton's Faith," *Christianity Today*, April

25, 1994, pp. 24-29.

[43]Ibid., p. 27.

[44]Ibid.; all quotes in the last two paragraphs are from p. 29.

[45]For a reading of Mother Teresa and her work that escapes liberal categories and can conceive of it as political, see Robert Inchausti, *The Ignorant Perfection of Ordinary Lives* (Albany: State University of New York Press, 1991), pp. 63-74.

[46]For a devastating illustration of just how hurtful it can be to imagine art (and culture) as an apolitical world unto itself, see Ray Müller's documentary *The Wonderful Horrible Life of Leni Riefenstahl* (Germany, 1993). Riefenstahl was the gifted director of *Triumph of the Will,* the Hitler-sponsored film of the massive Nazi congress in Nuremberg in 1934. *Triumph* is regarded by film historians as the greatest propaganda film ever made. Yet Riefenstahl, operating out of Arnold-like liberal assumptions on art, insists that her movie was not propaganda because there was no narrator offering "political" commentary and she herself was never interested in "politics."

[47]See Stephen Board, "Prophet Bayly," *Christianity Today,* June 20, 1994, pp. 40-41.

[48]Clayton, *Pleasures of Babel,* p. 8.

[49]Ibid., p. 9.

[50]Ibid., p. 27.

[51]Renato Rosaldo, *Culture and Truth: The Remaking of Social Analysis* (Boston: Beacon, 1989), pp. 25-26. Similar definitions are echoed throughout the fledgling field of cultural studies. See, for example, Clayton, *Pleasures of Babel,* p. 8, and Jenks, *Culture,* pp. 8, 157-58. For a wide-ranging discussion of culture anthropologically defined, see Richard A. Shweder and Robert A. LeVine, eds., *Culture Theory: Essays on Mind, Self and Emotion* (Cambridge: Cambridge University Press, 1984).

[52]Quote from Long, *Living the Discipline,* p. 9.

Chapter 5: The Church as Church

[1]H. Richard Niebuhr, *Christ and Culture* (New York: Harper Torchbooks, 1951), pp. 2-3.

[2]Obviously I borrow this chapter's subtitle from John Howard Yoder's influential work *The Politics of Jesus,* 2nd ed. (Grand Rapids, Mich.: Eerdmans, 1994). Yoder was one of the first theologians to crystallize the political aspects of Jesus' life and ministry and push their implications. In this chapter I will largely rely on more recent New Testament scholarship, particularly that of N. T. Wright and Ben F. Meyer. But it is important to emphasize that what follows is, in broad strokes, hardly an account put forward by a mere handful of theologians and biblical scholars. As Yoder makes clear, his 1972 book (the first edition of *Politics)* was *"then* a summary of the widely known scholarship of the time." Yoder especially made use of the work of Amos Wilder, Oscar Cullmann, Otto Piper, Paul Minear and Markus Barth. In his revised edition,

Yoder correctly notes that in the intervening decades since his book was first published, scholars now "less than ever . . . make Jesus apolitical" (pp. vii, x, 13-14). The list of active biblical scholars alone, which Yoder might cite as vivid proof but does not, includes, in New Testament studies, John Riches, Gerd Theissen, Wayne Meeks, William Herzog, Gerhard Lohfink, Ched Myers, Walter Wink, Marcus Borg, Richard Hays, E. P. Sanders and Richard Horsley, and in Old Testament studies, Walter Brueggemann, Paul Hanson, Christopher J. H. Wright, Patrick Miller and Norman Gottwald. For a helpful overview of some of the studies especially concerning politics and Jesus, see Ben Witherington III, *The Jesus Quest: The Third Search for the Jew of Nazareth* (Downers Grove, Ill.: InterVarsity Press, 1995), pp. 16-17, 100-102, 116-18 and especially 151-60.

Let me here also make it clear that in speaking of and emphasizing "politics" I am not attempting to make an ideology or political program alien to Christianity primary to and formative of the faith. On the contrary, my intention is diametrically the opposite. It is exactly by recovering its comprehensive cultural, social and political dimension that we may make Christianity primary to and formative of ideologies, worldviews, philosophies, psychologies, professions or any other potential competitors for our allegiance. What I am after, then, is not what theologian Arne Rasmusson calls a "mediating political theology"—a theology that mediates and tries to make Christianity palatable to a dominant non-Christian political system. Instead, like Rasmusson, I look for an "ecclesial theological politics," a politics or culture that is itself, first and finally, church-centered and theological. See Rasmusson's sophisticated and thorough treatment of this issue in his *The Church as Polis* (Notre Dame, Ind.: University of Notre Dame Press, 1995).

[3]N. T. Wright, "The New Testament and the 'State,' " *Themelios* 16, no. 1 (October/November 1990): 11.

[4]See Ben F. Meyer, *The Early Christians: Their World Mission and Self-Discovery* (Wilmington, Del.: Michael Glazier, 1986), p. 61.

[5]Roman occupation was "simply the mode that Israel's continuing exile had taken. . . . As long as Herod and Pilate were in control of Palestine, Israel was still under the curse of Deuteronomy 29" (N. T. Wright, *The Climax of the Covenant* [Minneapolis: Fortress, 1991], p. 141). See also his *The New Testament and the People of God* (Minneapolis: Fortress, 1992), pp. 268-72.

[6]For a helpful survey of these options as theological and political, see Yoder, *Politics of Jesus*. Meyer comments that much theology (I would note pietistic evangelicalism and existentialist neo-orthodoxy) has misconceived the career of Jesus "as an individualistic call to decision, in almost complete abstraction from its Jewishness and from the intra-Jewish historical context of religious competitors for Israel's allegiance (Pharisees, Zealots, Sadducees, Essenes, baptists . . .)" (*Early Christians*, pp. 43-44).

[7]Wright, *New Testament and the People of God*, p. 169.

[8]Ernst Troeltsch, *The Social Teaching of the Christian Churches,* trans. Olive Wyon (New York: Macmillan, 1931), 1:40.

[9]All quotations from Wright in this paragraph are from *New Testament and the People of God,* pp. 169-70.

[10]Yoder, *Politics of Jesus,* p. 28.

[11]Allen Verhey, *The Great Reversal* (Grand Rapids, Mich.: Eerdmans, 1984), p. 74.

[12]Charles P. Price and Louis Weil, *Liturgy for Living* (New York: Seabury, 1979), p. 21; Yoder, *Politics of Jesus,* pp. 206-7.

[13]Robert Banks, *Paul's Idea of Community* (Grand Rapids, Mich.: Eerdmans, 1988), p. 34.

[14]Wayne Meeks, *The Origins of Christian Morality: The First Two Centuries* (New Haven, Conn.: Yale University Press, 1993), p. 45.

[15]Wright, *New Testament and the People of God,* p. 120.

[16]Ibid., p. 350.

[17]See John H. Westerhoff, "Fashioning Christians in Our Day," in *Schooling Christians,* ed. Stanley Hauerwas and John H. Westerhoff (Grand Rapids, Mich.: Eerdmans, 1992), p. 280. Compare Wright: "The Christians, meanwhile, do not seem to have taken refuge in the defence that they were merely a private club for the advancement of personal piety. They continued to proclaim their allegiance to a Christ who was a 'king' in a sense which precluded allegiance to Caesar, even if his kingdom was not to be conceived on the model of Caesar's" (*New Testament and the People of God,* p. 355).

[18]Meeks, *Origins of Christian Morality,* p. 110. So far was early Christianity removed from its later liberal, individualistic incarnation that the eminent historian of antiquity Peter Brown comments that its appeal "lay in its radical sense of community" (*The World of Late Antiquity: A.D. 150-750* [New York: Harcourt Brace Jovanovich, 1971], p. 68). In another place he observes that the church was concerned to create a "society in miniature, a 'people of God'; its appeal lay in its exceptional degree of cohesion" (*Religion and Society in the Age of St. Augustine* [New York: Harper & Row, 1972], p. 136).

[19]Robert W. Jenson, *The Triune Identity* (Philadelphia: Fortress, 1982), p. 5.

[20]Ibid., p. 7.

[21]Ibid., p. 47.

[22]For a fuller account on this point, see my *Families at the Crossroads* (Downers Grove, Ill.: InterVarsity Press, 1993), pp. 9-26, 174-79.

[23]Matthew Arnold, *Culture and Anarchy: An Essay in Political and Social Criticism* (Ann Arbor: University of Michigan Press, 1965), p. 164.

[24]Meyer, *Early Christians,* p. 46.

[25]Ibid., p. 47.

[26]*New Testament and the People of God,* pp. 247-48. Elsewhere Wright remarks that Jewish theology was a "fighting doctrine." In the same vein, for the early church "the major issues at stake . . . were monotheism, idolatry, election,

holiness and how these interacted. And if that list sounds abstract, removed from the actual life-setting of actual churches, it is because we have forgotten, or have not yet learned . . . that precisely these 'theological' issues functioned as shorthand ways of articulating the points of pressure, tension and conflict between different actual communities, specifically, Jews and pagans" (*Climax of the Covenant*, pp. 125, 122).

[27]Meyer: "Neither the primitive Christian proclaimer nor the point and function of his proclamation is intelligible in historical terms apart from this biblical and ecclesial legacy" (*Early Christians*, p. 47).

[28]Ibid., pp. 38-39.

[29]See ibid., p. 65.

[30]See E. J. Tinsley, *The Imitation of God in Christ* (Philadelphia: Westminster Press, 1960), p. 177. As Tinsley eloquently puts it on the same page, Jesus was not simply "a copyist, but a creative artist, in relation to his nation's history."

[31]Wright, *New Testament and the People of God*, p. 225, n. 29. I have added Hollywood to Wright's list.

[32]See Meyer, *Early Christians*, pp. 60-61.

[33]Ibid., p. 64. See also Wright, *New Testament and the People of God*, pp. 306-7.

[34]God "sees that the only way of rescuing his world is to call a people, and to enter into a covenant with them, so that through them he will deal with evil. But the means of dealing with evil is to concentrate it in one place and condemn—execute—it there. The full force of this condemnation is not intended to fall on this people in general, but on their representative, the Messiah" (Wright, *Climax of the Covenant*, p. 239).

[35]Ibid., p. 151.

[36]On the significance of resurrection, see Wright, *New Testament and the People of God*, pp. 328-34.

[37]Meyer, *Early Christians*, p. 96. See also Wright, *New Testament and the People of God*, pp. 93, 96; *Climax of the Covenant*, pp. 150-51. The church as "new Israel" does not nullify God's election of "old Israel" and those within it who do not now believe on Jesus. I take this to be one of the main points of Paul's difficult argument in Romans 9—11. Put in terms applicable today, the existence of the church does not mean present-day Jews are no longer God's chosen people. God has not forgotten, and will never forget, this "Israel."

[38]Meyer, *Early Christians*, p. 43.

[39]John Milbank, *Theology and Social Theory* (London: Basil Blackwell, 1990), p. 388 (emphasis in original). Compare Tinsley: "The life of the Christian is the life of itinerant Israel over again, with the same trials and temptations (1 Cor 10:5-13), but the Christian now knows that what was being rehearsed in a preliminary way in the history of Israel was the life of Christ with his faithful followers. Because in Christ the Christians are the New Israel, their life is bound to be a series of variations on the theme of the 'Way' of the Old Israel as it has been summed up for them in Christ" (*Imitation of God*, p. 157).

[40]Gordon Lafer, "Universalism and Particularism in Jewish Law," in *Jewish Identity*, ed. David Theo Goldberg and Michael Krausz (Philadelphia: Temple University Press, 1993), p. 196 (emphasis added). Lafer's point is quite explicit in Jeremiah 12:15-16: "And after I [God] have plucked them [the nations] up, I will again have compassion on them, and I will bring them again to their heritage and to their land, everyone of them. And then, if they will diligently learn the ways of my people [i.e., the culture of Israel], to swear by my name, 'As the LORD lives,' as they taught my people to swear by Baal, then they shall be built up in the midst of my people."

[41]See George Lindbeck, "The Church," in *Keeping the Faith*, ed. Geoffrey Wainwright (Philadelphia: Fortress, 1988), pp. 193, 183. I am indebted to Inagrace Dietterich for calling my attention to Lindbeck's extraordinary essay.

[42]Wayne Booth, "Individualism and the Mystery of the Social Self," in *Freedom and Interpretation*, ed. Barbara Johnson (New York: BasicBooks, 1993), pp. 81, 87-88.

[43]Quoted from Philip Slater's *The Earth Walk* without further attribution in Lawrence Stone, *The Past and the Present Revisited* (London: Routledge and Kegan Paul, 1987), p. 325.

[44]Booth, "Individualism," pp. 78, 79.

[45]For a classic statement, see H. Wheeler Robinson, "Hebrew Psychology," in *The People and the Book*, ed. A. S. Peake (London: Oxford University Press, 1925), pp. 353-82. Robinson remarks that such doctrines as original sin are incomprehensible without a notion such as corporate personality. I would add that our thoroughgoing individualism also threatens to render incoherent the doctrines of atonement, of the church and even, most fundamentally, of the Trinity.

[46]Bruce J. Malina, *The New Testament World: Insights from Cultural Anthropology* (Atlanta: John Knox, 1981), pp. 54, 55 (emphasis in original).

[47]Charles Talbert, *Reading Corinthians: A Literary and Theological Commentary on 1 and 2 Corinthians* (New York: Crossroad, 1987), p. 31. Compare J. Paul Sampley: "Paul thinks of believers' relationship with Christ in terms of solidarity with, participation in, or belonging to Christ. . . . Those who have faith are one together in Christ. This solidarity with Christ is Paul's primary identification of believers." And: "Just as surely as one does not snub the workings of the Spirit, one does not disregard the community in one's life of faith." And: "Paul's great interest in the health and growth of the individual's faith is always set within his concern for the well-being of the community, and his commitment to community is always located within his conviction that God's renewal of the entire cosmos is under way." See his *Walking Between the Times: Paul's Moral Reasoning* (Minneapolis: Fortress, 1991), pp. 12, 43, 118.

[48]Booth, "Individualism," p. 79.

[49]Meeks, *Origins of Christian Morality*, p. 6.

Chapter 6: The Church as Worshiping Community

[1] William H. Willimon, *Peculiar Speech* (Grand Rapids, Mich.: Eerdmans, 1992), pp. 54-55.

[2] See the helpful comments of Howard Clark Kee, *Who Are the People of God? Early Christian Models of Community* (New Haven, Conn.: Yale University Press, 1995), pp. 131-34.

[3] Wayne A. Meeks, *The Moral World of the First Christians* (Philadelphia: Westminster Press, 1986), p. 145.

[4] Nancey Murphy, *Theology in the Age of Scientific Reasoning* (Ithaca, N.Y.: Cornell University Press, 1990), p. 164. She adds, "This is not to say, of course, that theories create what is seen, only that theoretical knowledge allows the observer to organize the raw data of sensation into intelligible patterns. It does leave open the possibility, however, that there may be more than one intelligible pattern." Stanley Fish makes this point in characteristically clear fashion: "The fact that the objects we have are all objects that appear to us in the context of some practice, of work done by some interpretive community, doesn't mean that they are not objects or that we don't have them, or that they exert no pressure on us. All it means is that they are interpreted objects and that since interpretations can change, the perceived shape of objects can change too." See *Doing What Comes Naturally* (Durham, N.C.: Duke University Press, 1989), p. 153.

[5] *Serpico* (directed by Sidney Lumet, 1973).

[6] Robert Inchausti, *The Ignorant Perfection of Ordinary People* (Albany: State University of New York Press, 1991), p. 56.

[7] Craig R. Dykstra, *Vision and Character* (New York: Paulist, 1981), p. 106.

[8] See John H. Westerhoff, "Fashioning Christians in Our Day," in *Schooling Christians,* ed. Stanley Hauerwas and John H. Westerhoff (Grand Rapids, Mich.: Eerdmans, 1992), pp. 272-73.

It is worthwhile to note that through much of the church's history Christians did make the liturgy the center of their lives. Historian Eamon Duffy has shown in abundant detail how the medieval English based all of life on the liturgy. As he writes, "Within the liturgy birth, copulation, and death, journeying and homecoming, guilt and forgiveness, the blessing of homely things and the call to pass beyond them were all located, tested and sanctioned. In the liturgy and the sacramental celebrations which were its central moments, medieval people found the key to the meaning and purpose of their lives." See *The Stripping of the Altars: Traditional Religion in England 1400-1580* (New Haven, Conn.: Yale University Press, 1992), p. 11; also pp. 11-52, 91-130.

[9] Aidan Kavanagh, *On Liturgical Theology* (New York: Pueblo, 1984), p. 178.

[10] For more on church as the Christian's primary family, see my *Families at the Crossroads: Beyond Traditional and Modern Options* (Downers Grove, Ill.: InterVarsity Press, 1993), pp. 67-88.

[11]See Robert A. Nisbet, *The Social Philosophers* (New York: Washington Square, 1973), pp. 80-81.

[12]Dale W. Brown, "An Anabaptist Theology of the Sacraments," presidential address presented at the Midwest Section of the American Theological Society, April 25, 1986, pp. 4-5.

[13]Ludwig Wittgenstein, *Tractatus Logico-Philosophicus*, trans. D. F. Pears and B. F. McGuinness (London: Routledge and Kegan Paul, 1922), no page number attributed; quoted in Kenneth J. Gergen, *The Saturated Self* (New York: BasicBooks, 1991), p. 5.

[14]Benjamin Lee Whorf, "Time, Space and Language," in Laura Thompson, *Culture in Crisis* (New York: Harper & Bros., 1950), p. 153.

[15]Nussbaum, "The Bondage and Freedom of Eros," *Times Literary Supplement*, June 1-7, 1990, no page number provided; quoted in Dennis Prager, "Judaism, Homosexuality and Civilization," *Ultimate Issues*, April-June 1990, p. 4. For confirmation of this point with reference to ancient sources, see Dale B. Martin, *The Corinthian Body* (New Haven, Conn.: Yale University Press, 1995), pp. 34, 177.

[16]See Willimon, *Peculiar Speech*, p. 65.

[17]William H. Willimon, *What's Right with the Church* (San Francisco: Harper & Row, 1985), pp. 94-97.

[18]See Margaret Visser, *The Rituals of Dinner* (New York: Penguin, 1991), pp. 1-2.

[19]Ibid., p. ix.

[20]For a fascinating review of anthropological literature on eating and discussion of how this literature relates to early Christian practices of eating, see John Dominic Crossan, *The Historical Jesus* (San Francisco: HarperSanFrancisco, 1991), pp. 303-53, 360-67.

[21]Kavanagh, *Liturgical Theology*, p. 34.

[22]See G. D. Cloete and D. J. Smit, eds., *A Moment of Truth* (Grand Rapids, Mich.: Eerdmans, 1984), p. vii.

[23]Brown, "Anabaptist Theology," p. 17.

[24]Visser, *Rituals*, p. 3.

[25]Ched Myers, *Binding the Strong Man: A Political Reading of Mark's Story of Jesus* (Maryknoll, N.Y.: Orbis, 1988), pp. 230, 361-64.

[26]Crossan, *Historical Jesus*, p. 341.

[27]For a discussion of forgiveness that is both theologically astute and grounded in the practice of the church, see L. Gregory Jones, *Embodying Forgiveness* (Grand Rapids, Mich.: Eerdmans, 1995).

[28]Stanley Hauerwas, *Christian Existence Today* (Durham, N.C.: Labyrinth, 1988), p. 91.

[29]Ibid., p. 96.

[30]Robin Gill, *A Textbook of Christian Ethics* (Edinburgh: T & T Clark, 1985), p. 296.

[31]Abraham Joshua Heschel, *I Asked for Wonder*, ed. Samuel H. Dresner (New

York: Crossroad, 1983), p. 20.

[32]Kavanagh, *Liturgical Theology*, pp. 148-49.

[33]I borrow the phrase, with adaptation, from Kavanagh, *Liturgical Theology*, p. 176.

Chapter 7: The Church as Parade

[1]Charles P. Price and Louis Weil, *Liturgy for Living* (New York: Seabury, 1979), p. 21.

[2]Timothy F. Sedgwick, *Sacramental Ethics* (Philadelphia: Fortress, 1987), p. 46.

[3]Ion Bria, ed., *Go Forth in Peace* (Geneva: World Council of Churches, 1986), pp. 38-46.

[4]Sedgwick, *Sacramental Ethics*, pp. 45-46.

[5]For this survey of liturgy's depoliticization, I am indebted to Aidan Kavanagh's wonderful account found in *On Liturgical Theology* (New York: Pueblo, 1984), pp. 103-15.

[6]Ibid., p. 89. For a Protestant treatment that also recognizes the primacy of (corporate) worship for theology, see Geoffrey Wainwright, *Doxology* (New York: Oxford University Press, 1980).

[7]Kavanagh, *On Liturgical Theology*, p. 91.

[8]And this, in turn, and certainly as in our day, mutates into emphasis on what the individual "feels" rather than emphasis on God's prevenient and graceful reality, reality there before—or even whether or not—an individual feels it. The tension is between an *ex opere operato* conception of the sacraments and liturgy, in which human response to God's salvific work is so downplayed that the sacraments degenerate into incantatory rites, and a kind of extreme free church voluntarism, in which the human response is so emphasized that it becomes primary. Then it is not so much a response to what God has already done and is already doing as an activity or emotion that will create the conditions in which God can save us.

[9]Kavanagh, *On Liturgical Theology*, p. 104. Eamon Duffy's *The Stripping of the Altars: Traditional Religion in England 1400-1530* (New Haven, Conn.: Yale University Press, 1992) has dozens of photographs showing how church architecture and decor were formerly utilized as theological instruction.

[10]Though I did not discover it until after I wrote this chapter, an essay by Ted Koontz marvelously parallels and develops several of the points made in the following exposition—right down to a discussion of Palm Sunday liturgy. See Theodore J. Koontz, "Christian Nonviolence: An Interpretation," as well as Michael G. Cartwright's response, "Conflicting Interpretations of Christian Pacifism," in *The Ethics of War and Peace: Religious and Secular Perspectives*, ed. Terry Nardin (Princeton, N.J.: Princeton University Press, 1996), pp. 169-96 and 197-213. I am grateful to Professor Cartwright for drawing these essays to my attention.

[11]The real problem, in my estimation, arises from the difficulty that most

Christians profess just war theory but actually adhere to a crusade perspective on war. The most intense arguments in practice tend to be between Christians who consider themselves pacifists and Christians who consider themselves adherents of the just war tradition. But if actual just war theory were more widely and deeply understood, the most intense arguments would be between pacifists allied with just war theorists against Christian crusaders. For an unusually candid, and therefore clarifying, exposition of the crusade position, see Harold O. J. Brown, "The Crusade or Preventive War," in *War: Four Christian Views*, ed. Robert G. Clouse, rev. ed. (Downers Grove, Ill.: InterVarsity Press, 1991), pp. 151-68.

[12]James Turner Johnson, *The Quest for Peace* (Princeton, N.J.: Princeton University Press, 1987), p. 52.

[13]David Hollenbach, *Nuclear Ethics* (New York: Paulist, 1983), p. 15.

Chapter 8: The Church as Listening Community

[1]Mary Ford, "Seeing, but Not Perceiving: Crisis and Context in Biblical Studies," *St. Vladimir's Theological Quarterly* 35, no. 2-3 (1991): 124. Ford continues: "That is why it is not the person who puts the context to one side, who claims to have *no* presuppositions, who can interpret correctly (for as modern science itself has demonstrated, it is not possible to be presupposition-less), but the person who works within this very context which provides *right* presuppositions." Exactly so.

I thank Stanley Grenz for drawing this article to my attention.

[2]It is interesting that the text notes that the reading was done "with interpretation. They gave the sense, so that the people understood the reading" (Neh 8:8). Thus it was recognized that the text could not speak for itself but demanded interpretation, and that the interpretation had best be communal.

[3]Stephen Toulmin, *Cosmopolis: The Hidden Agenda of Modernity* (Chicago: University of Chicago Press, 1990), p. 35 (emphasis added).

[4]*The Gods Must Be Crazy* (directed by Jamie Uys, 1981). Lest this fictional example be thought purely fanciful, Jackson Lears asks us to consider the meaning of magazine advertisements to the Abelam of New Guineau. The Abelam are known for their *tambarans,* multicolored sacred designs thought to embody powerful ancestral spirits and used to cover the outside of ceremonial houses. Somehow Western magazines found their way into Abelam villages, so that in 1963 British anthropologist Anthony Forge observed splashy advertisements of "the Spam and sweet corn and honey-baked ham type" pasted on a ceremonial house. In Forge's words, "Inquiries revealed that the Abelam had no idea of what was represented but thought that with their bright colours and incomprehensibility the selected pages were likely to be European tambarans and therefore powerful." See Lears, *Fables of Abundance: A Cultural History of Advertising in America* (New York: BasicBooks,

1994), p. 1.

[5]Steven Waldman, "The Tyranny of Choice," *The New Republic,* January 27, 1992, p. 23.

[6]Robert N. Bellah et al., *Habits of the Heart* (Berkeley: University of California Press, 1985), pp. 221, 235.

[7]On this point see N. T. Wright, *The New Testament and the People of God* (Minneapolis: Fortress, 1992), p. 60.

[8]John Calvin, *Institutes of Christian Religion,* trans. Ford Lewis Battles, ed. John T. McNeill (Philadelphia: Westminster Press, 1960), 4.1.1 (p. 1012), 4.1.4 (p. 1016).

[9]Calvin *Institutes* 4.1.10 (p. 1024).

[10]Thus the Lutheran theologian Helmut Thielicke affirms that *sola Scriptura* makes sense only if it implies an "active Word that comes to us, strikes us, and summons us to a new being." See *The Evangelical Faith,* trans. Geoffrey W. Bromiley (Grand Rapids, Mich.: Eerdmans, 1974), 1:199-200. See also the significant treatment of Karl Barth, *Church Dogmatics* 1/2, trans. G. T. Thomson and Harold Knight (Edinburgh: T & T Clark, 1956), pp. 710-22. Calvin's affirmation of the inseparability of the truth of the written words from the witness of the Spirit comes in his *Institutes* 1.7 (pp. 74-81).

[11]*Catechism of the Catholic Church* (Liguori, Mo.: Liguori, 1994), par. 108 (p. 31). The quote comes from St. Bernard. The Catechism elaborates in the same paragraph, "If the Scriptures are not to remain a dead letter, Christ, the eternal Word of the living God, must, through the Holy Spirit, 'open [our] minds to understand the Scripture.' "

[12]Karl Barth: "The Word of God has surrendered itself so fully to the need of interpretation that some mediation is always necessary. There is no one who as hearer of the Word does not also and necessarily live by the service of such mediators. They may perhaps be remote from him. They may not be known to him as such. But they are in fact effectual, and they have intervened between the scriptural word and himself, and performed for him the service of interpretation and application. We can declare positively that the Church as a whole is an organisation which exists for this mediatorial work. For this reason no member of the Church can remain unconcerned, idle and inactive in face of this duty. If the interpretation of Scripture is not the concern of a special office but of the whole Church, no member of the Church can remain mere spectator of what is or is not undertaken by this office to this end" (*Church Dogmatics* 1/2, p. 714).

[13]John Howard Yoder, *The Priestly Kingdom* (Notre Dame, Ind.: University of Notre Dame Press, pp. 24-25).

[14]Walter J. Ong, *Orality and Literacy: The Technologizing of the Word* (London: Routledge, 1982), p. 11. For a brief overview of the history of orality and writing, see Raymond Williams, *The Sociology of Culture* (1981; reprint Chicago: University of Chicago Press, 1995), pp. 94-95, 109-10.

[15]Ong, *Orality,* p. 32.

[16]Ibid., pp. 43-44, 78.

[17]Ibid., p. 69.

[18]On secondary orality, see ibid., pp. 1, 136 and throughout.

Seeing promise in secondary orality, I do not intend to naively baptize it. Not least through the growth and expanded use of computer technology, it does present potential peril of increased privatization and even gnosticism. Novelist William Gibson gets at these possibilities succinctly when he reflects on a character: "For Case, who'd lived for the bodiless exultation of cyberspace, [to be disconnected from computerized, worldwide networks] was the Fall. In the bars he'd frequented as a cowboy hotshot, the elite stance involved a certain relaxed contempt for the flesh. The body was meat. [Unhooked from cyberspace,] Case fell into the prison of his own flesh" (*Neuromancer* [New York: Ace Books, 1984], p. 6). Much depends on exactly how Christians respond to and appropriate these brave new technologies. Yet I think it a gross error to imagine computer technologies as somehow sinister and writing as pristine. As Walter Ong points out, writing too is a technologizing of the word, and Plato in fact voiced the same objections to writing that are today voiced against computers, such as the destruction of memory (*Orality,* pp. 79-81).

[19]Toulmin shows how print-based culture turned away from four kinds of practical knowledge—the oral, the particular, the local and the timely—in *Cosmopolis,* pp. 30-36.

For a groundbreaking exposition of reading in community, see Stephen E. Fowl and L. Gregory Jones, *Reading in Communion: Scripture and Ethics in Christian Life* (Grand Rapids, Mich.: Eerdmans, 1991).

[20]Jacques Ellul, *The Humiliation of the Word,* trans. Joyce Main Hanks (Grand Rapids, Mich.: Eerdmans, 1985), pp. 44-45. Likewise, Donald Bloesch helpfully notes, "In biblical understanding sight is related to covetousness; what we see we can master or control. Hearing, on the other hand, is associated with faith, for we are then wholly dependent on the speaker and our condition is one of waiting rather than strategic planning." See *A Theology of Word and Spirit: Authority and Method in Theology* (Downers Grove, Ill.: InterVarsity Press, 1992), p. 98. On pages 94-102 Bloesch provides an excellently balanced discussion of word and image, not succumbing to unnuanced iconoclasm as do some strongly Reformed treatments (such as Ellul's).

[21]Which is emphatically not to deny that God's Word involves or entails important propositional claims. Francis Watson has noted that the talk of revelation of God or Christ as an "event" has sometimes misleadingly suggested that we can altogether avoid propositional knowledge. As Watson puts it, "We cannot know God without knowing about God; knowing about God is a necessary although not sufficient condition for knowing God" (Watson, "Is Revelation an 'Event'?" *Modern Theology* 10 [1994]: 388, as quoted in

Gerard Loughlin, *Telling God's Story: Bible, Church and Narrative Theology* [Cambridge: Cambridge University Press, 1996], p. 180.) Similarly, Stanley Hauerwas remarks, "It has become popular to say that revelation is not concerned with propositions, but is instead the self-disclosure of God. Thus many speak of 'revelatory events'—the 'Exodus event' or the 'resurrection event.' They often wish to suggest that revelation does not make claims about what happened, but about the meaning of what happened. In contrast, it is my contention that revelation involves propositional claims, none of which can be isolated by themselves, but are intelligible only as they form a coherent narrative." See *The Peaceable Kingdom: A Primer in Christian Ethics* (Notre Dame, Ind.: University of Notre Dame Press, 1983), p. 66.

[22]I draw this reading of John from Anthony C. Thiselton, *New Horizons in Hermeneutics* (Grand Rapids, Mich.: Zondervan, 1992), p. 69. The theme of embodiment is perhaps even stronger in the writings of Paul. Charles H. Talbert helpfully casts Paul's understanding of the body of Christ in the terms of corporate personality: "Just as Israel could serve as the name of an individual (Jacob) or a community (the people of Israel descended from the individual and identified with him), so could 'Christ' (e.g., Phil 2:11, the individual; 1 Cor 12:12, the corporate personality). . . . Paul is saying then that individual Christians in their corporeal existence are the various body parts of the corporate personality personality of Christ through which the life of Christ is expressed." See Talbert's *Reading Corinthians* (New York: Crossroad, 1987), p. 31.

[23]Joseph T. Lienhard makes this point quite effectively when he writes that the Bible exists "in" though "not under" the church. Exactly where in the church does it exist? "The answer, I believe, is: it exists, first and most importantly, in worship. The words of the Bible are not proclaimed in worship on Sunday, and every day, because scholars have written books about them; scholars write books about the Bible because its words are proclaimed in the Church. Luke's beautiful account of the two disciples on the road to Emmaus is one of the earliest witnesses to the Eucharistic liturgy: first the Scripture is explained, and then bread is broken." See his *The Bible, the Church and Authority: The Canon of the Christian Bible in History and Theology* (Collegeville, Minn.: Liturgical, 1995), p. 101.

[24]See again Thiselton, *New Horizons,* pp. 70-71.

[25]On orality and apprenticeship, see Ong, *Orality,* pp. 9, 43. These thoughts on application manuals arising through the breakdown of community I owe partly to conversations with my friend James Sire.

[26]Nicholas Lash, *Theology on the Way to Emmaus* (London: SCM Press, 1986), p. 42. See also Michael G. Cartwright, "The Practice and Performance of Scripture: Grounding Christian Ethics in a Communal Hermeneutic," *Annual of the Society of Christian Ethics* (Washington, D.C.: Georgetown University Press, 1988), pp. 31-53. Cartwright's essay expounds on an epigraph from

Max Horkheimer (*Kritische Theorie,* vol. 1) that neatly captures the central concerns of this book: "Religion had so long been robbed of clear, specific content, so formalized, adapted, and spiritualized, and shifted to the inner-most subjectivity of the subject, that it was compatible with any act and any public praxis that was customary in this atheistic reality."

[27]Lash, *Theology on the Way,* pp. 42-43.

[28]Wright, *New Testament and the People of God,* p. 140. See also his "How Can the Bible Be Authoritative?" *Vox Evangelica* 21 (1991): 7-32.

[29]Wright, *New Testament and the People of God,* p. 140. Walter Brueggemann is drawn to the metaphor of drama for similar reasons. He writes, "I find this notion of drama with its playful open-endedness to be an appropriate counterpart to the epistemology of postmodernity because drama in life and faith, as drama in theater, need not be so imperialistic and dare not be so absolute. Drama need not claim to voice or enact the whole of truth, but can play with, probe, and explore one moment of truth with patience and courage. It intends, moreover, that this fully exposed moment of enactment should be an opening and a sacrament of everything larger, though it does not claim to grasp all that is larger." See *Texts Under Negotiation: The Bible and Postmodern Imagination* (Minneapolis: Fortress, 1993), p. 65.

[30]Wright, *New Testament and the People of God,* p. 142.

Chapter 9: The Church as World

[1]For examples of such criticisms, see Wilson D. Miscamble, "Sectarian Passiv-ism?" *Theology Today,* April 1987, pp. 69-77, and J. Philip Wogaman, *Christian Perspectives on Politics* (Philadelphia: Fortress, 1988), pp. 33-52.

[2]Richard R. Topping, "The Anti-foundationalist Challenge to Evangelical Apologetics," *Evangelical Quarterly* 63, no. 1 (1991): 45. Helpful overviews of foundationalism can be found in Jonathan Dancy, *Introducion to Contemporary Epistemology* (Oxford: Basil Blackwell, 1985), and John E. Thiel, *Nonfounda-tionalism* (Minneapolois: Fortress, 1994).

[3]Jeffrey Stout, *The Flight from Authority* (Notre Dame, Ind.: University of Notre Dame Press, 1981), p. 46. A more detailed account of the historical situation and its results is provided in the first two chapters of Stephen Toulmin, *Cosmopolis* (Chicago: University of Chicago Press, 1990), pp. 1-87. Unfortu-nately, both Stout and Toulmin simplify historical matters to the detriment of ecclesial institutions and to the advantage of the emerging nation-state. They adhere to what has become more or less the standard account, that the modern state arose to keep peace among warring religious tribes. In an important corrective essay, William T. Cavanaugh argues that this account "puts the matter backwards." "The 'Wars of Religion' were not the events which necessitated the birth of the modern State; they were in fact themselves the birthpangs of the State. These wars were not simply a matter of conflict between 'Protestantism' and 'Catholicism,' but were fought largely for the

aggrandizement of the emerging State over the decaying remnants of the medieval ecclesial order." See his " 'A Fire Strong Enough to Consume the House': The Wars of Religion and the Rise of the State," *Modern Theology* 11, no. 4 (October 1995): 397-420 (quote from p. 398).

[4]Lorraine Daston, "Baconian Facts, Academic Civility and the Prehistory of Objectivity," in *Rethinking Objectivity*, ed. Allan Megill (Durham, N.C.: Duke University Press, 1994), pp. 52-53.

[5]Stephen Toulmin, *The Uses of Argument* (Cambridge: Cambridge University Press, 1958), pp. 249, 127. Descartes is quite explicit about mathematics's appeal and influence on his work. In the first chapter of his *Discourse* he comments, "Above all I enjoyed mathematics, because of the certainty and self-evidence of its reasonings," and "I was astonished that on such firm and solid foundations nothing more exalted had been built." In the second chapter he explains that since "only the mathematicians have been able to arrive at proofs, that is to say, certain and evident reasons, I had no doubt that it was by the same things which they had examined that I should begin." And in chapter 5 he writes, "I have always remained firm in my resolution . . . not to accept anything as being true which did not seem to me more clear and certain than had previously the demonstrations of the geometers" (*Discourse on Method*, trans. F. E. Sutcliffe [London: Penguin, 1986], pp. 31, 41-42, 61).

[6]These three characteristics may share affinities. Stanley Hauerwas has pointed out to me that *individual* was a term first used in mathematics, to denote a "free-standing entity."

Though I have tried to imply disclaimers, it may be worthwhile to explicitly point out at this juncture that I am aware the word *foundationalism* hardly has a single, univocal meaning. So it is that there are some important Christian thinkers, perhaps most notably Alvin Plantinga and William Alston, who call themselves foundationalists but are certainly not foundationalists of the sort described in these pages.

[7]Toulmin, *Cosmopolis*, p. 178.

[8]Toulmin, *Uses of Argument*, p. 183.

[9]C. S. Lewis, *Mere Christianity* (New York: Macmillan, 1960), p. 17.

[10]David S. Cunningham powerfully argues that persuasion is essential to Christian theology because people move among different, and competing, standards. "Most of our arguments take place precisely because we have no general agreement about the rules of the game; and the absence of such universally accepted conventions makes persuasion essential." See his *Faithful Persuasion: In Aid of a Rhetoric of Christian Theology* (Notre Dame, Ind.: University of Notre Dame Press, 1990, 1991), p. 154.

[11]See Joseph J. Kotva, Jr., "Christian Virtue Ethics and the 'Sectarian Temptation,' " *Heythrop Journal* 35 (1994): 38.

[12]For an excellent and much more detailed look at several of the themes to

follow, see J. Richard Middleton and Brian J. Walsh, *Truth Is Stranger Than It Used to Be: Biblical Faith in a Postmodern World* (Downers Grove, Ill.: InterVarsity Press, 1995).

[13]Old Testament scholar Christopher R. Seitz observes that Israel, along with humanity in general, is created in the image of God *and* liable to the effects of the Fall. "Whatever happened to the divine image in Adam [with the Fall] extends in equal measure both to Israel and to the other nations. God's special people do not live longer, jump higher, or fail to disappoint just as profoundly; the opposite may well be true. What marks them out is that God will speak to them in a special and persistent way, or to individuals among them who will pass on what they know even when the tongue sticks or Tarshish seems like a safe place to hide from the potent words of God." See "Human Sexuality: Viewed from the Bible's Understanding of the Human Condition," *Theology Today* 52, no 2 (July 1995): 238.

[14]Tremper Longman III and Daniel G. Reid intriguingly observe that Exodus shows God's power on behalf of Israel, while Exile shows God's power working *against* (and so punishing) Israel. See their *God Is a Warrior* (Grand Rapids, Mich.: Zondervan, 1995), p. 52. The theological point of God's engagement with Israel, it would seem, is not any specialness innate to Israel, but is instead the demonstration of God's character and power.

[15]I borrow this excellent contrast from Robert Inchausti, who deploys it in considering the "personal" moral failures of Martin Luther King Jr. See Inchausti's *The Ignorant Perfection of Ordinary People* (Albany: State University of New York, 1991), p. 85.

[16]For an intriguing early essay that explores the potential of the church in diaspora, see George A. Lindbeck, "The Sectarian Future of the Church," in *The God Experience*, ed. Joseph P. Whelan (New York: Paulist, 1971), pp. 226-43.

[17]James S. Ackerman, "Jonah," in *The Literary Guide to the Bible*, ed. Robert Alter and Frank Kermode (Cambridge, Mass.: Harvard University Press, 1987), p. 235.

[18]Fyodor Dostoevsky, *The Brothers Karamazov*, trans. Richard Pevear and Larissa Volokhonsky (San Francisco: North Point, 1990), p. 29.

[19]Barth, *Church Dogmatics* 4/3/1, trans. G. W. Bromiley (Edinburgh: T & T Clark, 1961), p. 115.

[20]Ibid., p. 119.

[21]Ibid., p. 117.

[22]Kotva, "Christian Virtue Ethics," p. 44.

George Hunsinger, commenting on the passage in Barth from which I have been drawing, helpfully clarifies exactly in what sense Christianity is exclusivist: "[Barth's position] holds that one scheme of theological doctrines (Christianity), taken as a whole, is true in a way that no other such scheme, taken as a whole, can be. Indeed, when taken as a whole, any other such scheme, regardless of its form—whether secular or religious, theoretical or practical, implicit or explicit—can only be regarded as false. Any such scheme when taken as a whole can only be false, because (by definition) it organizes itself around some central doctrines other than those concerning Jesus Christ as he is attested for us in Holy Scripture. Any unified and differentiated theological scheme or whole, organized around a different controlling center, can only stand in contradistinction to (and in competition with) Christianity as an alternative scheme of truth." See *How to Read Karl Barth* (New York: Oxford University Press, 1991), p. 278.

[23] *The Apostolic Tradition of Hippolytus,* sorting out potential inquirers to the faith, flatly commands, "If a man is an actor or pantomimist, he must desist or be rejected" (trans. Burton Scott Easton [N.p.: Archon Books, 1962], pt. 2 [p. 42]).

[24] The epigraph to Eberhard Arnold, *Why We Live in Community* (Farmington, Penn.: Plough Publishing House, 1995).

[25] See Barth, *Church Dogmatics* 4/3/1, pp. 126-28.

[26] Ibid., p. 124.

Chapter 10: The Church as Mission and Message

[1] David J. Bosch, *Transforming Mission: Paradigm Shifts in Theology of Mission* (Maryknoll, N.Y.: Orbis, 1991), pp. 205-6.

[2] Ibid., p. 205. "The same was true of the Byzantine Church, only more so" (p. 205).

[3] Ibid., pp. 221-22.

[4] Columbus, "Journal," December 24, 1492; quoted in Tzvetan Todorov, *The Conquest of America* (New York: HarperPerennial, 1982), p. 43.

[5] Columbus, "Journal," November 6, 1492; quoted in Todorov, *Conquest,* p. 50.

[6] Columbus, "Letter to the Sovereigns," September 1493; quoted in Todorov, *Conquest,* p. 47.

[7] Columbus, "Journal," November 27, 1492; quoted in Todorov, *Conquest,* p. 43.

[8] Kirkpatrick Sale, *The Conquest of Paradise* (New York: Alfred A. Knopf, 1990), pp. 153-54; quoted in James W. Loewen, *Lies My Teacher Told Me* (New York: New Press, 1995), pp. 51-52. (Emphasis added.)

[9] See Frances Kartunnen, *Between Worlds* (New Brunswick, N.J.: Rutgers University Press, 1994), p. 88.

[10] Palacios Rubios, *Requerimiento* (1514); as quoted in Todorov, *Conquest,* p. 147. See also Loewen, *Lies,* p. 34.

[11] Bosch, *Transforming Mission,* p. 246. The two missions were the French Protestant excursion to Brazil (1555) and the mission to the Lapps promoted by the king of Sweden (begun in 1559).

[12] Ibid., p. 259.

[13] Ibid., p. 260.

[14] Ibid., p. 204. Jürgen Moltmann contends that in Constantinian evangeliza-

tion "not the church but the emperor 'evangelized' by subjecting the peoples to his Christian empire." Under such a rubric, Christians did not spread the gospel "in order to awaken faith" but instead "spread the kingdom of Christ in order to rule the world in God's name." See his "Christianity in the Third Millennium," *Theology Today* 51, no. 1 (April 1994): 85.

[15]For Bosch's treatment of Pietism, see *Transforming Mission,* pp. 253-55.

[16]Quoted in Todorov, *Conquest,* p. 151.

[17]Frank E. Sugeno, "Evangelism: Avoiding the Errors of the Past," *Anglican and Episcopal History* 60, no. 3 (September 1991): 283. More mischievously, but with considerable accuracy, Harold Bloom comments, "Revivalism, in America, tends to be the perpetual shock of the individual discovering yet again what she and he always have known, which is that God loves her and him on an absolutely personal and indeed intimate basis." See *The American Religion* (New York: Simon & Schuster, 1992), p. 17.

[18]From Whitefield's sermon "The Lord Is Our Light," in John Gillies, *Memoirs of George Whitefield* (New Haven, Conn.: n.p., 1834), p. 588; quoted in H. Richard Niebuhr, *The Kingdom of God in America* (New York: Harper Torchbooks, 1937), p. 120.

The individualism implicit in revivalism was a point of contention in an important nineteenth-century debate between theologians John Nevin and Charles Hodge. Hodge stressed "the personal and individual relationship of the believer with Christ, while Nevin made the church an indispensable mediator of Christian experience." Thus Nevin "attacked 'revivalism' as unchurchly, self-centered and incapable of establishing real union with Christ. Hodge remained neutral." See Linden J. De Bie, "Real Presence or Real Absence? The Spoils of War in Nineteenth-Century American Eucharistic Controversy," *Pro Ecclesia* 4, no. 4 (Fall 1995): 438-39.

[19]Bosch, *Transforming Mission,* p. 282.

[20]George Marsden, *Fundamentalism and American Culture* (Oxford: Oxford University Press, 1980), p. 38. For documentation and other comments on such attitudes, see also pp. 32, 49, 91, 207, 211.

[21]Niebuhr, *Kingdom of God in America,* p. 181. Marsden similarly observes, with the nineteenth century in mind, "The characteristic American response to secularization was to bless its manifestations—such as materialism, capitalism, and nationalism—with Christian symbolism" (*Fundamentalism,* p. 49).

At another place in his still important book, Niebuhr contrasts revivalistic individualism with the biblical vision of the kingdom, writing that early American Protestants thought of the promise of the kingdom not as "in the first place . . . a warless world wherein lions and lambs would lie down together, or of plenty which every man might enjoy in tranquility beneath his own vine and fig tree. They thought rather of the cleansing of the inward parts or the restoration to man of inner harmony, of the elimination of the war in the members, whence all other wars and fightings came" (p. 91).

[22]For an extended discussion, with examples and documentation, see Douglas G. Webster, *Selling Jesus* (Downers Grove, Ill.: InterVarsity Press, 1992). For profound theological criticism, see Philip D. Kenneson, "Selling [Out] the Church in the Marketplace of Desire," *Modern Theology* 9, no. 4 (October 1993): 319-48.

[23]Ben F. Meyer, *The Early Christians: Their World Mission and Self-Discovery* (Wilmington, Del.: Michael Glazier, 1986), p. 145.

[24]Note that the similar but nonidentical list of Colossians 3:11 cites the categories of circumcised and uncircumcised, barbarian and Scythian (an ancient nomadic people understood as the ultimate barbarians).

[25]Meyer, *Early Christians,* p. 182.

[26]Bosch, *Transforming Mission,* p. 191. He further notes, "The testimonies of enemies of the church (such as Celsus and Julian the Apostate) frequently mentioned the extraordinary conduct of Christians, often with reference to the fact that this conduct had been a factor in winning people over to the Christian faith" (p. 192).

[27]William J. Abraham, *The Logic of Evangelism* (Grand Rapids, Mich.: Eerdmans, 1989), p. 81.

[28]Ibid., p. 96.

[29]I am here adapting, theologically and evangelistically, the approach to persuasion suggested by Barbara Herrnstein Smith in her "The Unquiet Judge: Activism Without Objectivism in Law and Politics," in *Rethinking Objectivity,* ed. Allan Megill (Durham, N.C.: Duke University Press, 1994), p. 301.

[30]Stanley Fish, *There's No Such Thing as Free Speech* (New York: Oxford University Press, 1994), pp. 215-16.

[31]Philip D. Kenneson, "There's No Such Thing as Objective Truth, and It's A Good Thing, Too," in *Christian Apologetics in the Postmodern World,* ed. Timothy R. Phillips and Dennis L. Okholm (Downers Grove, Ill.: InterVarsity Press, 1995), p. 162.

[32]Kartunnen, *Between Worlds,* p. 13. "For a brief time the mainlanders were uncertain about what sort of food the Spaniards might eat, whether the horsemen were separable from their horses, and whether they could be wounded" (p. 5).

[33]Noted by Bartolomé de Las Casas, *Historia de las Indias* 3.145; quoted in Todorov, *Conquest,* p. 90.

[34]George A. Lindbeck, *The Nature of Doctrine* (Philadelphia: Westminster Press, 1984), p. 64.

[35]Ibid.

[36]John Milbank writes that Christianity "from the first took the side of rhetoric against philosophy and contended that the Good and the True are those things of which we 'have a persuasion,' *pistis,* or 'faith.' We need the stories of Jesus for salvation, rather than just a speculative notion of the good,

because only the attraction exercised by a particular set of words and images causes us to acknowledge the good and to have an idea of the ultimate *telos*. *Testimony* is here offered to the Good, in witnessing that also participates in it. This commitment to a rhetorical, and not dialectical path to the Good opens out the following implication: only persuasion of the truth can be non-violent, but truth is only available through persuasion. Therefore truth, and non-violence, have to be recognized simultaneously in that by which we are persuaded" (*Theology and Social Theory* [London: Basil Blackwell, 1990], p. 398).

[37]See the discussion in Todorov, *Conquest*, pp. 179-81.

[38]I here paraphrase Robert Inchausti, who in his context is discussing nonviolence and not evangelism. See his *The Ignorant Perfection of Ordinary People* (Albany: State University of New York Press, 1991), pp. 130-31.

Chapter 11: The Church as a Way of Life

[1]On culture as "signifying system," see Raymond Williams, *The Sociology of Culture* (1981; reprint Chicago: University of Chicago Press, 1995), p. 13.

[2]See again ibid., pp. 27, 207-10.

[3]Ion Bria, ed., *Go Forth in Peace* (Geneva: World Council of Churches Mission Series, 1986), pp. 38-46.

[4]In much that follows I am deeply indebted to John Howard Yoder, "*Christ and Culture:* A Critique of H. Richard Niebuhr," unpublished paper, 1976. After the completion of this chapter, Yoder's important essay was published as "How H. Richard Niebuhr Reasoned: A Critique of *Christ and Culture*," in *Authentic Transformation*, ed. John Howard Yoder et al. (Nashville, Abingdon, 1996), pp. 1-74.

[5]James Wm. McClendon Jr., *Systematic Theology: Ethics* (Nashville: Abingdon, 1986), p. 231.

[6]These examples can be easily complicated, but that in itself emphasizes the cultural qualities of actual, lived Christianity. For instance, there was a time when Christian rock musicians could not be imagined, because there was a time when there was as yet no rock music at all. Even now some Christians reject rock music and its making. And though we might count on most Christians to reject pornography, we are assured of an argument about what, exactly, is pornographic. Those rejecting rock music regard it as pornographic. Are the painted nudes in a museum pornographic? What of the disrobed actor so completely self-revelatory at the neighborhood cinema? No general, once-for-all rules are sufficient to answer these questions. Once more, as always, we are pulled back to the concrete, the timely, the particular, the local—in short, the cultural.

[7]I try to set forth what this means at some length in *Families at the Crossroads* (Downers Grove, Ill.: InterVarsity Press, 1993).

[8]Most of these examples are drawn from James W. Loewen, *Lies My Teacher*

Told Me (New York: New Press, 1995), pp. 36, 59, 103-5.

[9]Stanley Fish has written acutely on the pitfalls of the entire inside-outside language when referring to cultural change. He notes that it is only from the perspective of a particular community that anything or anyone is "inside" or "outside." The "status as a something or someone outside is conferred by the very community from which he is supposedly distinct; his is an *interpreted* outside, and forms along with other items and persons a general background of irrelevance that defines and is defined by the sense of relevance that informs the community, telling it what it must pay attention to and what it can afford to ignore." Consequently, when a person or event or object becomes part of an interpretive community, it is absorbed or adopted from the inside out. In Fish's words, "When the sense of relevance changes—when the community is persuaded . . . that its project requires the taking into account of what had hitherto been considered beside the point or essential only to someone else's point—the boundaries of outside/inside will have to be redrawn *from the inside.*" Far from being a stagnant, self-enclosed entity, then, an interpretive community or culture "is always engaged in doing work, the work of transforming the landscape into material for its own project; but that project is then itself transformed by the very work it does." See *Doing What Comes Naturally* (Durham, N.C.: Duke University Press, 1989), pp. 148, 150.

[10]The "narrative" language is found in McClendon, *Systematic Theology: Ethics,* p. 143. The "code" language comes from Robert Scholes, *Textual Power* (New Haven, Conn.: Yale University Press, 1985), p. 163. (I am grateful to David Wright for drawing Scholes's essay to my attention.)

[11]Scholes, *Textual Power,* p. 162.

[12]I borrow and adapt the ship metaphor from Jeffrey Stout, *Ethics After Babel* (Boston: Beacon, 1988), pp. 57-59.

[13]For excellent commentary along these lines regarding the world religions, see the essays by John Milbank and Kenneth Surin in *Christian Uniqueness Reconsidered,* ed. Gavin D'Costa (Maryknoll, N.Y.: Orbis, 1990), pp. 174-212.

[14]Michael Goldberg, *Jews and Christians, Getting Our Stories Straight* (Nashville: Abingdon, 1985), p. 222.

I cannot overemphasize that the living God and actual God-shaped community are primary to and pervade or enliven the five other "steps" that follow. Indeed, the "step" language is misleading if it suggests stages or fundamental processes that, once accomplished, can be left behind, much as the child who has learned to walk abandons the crawling stage. The following five steps (with the exclusion of the last) are resonant with those who tend to treat Christianity as a worldview or set of propositions, but Christianity is much more than a worldview or collection of cognitive beliefs. This has been wonderfully expressed by Gregory A. Clark, who notes that "philosophy itself is a form of spirituality (or a process of conversion)" if "spirituality" is understood as "one's turning and moving toward truth or supreme goodness, one's orientation toward that which satisfies our intellect and gives happiness. The spiritual life will take different forms, according to what people identify as 'truth' or 'the supreme good.' It will also vary with the resources one has to move along toward" the truth or the good. Accordingly, "the proper goal of Christian philosophy" is not to antecedently and abstractly establish the credibility of Christianity, but to provide "Christian description of Christian experience." And: "For the Christian, the practices that Christian philosophy presupposes may include, or even be identified with, prayer, meditation, celebrating the Eucharist, feeding the poor, healing the sick, casting out demons, preaching a sermon and confession. Christians have traditionally worked out their reflections on the nature of the God they worship and their understanding of truth in these contexts, rather than in essays or papers delivered at conferences." See Clark, "The Nature of Conversion: How the Rhetoric of Worldview Philosophy Can Betray Evangelicals," in *The Nature of Confession: Evangelicals and Postliberals in Conversation,* ed. Timothy R. Phillips and Dennis L. Okholm (Downers Grove, Ill.: InterVarsity Press, 1996), pp. 210-11.

[15]I say more on translatability, drawing from Alasdair MacIntyre, in "How Firm a Foundation: Can Evangelicals Be Nonfoundationalists?" in *The Nature of Confession: Evangelicals and Postliberals in Conversation,* ed. Timothy R. Phillips and Dennis L. Okholm (Downers Grove, Ill: InterVarsity Press, 1996), pp. 81-92.

[16]For comments on Hebrews and Jewish-Christian apocalypticism, I draw on George Eldon Ladd, *A Theology of the New Testament* (Grand Rapids, Mich.: Eerdmans, 1974), pp. 572-74; the direct quotation comes from p. 574. I have also had these thoughts on eschatology helpfully crystallized by James Burtness, *Shaping the Future: The Ethics of Dietrich Bonhoeffer* (Philadelphia: Fortress, 1985).

For an excellent exposition of the Greek philosophical take on time, and how this affected Greek theology, see Robert W. Jenson, *The Triune Identity* (Philadelphia: Fortress, 1982), pp. 58-61.

[17]John Milbank, *Christianity and Social Theory* (London: Basil Blackwell, 1990), p. 388.

[18]Stanley Fish, *Is There a Text in This Class?* (Cambridge, Mass.: Harvard University Press, 1980), p. 193. I need hardly add, but will, that Fish is not a professing Christian. What he has, perhaps through his study of John Milton, is a fine sense of how the eschatological affects epistemology. See for example his essay "Unger and Milton," in *Doing What Comes Naturally,* pp. 399-435.

[19]Once more I shamelessly poach, this time paraphrasing and elaborating on Frank Lentricchia, *Criticism and Social Change* (Chicago: University of Chicago Press, 1985), p. 12.

Perhaps the best example I know of this kind of life-changing and life-sustaining Christian worship is provided by the African-American church. The black American church has animated and led a community subjected to incredible suffering, enabling that community on Christian terms to engage life "as both a carnival to enjoy and a battlefield on which to fight. Afro-American Christianity promotes a gospel which empowers black people to survive and struggle in a God-forsaken world." The quote is from Cornel West's excellent essay "Subversive Joy and Revolutionary Patience in Black Christianity," found in West, *Prophetic Fragments* (Grand Rapids, Mich.: Eerdmans, 1988), pp. 161-65.

Chapter 12: The Church as a Community of Friends

[1]On this subject, Hendrik Berkhof, *Christ and the Powers,* trans. John H. Yoder (Scottdale, Penn.: Herald, 1962, 1977), still repays study. Robert E. Webber and I discuss this view of the principalities and the powers at length in *People of the Truth* (Harrisburg, Penn.: Morehouse, 1988, 1993), pp. 22-34.

[2]See Wendell Berry, *Sex, Economy, Freedom and Community* (New York: Pantheon, 1992), pp. 117-73.

[3]Robert Inchausti, *The Ignorant Perfection of Ordinary People* (Albany: State University of New York Press, 1991), p. 4.

[4]Ibid., p. 141.

[5]John Fiske (*Power Plays, Power Works* [London: Verso, 1993]) writes, "Language is a crucial site of struggle, for of all of our circulation systems it is the one with the widest terrain of operation. It works extensively across the globe and across the nation to spread its own preferred ways of thinking, and intensively to carry the same cultural work into the innermost areas of consciousness" (p. 31).

[6]Inchausti, *Ignorant Perfection*, p. 63.

[7]The idea of living "out of control" is wonderfully and inspiringly discussed by Stanley Hauerwas in his *The Peaceable Kingdom* (Notre Dame, Ind.: University of Notre Dame Press, 1983), esp. pp. 105, 135-51.

[8]See John McKnight, *The Careless Society* (New York: BasicBooks, 1995), pp. x, 167.

[9]McKnight observes, "The surest indication of the experience of community is the explicit common knowledge of tragedy, death and suffering. The managed, ordered, technical vision embodied in professional and institutional systems leaves no space for tragedy; they are basically methods for production. Indeed, they are designed to deny the central dilemmas of life," whereas "to be in community is to be a part of ritual, lamentation, and celebration of our fallibility" (*Careless Society,* pp. 171, 172).

[10]James MacMillan's *Cantos Sagrados* are included on his *Seven Last Words from the Cross* (New York: Catalyst, 1995).

[11]See Inchausti, *Ignorant Perfection*, pp. 20-21.

[12]Michel de Certeau, *The Practice of Everyday Life,* trans. Steven Randall

(Berkeley: University of California Press, 1984), p. xiii (first emphasis in the original, second emphasis added).

For beautiful evidence of how the indigenous population adapted and enriched Spanish Catholicism and music, I recommend Joel Cohen's album *Nueva España: Close Encounters in the New World, 1590-1690* (Germany: Erato Disques, 1993).

[13]James C. Scott, *The Weapons of the Weak: Everyday Forms of Resistance* (New Haven, Conn.: Yale University Press, 1985), p. 350.

[14]Walter Brueggemann, *Finally Comes the Poet* (Minneapolis: Fortress, 1989), pp. 114, 113-14.

[15]See John Dominic Crossan, *The Historical Jesus: The Life of a Mediterranean Jewish Peasant* (San Francisco: HarperSanFrancisco, 1991), p. 29.

[16]Walter Wink, *Engaging the Powers* (Minneapolis: Fortress, 1992), pp. 178, 179 (see the whole of chapter six, pp. 175-93).

[17]Such a *Christus Victor* understanding of the atonement has long plagued theologians on ethical grounds. For instance, could Jesus—the truth incarnate—really have intentionally deceived Satan? My wording tries to avoid such quandaries, but for a full and cogent response to these concerns, see Thomas N. Finger, *Christian Theology: An Eschatological Approach* (Nashville: Thomas Nelson, 1985), 1:317-24, 331-38. Like Finger, I do not wish to deny the validity and importance of other "models" of the atonement.

[18]In *After Virtue* (Notre Dame: University of Notre Dame Press, 1981), p. 187. MacIntyre calls a practice "any coherent and complex form of socially established cooperative human activity through which goods internal to that form of activity are realized in the course of trying to achieve those standards of excellence which are appropriate to, and partially definitive of, that form of activity, with the result that human powers to achieve excellence, and human conceptions of the ends of goods involved, are systematically extended."

[19]McClendon, *Systematic Theology: Ethics* (Nashville: Abingdon, 1986), p. 173.

[20]MacIntyre, *After Virtue*, pp. 26-27, 30-32, 74-78, 85-87.

[21]In Stanley Hauerwas, *A Community of Character* (Notre Dame, Ind.: University of Notre Dame Press, 1981), p. 231, n. 12.

[22]McKnight, *Careless Society*, pp. 178-79.

[23]Iris Murdoch, "The Sublime and the Good," *Chicago Review* 13 (Autumn 1959): 54; quoted in Stanley Hauerwas, *Vision and Virtue* (Notre Dame, Ind.: University of Notre Dame Press, 1981), pp. 38-39.

[24]Rowan Williams, *Resurrection* (New York: Pilgrim, 1984), p. 90.

[25]*The Book of Common Prayer* (New York: Church Hymnal Corporation/Seabury, 1979), p. 363.

Index